Christina Crawford worked as an actress from 1959 to 1972, appearing in numerous summer stock productions, several films, a soap opera and on television.

She then went back to university and in 1975 took a Master's degree in Communication Management. She has since worked in the public relations department of a large company handling corporate communications, including film and videotape productions. With her writer-producer husband she has formed a company to promote literary and entertainment ventures.

In a recent interview in the *New York Times Book Review*, Christina Crawford described the beginnings of the book that has become a worldwide bestseller:

'In the summer of 1977 I reached a point in my life where it was time to write the truth. I was 37 then and had been a public figure since I was a baby. I wanted to tell what it was like growing up as a Hollywood child – including the child abuse ...'

Christina Crawford

Mommie Dearest

A MAYFLOWER BOOK

GRANADA
London Toronto Sydney New York

Published by Granada Publishing Limited in 1980
Reprinted in 1981

ISBN 0 583 13066 6

First published in Great Britain by
Hart-Davis, MacGibbon Ltd 1979
Copyright © Christina Crawford 1978

Granada Publishing Ltd
Frogmore, St Albans, Herts AL2 2NF
and
36 Golden Square, London W1R 4AH
866 United Nations Plaza, New York, NY 10017, USA
117 York Street, Sydney, NSW 2000, Australia
100 Skyway Avenue, Rexdale, Ontario, M9W 3A6, Canada
61 Beach Road, Auckland, New Zealand

Made and Printed in Great Britain by
Richard Clay (The Chaucer Press) Ltd
Bungay, Suffolk
Set in Linotype Granjon

Granada ®
Granada Publishing ®

This book is dedicated with love to
Bernie and Mildred, who helped me find my way,
my brother Chris, who shared much of the journey with me,
and my beloved husband, David, who made it all worthwhile.

ACKNOWLEDGMENTS

Style Many friends have made very special contributions to my life and to this book. I want to acknowledge them with love and gratitude:

My husband, C. David Koontz, for his incredible tenacity, good judgment, and consistent caring; my stepson, David, for his patience and good humour; my brother, Christopher Crawford, for his valuable assistance and friendship. *Ref*

Bernard Berkowitz and Mildred Newman, for encouragement and help in launching this entire project.

Lynn Nesbit, for being the best agent imaginable, and Stephen Sultan, for his persistence.

Judy Feiffer, my first editor, who guided me through the difficult moments with insight, sensitivity, and courage, and Howard Cady, who handled the task of being my second editor with graciousness.

Cheryl Levine, for her determination and assistance in typing the original manuscript, and Teresa Joseph, for her wisdom and professional expertise. *Ref*

Nicki Bailey and Margaret Lee Chadwick, for nearly a lifetime of friendship and faith in my ability.

Jerome Pickman, Douglas Fairbanks, Jr, and Phillip Terry, for sharing remembrances.

Martin Leaf, my attorney, for his professional skill and friendship.

Linda Rose, for her generosity, love, and a home-away-from-home.

Photoplay magazine, for permission to use photographs originally printed in their publication.

PART
ONE

ONE

DEAD. Joan Crawford. New York City. 10 May 1977, at 10 A.M. Eastern Daylight time. Official cause of death: coronary arrest.

As the wire services sped the news around the world we heard a brief obit on the all-news radio station on our way to the airport.

The only time so far that I had cried was when an old fan called to tell me about the TV news station coming to film souvenirs of her old clothes, ankle-strap shoes, and the photographs of her in his living room. He asked if he could have her dog.

She's barely cold and someone wants the dog! The rage made me shake and tears spilled down my face, yet somehow my voice sounded ever polite until I hung up the phone.

Eng.

Superstar is dead. Now the closet door will open and every weirdo in America will be on parade waving the faithful notes signed 'God Bless . . . Joan.' I cried. But it wasn't sorrow, it was anger. A flash of the old rage like one of those violent Eastern thunder-and-lightning storms that sweep across the sky and are gone.

Eng.

I had a terrible headache and felt sort of shaky inside, but there were no tears. David held my hand and I felt his strength slowly calm me. Somehow if I could just hold on to his hand, I could make it through this.

It was dawn when we landed in New York. Outside the baggage claim area a dark-haired man with a slight accent asked if we wanted a taxi. I said yes and he took our bags. There were no yellow cabs in sight. David and I followed him to a black limousine parked at the kerb. I looked at David and smiled. Well, why not? Twenty bucks was fair enough and it would be a nice change for us. As we drove through Queens, the dirty old buildings, the knee-deep potholes, the elevated subway trains rattling overhead, and the people pushing their way through another day made me feel deeply relieved we didn't live in the city.

My brother Chris arrived at the hotel about ten-thirty. He looked older and much thinner. Hard times and trouble were so clearly evident that he may as well have been carrying a sign. We held each other in greeting and consolation and a kind of understanding that went back thirty years deep into childhood. 'I'm really glad you're here,' is all I said. It was very tough for him. Chris hadn't been included in any family event since he was fifteen years old. The four of us kids had always been in touch, but privately. Mother had barely mentioned his name for the last nineteen years. Now that she was dead we were all together again. Actually, he lived only about a hundred miles from New York City, but it was like another world out there. He had found his town now, he belonged there. He knew almost everyone, married, and owned a house . . . did his job . . . had been a volunteer fireman . . . found a place for himself after coming home from Vietnam. I really love Chris.

We drank black coffee out of slightly soggy paper cups from the delicatessen around the corner and he took another aspirin. David had changed into his blue suit and my heart overflowed with pride. What a terrific man, this husband of mine. I'm the luckiest woman in the whole world.

At noon the three of us took a taxi to the Drake Hotel. There we were to meet the lawyer, the secretary, and one sister, Cathy, with her husband.

The greetings were strained. Everyone was being polite, but there were other feelings beneath all that niceness. Words seemed hollow and as I looked from face to face I sensed something strange. Chris sat across the room from the secretary. Years ago they had been enemies. But now Chris just smoked his cigarettes and watched. My sister's husband talked and

12

talked about 'Joan' this and 'Joan' that, rambling along nervously oblivious.

Nothing had been written down before Mother's death regarding the funeral arrangements except that she wanted to be cremated. I thought it was odd that someone so fanatically well organized should have left all these details to anyone else, let alone to a group decision. Nevertheless, that was it. Somehow we had to make the decisions right away. There we were, a disparate group, to say the least, deciding how to arrange the formality of burying our mother. Never in any of our past experiences had we decided anything in relation to her except how we would each live our lives. As the hours dragged on, it became painfully clear what some of those life decisions had been.

Then, during one of the many phone calls to Campbell's funeral home, a strange expression came over the lawyer's face as he listened to the voice on the other end of the line. It was the only emotional display I saw on his face during the entire time and it was just a look of surprise.

'Your mother has been embalmed. You may see her if you want to.' He said it straight and without emphasis. He assured us it wasn't an order he had given because he knew she was to be cremated. There was to be no autopsy; that had been decided before my arrival.

Whatever the reason, there she was: embalmed at Campbell's. Strange. In fact it was all beginning to take on a spacy, weird feeling. I had to keep in direct contact with David to maintain my sense of reality, which kept threatening to fade out.

We were like a sequestered jury. Decisions had to be made and no matter how much anyone wanted either to back out or to take over, a kind of ritualistic primitivism prevented autocratic rule. We all had to participate and cast our vote.

The secretary and my sister seemed to feel that they had an inside track to Mother's thinking. Chris, I think, had vowed to keep his mouth shut as long as possible. David had never met Mother and was being quietly diplomatic. My sister's husband jabbered on and on about their close relationship with 'Joan'. I could feel my anger rising again.

The funeral home on Eighty-first Street was just what you'd imagine it to be. It seemed more like a movie every minute. The men there were dressed exactly right. They looked and sounded like undertakers. It was quiet and people spoke softly. There was a muffled quality to everything. I was beginning to feel very tired and a little sick to my stomach. I held on to David's hand whenever I could. He was my life and my reality in the midst of this. My sister was asked to sign the papers and then she and I went to a room upstairs where we chose the plain brass urn without any grapes or goddesses on it. There would be no inscription either.

When we returned downstairs, Chris and my other sister, Cindy, had arrived. The little blue room with its love seats and small chairs was full. The moment had come.

A man from Campbell's asked who would like to see Mother. For the first time a complete silence surrounded all of us. It was almost as though no one could even breathe. We looked at one another. What thoughts must have been careering around in each brain! Cathy said no. Cindy shook her head no. Chris swallowed hard and looked quite pale. He said no. The man from Campbell's looked directly at me, expressionless. Almost inaudibly I said, 'I'd like to see her.' He opened the door and I followed him to the small elevator. We entered and the door closed very softly.

There was not much room in the elevator so we stood only two feet apart. He started telling me how beautiful she looked, and his own face was quite radiant as he described how hard he'd worked from some of his favourite photographs of her. I found myself completely caught up in his story. I realized in a strange flash of understanding that, for a moment, he'd thought that no one would see what he'd done, that no one would be there to appreciate his work of art. He seemed almost grateful and his eyes sparkled. I stared at him in genuine fascination. I had never known anyone who did this for a living.

It seemed like a very long time that he and I were bound together in this special exchange. I was to be the final audience.

The little elevator stopped on the second floor. He led the way again, down a short hallway past the room with the satin-lined coffins where my sister and I had chosen the urn just a few minutes before. At the end of the hall there was a large room. The door was open but the lights were off. He stepped aside to let me by and I walked slowly because I wasn't sure where we were going. The lights went on and startled me. I looked straight ahead with a terrible fright. There she was, not ten feet away from me, lying on a table . . . dead.

'May I be alone, please,' I whispered. My knees felt weak and my hands were shaking. I heard the man walk down the hallway. I stood there, alone. A lump filled my throat and tears covered my eyes. I looked and looked and looked. That's my mother on that table and she's really dead. Somehow I absolutely had to know that. Somehow I had to take this terrifying time alone to make that real – to know for myself that death was real even if much of life hadn't been. To make sure of that reality, I gave myself this time alone with her at the very end so that I could go on. It was a very fragile feeling. I was scared. I mean really scared. Scared beyond anything I'd ever known before. I didn't know what to do. I was still standing at the doorway to the room. I hadn't moved. There was no one here with me. This was my time. I didn't have to worry about keeping anyone waiting, or what anyone else thought. It was just the two of us. Mother and me . . . alone for the very last time. An incredible wave of sadness washed over me. My mouth was trembling and my eyes filled with tears that hadn't yet fallen free. I swallowed a couple of times and heard myself say, 'Mommie . . . oh Mommie . . . I loved you so much . . .' The tears inched down my face and I wiped a few away.

I walked up to the table and stood next to her. Her eyes were closed. They had done a good job with the makeup. Her face looked quite natural, surprisingly so. Her hair was short and brushed back from her face. It was grey. Her hands were resting on a cream-coloured satin comforter that covered her, and she had been dressed in a pale salmon-coloured silk kimono wrap. Her nails were polished, and she even had lipstick on. As I looked carefully at her almost inch by inch, I noticed how terribly thin she was. In truth, she had wasted away to nothing, to skin and bones. It dawned on me in that moment that coronary arrest was not the whole story, not the whole story at all. It takes a long time to become that thin. There was hardly anything left to her at all. But her face was indeed her face and I looked at her a long time. I had never seen a dead person before. At any moment I expected her to open her eyes and say, 'Tina'. For a split second I even wondered if she'd scold me or have something to say about the way I was dressed.

As I stood before my mother for this last time I realized there could be no further exchange between us. Throughout all our years together, I was never absolutely sure of the reception I was going to get from her. I never knew whether it would be a big hug of loving affection or a verbal slap in the face.

Though I felt no trace of guilt or regret about our long and often turbulent relationship, I did feel an enormous surge of loneliness that this silence was the end of it all. I had not seen her in several years, but I had imagined that we might have one last talk, that somehow she might know before the end of her life who this eldest daughter of hers really was and perhaps even take some measure of pride in what had evolved out of our chaotic relationship. I remembered how she'd insisted that I make an appointment to see her even when we were together every day. I looked down at this painfully thin woman with sadness, thinking of the way she'd regimented her life in order to avoid really living it. She'd become so afraid of spontaneity, of anything she couldn't directly control.

Now, I had an overwhelming need to feel her strong embrace, remembered from the far reaches of my childhood, just one last time. Instead, I reached over and touched her hand. It was cold. Mother had very strong hands and prided herself on a straight-forward handshake. Her hands were now very thin, her wrists little more than bones.

I don't know how long I stood there thinking about her, about me, about the two of us locked in a duel of wits and will all these years. I was the first child, her precious, beautiful princess of a daughter, the golden-haired baby she wanted so much. May-be it was a stroke of eternal justice that I should have the courage to be the last, to be with her for a while in death. This final appointment with my mother was one she had not made and she could not change.

'I know you're not really here with me any more, Mother . . . I know your soul is gone already . . . I just want to tell you that I love you . . . that I forgive you. You know I forgave you long ago. We had so much pain together, you and I, but now, Mother,

16

God has set us both free. God has set you free to begin another journey. I pray the next one has less anguish. God has set us free, Mommie dearest. Go in peace.'

I could hear the sobs now. They were mine.

I knew it was time for me to go. I leaned over and kissed her forehead gently. 'Goodbye, Mother. Goodbye . . . and I love you.'

I wiped my face with the back of my hand and put on my dark glasses. Then I turned and left her.

As we walked down the stairs, I managed to tell the man from Campbell's that she looked beautiful. He had done a good job.

TWO

Hollywood in the 1920s was already a town of folklore and the focus of national fantasy.

In those days the silent-screen stars built magnificent estates up in the hills that were copies of European castles or English manor houses and even Mediterranean villas. The European influence was very strong and artisans were imported from Europe to create hand-painted ceilings, intricate tile mosaics, hand-carved cornices, doors, banisters, and all the lavish decorations that adorned these modern-day royal abodes. There was as yet no income tax. The studios paid their stars enormous sums. Mary Pickford, Charles Chaplin, and others were reportedly getting a million dollars a year, tax-free. Lesser luminaries may not have been overnight millionaires, but certainly they had no thoughts of poverty. Most spent their newly acquired and seemingly never-ending supply of money on gratifying whatever whim occurred. But these stars were also tied to Hollywood studios, working a six-day week, turning out full-length feature films in a month. Their spending was attuned to local self-indulgence: palatial mansions, expensive cars, lavish pool parties, and jewellery.

A large staff was required to run the silver-screen palaces but getting servants was no problem. After the artisans and builders left, the servants were also imported from European countries, where they had been properly trained by families of inherited wealth and longer-standing noble lineage. Despite their money and fame, the majority of stars had recently come from ordinary families and small towns. They had no idea how to be the grand ladies and gentlemen of their own dreams, so they copied what they had heard about the established Eastern families of the industrial revolution and were particularly fond of the more eccentric ways of European nobility. Some even copied characters from their own movies. But in order to achieve those elegant fantasies with any semblance of authenticity, someone in the newly constructed Southern California palaces had to know which fork went where, how to run the household, plan the menus, choose the linens, and serve the wine. The simplest solution, indeed, was for them to import servants to run the houses as they had earlier imported the artisans to build them. So, for the next thirty years the English butlers and nannies, the Scandinavian, German, French, and Italian cooks, maids, and chauffeurs, the Japanese gardeners, and the Filipino houseboys streamed into Los Angeles to teach their royal employers how to live like ladies and gentlemen.

No matter how much money they made, though, actors and Jews were rarely allowed to live in the most fashionable residential districts of the time. The establishment frowned on these nouveaux riches movie people and found ways to exclude them from their neighbourhoods, their private clubs, and their golf courses. It was natural, then, for these latter-day gods and goddesses of the silent silver screen to find their way into the vacant hillsides of Hollywood and a few years later move even further west to build a separate city of their very own called Beverly Hills.

From small towns all over America young hopefuls came to join the silver-screen phenomenon. Winners of dance contests and beauty pageants, anyone who'd made a mark in anything vaguely resembling show business – they all flocked to Hollywood in a steady stream. When they arrived they found themselves in fierce competition with more seasoned veterans of Broadway chorus lines and vaudeville. Still they came, each with a couple of dollars and a suitcase full of dreams.

Hollywood was also a small town in the twenties. If you could figure out how to get there, you could figure out how to meet

19

people. That wasn't the problem. The problem was how to get into the movies.

It was customary to line up in front of the casting offices at the studios in the morning. If there was actually a picture casting bit parts and extras, then there was the possibility of work. And if there wasn't any work, it was the best way to find out what was going on at the other studios. Mother told me that actors got paid five dollars a day, which included the wardrobe they wore before the camera, unless it was a costume picture, and there was no such thing as an eight-hour day. There was no overtime pay and there were no unions. She also told me that it was common practice for actors to kick back two or three dollars out of the five they were paid. If they didn't kick back, they didn't work that studio the next time a picture was casting. You worked for two or three dollars a day or you didn't work at all.

But whether you had to line up at the studio casting offices or were fortunate enough to have a studio contract, if you wanted to be a movie star you worked diligently at the next most important part of creating a career: 'being seen'. Being seen had different echelons to it which depended largely on how much money could be spent on personal progress. Being seen first meant getting invited to the best possible parties you could manage and then working even harder to get yourself invited to the right parties. Being seen also meant having your name appear in the gossip columns, which necessitated going somewhere with people better known than yourself, no matter who they were and regardless of what you thought of them. Being seen meant making sure that the way you looked attracted attention – almost any kind of attention, so that in addition to the beautiful people, the successful people, there was always an ample contingent of the outlandish and the freaky – usually the ones either on their way up or on their way out. Being seen meant spending hours dreaming up schemes of noticeable behaviour patterns and idiosyncrasies of every conceivable kind. Entrances and exits were elaborately planned one-act plays designed to enhance 'being seen' – to ensure that heads would turn and that people would inquire as to the identity of the player. If you didn't start out with easily accessible neurotic behaviour, you simply created some. If you couldn't afford real glamour, you became outrageous. Anything worked if you were noticed. Here was a totally separate reality with its own set of values that had nothing to do with the rest of the world. Here, as nowhere else, make-believe was real.

It didn't matter for an instant how you got where you were going because the studio publicity departments would make up their own stories for the public once you officially arrived. Everyone was after the same thing: *stardom*. They would claw and fight or screw anything that walked to get there one step ahead of you. There was no protection from the kickbacks or the famous casting couches, and no one felt bad if you didn't make it. If you failed that was just one less body in competition for the attention and the pictures. Fairness and morality were irrelevant. They had been left behind for care and safekeeping in all the little towns across America.

It was contended that the absolute mark of local social acceptance could only be bestowed by one Hollywood invitation. Among the many luminaries that sparkled brilliantly, none were more awesome than the unofficial royal family of Hollywood, the publicity-appointed king and queen of Tinsel Town, Douglas Fairbanks and Mary Pickford. An invitation to Pickfair, as their estate was known, was universally acknowledged as the only legitimate indication that one had attained recognition in Hollywood.

Billie Cassin had changed her professional name back to her original name Lucille LeSueur before she arrived in Hollywood in January 1925, as one of the lucky newcomers. She already had a signed MGM contract. During the day at the studio she did the usual stand-in and bit parts while at night she danced in exhibition contests with various partners and finally with a serious beau, Mike Cudahy of the Chicago meat-packing family.

She made close friends with the studio publicity department, posing for every outlandish publicity gimmick. She made herself available on a moment's notice at a time when the big female stars on the Metro lot were becoming increasingly disenchanted with the insatiable publicity mill, even refusing to sit for any still pictures. That publicity churned out month after month created a national excitement about the young starlet, Lucille LeSueur, before she'd been given an opportunity to display her acting skills to any extent in a movie. The unsung heroes of her career were the nameless troops of the MGM publicity department. Many of them devoted their lives to creating the fabulous fantasies of stardom for the rest of the world. Mother never forgot her allegiance to them. As one elderly publicist said after her death: 'She had four marriages which only lasted three years each, but I've loved her for more than forty years.'

She became Joan Crawford a year later through a movie magazine 'name-the-star' contest sponsored by MGM. She hated her new first name so much that she called herself 'Jo-ann' at the studio for several years. She said that Crawford sounded like 'crawfish' and she hated that, too. Although formally and professionally she took the name Joan Crawford, privately with her old friends and anyone new she cared about, she called herself Billie for many years.

It was 1926. She diligently began putting this new creature called Joan Crawford together as a total movie star. Every facet of her being was remodelled, leaving at least the mannerisms and former physical appearance of Lucille LeSueur behind. From 1925 to 1928 she appeared in over twenty films. But it wasn't until *Our Dancing Daughters*, which was released in 1928, that she finally tasted stardom.

A year later she married the prince of Pickfair, Douglas Fairbanks, Jr. The columnists acknowledged the union with mixed reviews. True, it seemed to be a love match but it was no secret in Hollywood that Joan Crawford never ceased trying to better herself or that she was already an accomplished social climber.

While courting, the young couple was under constant pressure from the press on one side and his influential family on the other.

But Joan Crawford had spunk, she was not one to give up without a fight. She had pursued Douglas for over a year after first seeing him on the opening night of his first major part in a Broadway hit called *Young Woodley*. She'd written him a fan letter and followed that up with a picture of herself signed 'Billie'. She was the one who encouraged Douglas to stand up against the combined family pressures, and it was her strong character that turned what otherwise might have been only a brief romantic interlude into a full-fledged marriage. The wedding did not have the approval of Douglas Fairbanks, Sr, or of stepmother Mary Pickford, but the young couple were married anyway in the rectory of a Catholic church according to the wishes of the bride, who considered herself a Catholic.

This was a time of major transition for Joan Crawford. Her dreams were all coming true. Behind her were the days of struggle. Ahead were the unlimited horizons of wealth and stardom. She had a new name, a new husband, a whole new world. She was the American dream. She embraced the Cinderella fairy tale as an embodiment of her own life. She had a natural flair for dramatization, which was to become an integral part of the creation of her new public image. However, what started as perhaps harmless inclination towards fantasy became what her friends later called an incorrigible exaggeration of each facet of her past. Sometimes her stories painted her early life as overly humble and poor, while other times these same incidents were spiced with innuendos of being madly sought after by the great men of the New York theatre. Only those who had known her since her teenage years could distinguish fact from fiction.

Overcoming obstacles by virtue of her willpower and determination appealed to her sense of drama and coincided neatly with the roles the studio gave her to play. Her triumphs seemed greater if the barriers placed in her way appeared to be insurmountable. Success was sweeter if the road was tougher.

Perhaps that is why she perpetuated the stories of not being welcome at Pickfair, saying publicly that she didn't think her new in-laws ever really liked her and that she always felt uncomfortable, ill at ease with them. Other accounts recall the in-laws as patronizing, perhaps, but not overtly unkind.

Regardless of these problems, real or embellished, her career continued to skyrocket. During the next four years she made over a dozen more films. She acquired polish and she credited Douglas with her good manners and taste.

The remake of *Rain*, released in 1932, was a dismal failure. In her portrayal she had allowed herself a sort of nakedness and vulnerability. She was striving for something more than just glorious costumes and stereotypical glamour. But the public and critics alike responded with mixed feelings to this departure in

Joan Crawford's public image. Simultaneously, the newspaper columns and movie magazines reported that the Fairbanks marriage was saddened by a miscarriage.

It may have been true that the young star in her late twenties had a miscarriage. However, years later Joan Crawford was bitterly outspoken and told at least one close friend that she'd really had an abortion.

In those days it was barely acknowledged by the studio publicity departments that their stars were married, never mind having babies! If it was unglamorous to have a baby, it was unthinkable to be called a grandmother. It simply wasn't done, it had never been done, and it probably shouldn't start now. This was hardly the era of dowager queens.

Whether abortion or miscarriage, the results were the same. There were neither children nor grandchildren from this marriage and it ended in the spring of 1933.

Although she was reportedly unable to have children, Joan Crawford was otherwise the incarnation of perfect health. She was a good athlete, suntanned and vibrant, didn't drink but was a cigarette smoker. She had achieved total stardom now, so she appeared in two or three starring vehicles a year with top billing. Competition at Metro continued to be fierce, but she won more battles for scripts than she lost. After her marriage to Fairbanks failed she devoted herself to her career and to her first love affair with Clark Gable. In Gable she said she'd found her match. He was a man big enough, charming enough, and strong enough to deal with her spirit, her drive, and her ambition. But he was also a married man and any permanent liaison was impossible.

Her brother Hal had divorced his wife of only a few years, leaving her with a baby girl. It was during this time that Joan Crawford considered adopting her niece and namesake, Joan. Although the incident received a good deal of publicity, the adoption never went through.

Then in October of 1935 she remarried. This time it was to Franchot Tone.

Franchot was the epitome of the cultured, well-educated gentleman. His family tree went all the way back to the American Revolution, and he had ancestors who were master silversmiths rivalling Paul Revere. He was from the Eastern establishment as far as Joan Crawford was concerned, and had also made substantial achievements through his membership in the famous Group Theater and in Broadway plays. Not only did he have breeding, impeccable taste, and a respected family, he was also an intellectual and considered an 'actor's actor'. They made several films together before and after they were married, but Franchot never became a real Hollywood star.

Mother said she was fascinated by his stories of the Group Theater and acting lessons patterned after those of the great Russian director Stanislavsky. Having never taken formal lessons in anything but singing and dancing, she badgered him to teach her what he'd learned. She told one hilarious story about the time he agreed to teach her 'method acting'. Her big eyes followed his every move and noted each gesture. As she listened attentively to the instructions, her heart sank.

Franchot had obviously decided to start at the very beginning. Although he was not normally given to practical jokes, that could be the only explanation for what was to follow. As the details unravelled it became clear. What Franchot wanted was for her to be a carrot! She was to stand like a carrot, think like a carrot, and feel like a carrot. For several minutes she stared at him in total silence while the full impact of what was expected of her crept through her consciousness. It was not what she had anticipated. However, she was determined to give it a try. Slowly she rose to her feet and took her position as a carrot. No one will ever know the extent of her performance as the ill-fated carrot because at this point in the story she burst into laughter. She said that she told Franchot she thought this was ridiculous. She was never going to be cast as a carrot and she couldn't imagine how in the world this could possibly help her career or get her better parts. That was the end of the acting lessons.

She and Franchot lived in her Brentwood house. Together they finished the remodelling she had begun, and her friend William Haines decorated it in a combination of modern and antique furniture. Franchot had contributed his beautiful family silver, including a massive antique tea service. The formal dining room had shelves built into one whole wall to provide a permanent display case for the exquisite pieces.

It was during the years of this marriage that Mother became a

25

wine connoisseur and learned about gourmet foods. Franchot taught her to appreciate fine art and classic literature. Her dinner parties were now impeccable. The long dining room table, which could easily seat twenty, was set in the most formal manner of Europe with linen, silver, and crystal all co-ordinated to create a perfect elegance. In the front basement there was a locked wine cellar stocked floor to ceiling with the finest wines money could buy. The 'jazz baby' turned slick sophisticated movie star was finally becoming a lady.

She was a big star when she married Franchot and he was considered just a leading man. Despite her box-office setback during the next few years, she remained a star and he made little progress towards becoming one. It was a disappointment to her and a serious disadvantage for him. It became painfully clear that he missed New York, the theatre, and his own way of life. He constantly lived in the shadow of her stardom even though he was a well-known and respected actor.

When Franchot's friends from the East came to Hollywood they headquartered at his house. Some actually stayed there, but others would just hang out around the pool. Franchot and his New York buddies would sit around for days on end drinking and talking about the 'good old days'. But when MGM friends of Mother's and the ever-present publicity folk gathered for an afternoon of gossip and shop talk, Franchot seemed uncomfortable and out of place. Mother said she couldn't relate to most of the New York people. She was too busy trying to salvage her own sinking career and had no time for drunken merrymaking. Her last big box-office year was 1936. She knew the pictures Metro assigned her were getting progressively more shallow and less successful with the public.

She was fighting for her professional life. She was busier working than Franchot and it irritated her enormously that he wasn't more ambitious. Then there were Franchot's little flirtations, which always threatened to turn into affairs. The personal and professional gap between them grew.

This marriage had not produced any children either, and when she actually caught Franchot having an affair with another woman she threw him out of her house. The divorce was final in April of 1939.

If her marriage to Fairbanks can be said to have given her a mark of acceptance and respectability, the marriage to Franchot gave her culture and elegance. She kept the silver and the antiques and added periodically to the wine cellar. She planned superb dinner menus and artfully arranged the place cards which designated careful seating arrangements. Her library shelves were adorned with beautiful collections of rare and esoteric leather-bound books, some of which she had taken the time to read. She still read the 'funny papers' and liked cookies with butter on them, but she was, at long last, a lady.

Mother found herself alone again in a huge, empty twenty-two-room house after two unsuccessful marriages, numerous attempts to have children, and fourteen years in pictures. And she wasn't getting any younger. Publicly her birth date was reported as 23 March 1908, but Grandmother told me that she was actually born in 1904. That made her closer to thirty-five in 1939 when I was delivered to her.

My official papers simply say 'girl' born on Sunday afternoon, 11 June 1939. My real mother was a student and my father a sailor, and neither of them wanted to take responsibility for me. So, I travelled from Hollywood Presbyterian Hospital to a baby broker to 426 North Bristol Avenue when I was only a few weeks old.

In no time at all I was a chubby, smiling baby named Joan. My towels were monogrammed 'Joan'. The silver picture frame with my birth statistics is monogrammed 'Joan', and the small Bible given to me as a baby says "To little Joan". Only a few weeks old and I was to be Joan Crawford, Jr. An awesome responsibility.

Mother and I were absolutely inseparable. She took me with her wherever she went. I slept in her dressing rooms and on the studio sound stages. I travelled in the car with her from the time I was only a few months old. She saved every bit of hair cut from my head, every tooth from my mouth. All were carefully sealed in envelopes and labelled in her generous handwriting. There were gifts for which she wrote little notes – 'to my beautiful infant' ... 'I love you my darling, beautiful child' – notes I could not read and only she knew about and saved.

 During the months of my infancy she showered me with the pent-up outpouring of love and affection that had been stifled in

27

her for so many years. Better still, she didn't have to share me with anyone; I was hers alone. She was my 'Mommie dearest', the wellspring from whence all love and affection flowed, and I was her longed-for golden-haired girl. She named me after herself and through the lavish affection, attention, and adornment she showered upon me, she made up for some of the poverty of her own childhood. I was to be the best, the most beautiful, the smartest, quickest, most special child on the face of the earth. I wanted for nothing: toys, clothes, and baby jewellery. She was constantly holding me and looking at me and trying to make my sparse hair grow into long golden ringlets. Whenever she didn't take me to the studio, she would rush home in time to feed me and give me my bath. She would sing lullabies to me and rock me to sleep.

In truth, I was adorable. I also became quite spoiled. I had everything. My nurse played endlessly with me and took care of me. My adoring, indulgent mother couldn't resist giving me anything I asked from her. In return, she had my total devotion. The sun rose and set on my beloved Mommie dearest. Her laughter was the music of my life, and the sound of her heart beating as she held me close to her made me feel safe and quiet. I sobbed whenever she left me even for a little while. I clung to her skirts if there were new people around. I learned very quickly to be adorable for company. I was very bright and seemed to know what pleased the big people. Everyone cooed over me and said what an absolutely beautiful child I was. I learned to walk and talk very rapidly.

We travelled extensively the first year of my life. When I was just three months old Mother took me to New York with her on the train. She kept an apartment in the city near the East River and every day my nurse, Aunt Kitty, took me for a stroll in my baby carriage.

Then in May 1940, Mommie drove with me to Las Vegas, Nevada, where she legally adopted me. The laws of the state of California did not then permit a single woman to adopt children. So I was eleven months old before my mother made these arrangements in Las Vegas. At some point before the final papers were signed, she had come to the conclusion that Joan Crawford, Jr, was not exactly fitting. She chose a new name for me and the adoption papers recorded that name as Christina Crawford.

In exchange for their more liberal adoption laws and a substantial fee, the state of Nevada attempted to provide some measure of future protection for the children adopted by single parents. Since my mother was an unmarried woman, if anything should happen to her there would be no one to provide for me. It was decided that a trust fund should be set up in my name. The court felt assured that this compromise was in the best interests of all concerned and dispatched its duty accordingly. During my early childhood I heard numerous references to this trust fund. Mommie said she periodically put the gifts of money her friends sent to me on special occasions in that trust.

For a reason I've never discovered, we went from Las Vegas to Miami, Florida. Curiously, Mommie had never mentioned our going to Miami. I discovered that we had been there for a period of several weeks only when I went to Miami to do my first picture in 1960, nearly twenty years later. There I was interviewed by a woman reporter who told me that she had interviewed my mother twenty years before and that she'd originally met me as a small baby. She didn't seem to have any explanation for our trip, either, except that my mother had said at the time that she was on a much needed vacation. It wouldn't seem so peculiar except that we *drove* the entire way. There were no freeways and it was most unusual for a woman alone with an eleven-month-old baby to drive nearly three thousand miles. But that is evidently what we did.

From Miami we went to New York City, where I celebrated my first birthday. The New York contingent of fans and a few close family friends were at the small party. I was dressed in an organdy pinafore and by then had a full head of blonde ringlets. The fans were specifically forbidden to take pictures of me, but somehow they managed to hide their cameras and snap the contraband photos anyway.

During our stay in the East, Mommie took me to visit some Christian Science friends who owned a beautiful dairy farm in upstate New York. From there we went to visit Helen Hayes and her family in Nyack, New York, before returning to California.

Strange Cargo and *Susan and God* had both been released in 1940. In *Strange Cargo* my mother was again teamed with Clark

Gable. Even though I was very young I remember Gable's visits to the house during the next two years. He seemed like a giant to me and had the most wonderful hearty laugh. Mommie and he resumed their romance, but again it was not destined to be a lasting romantic relationship. She once said that Gable was only interested in women who weren't available. Then there were her own problems with the relationship. As much as she yearned for and was attracted to strong men, deep down inside she only wanted men she could dominate. That definitely was *not* Clark Gable. He was known as a man's man, a sportsman, and quite a lover. Gable had a spirit and a verve for living that set him apart. Although their love affair was relatively brief, Mommie spoke of Gable with a special fondness and respect for the rest of her life. When asked by interviewers who was her favourite leading man or male Hollywood star, she put Gable at the top of the list. Maybe it was because she never did manage to outshine him professionally nor dominate him personally that she retained her respect and love for him over a span of nearly thirty years.

During 1941 and 1942 she made two pictures a year under her Metro contract. But though she continued working, she knew that her career was in serious trouble. She couldn't get any good scripts. Her pictures were not doing well at the box office. She had been a big star now for over twelve years, but another major transition was looming ominously on the horizon.

At the time she didn't say much about her feelings, but many years later in an interview she talked quite frankly about how badly it had hurt her feelings that the studio and the public preferred the younger pin-up stars of the war years such as Lana Turner and Betty Grable. Metro was the only real home she had ever known. Louis B. Mayer was more a father to her than anyone from her own childhood days. She had literally grown up on the MGM lot. She was closer to the crew, office staff, and fellow actors than she'd ever been to her own family.

Finding herself a 'has-been' at the age of about thirty-seven was a shock. Having to leave her home at MGM was a bereavement. She was never quite the same again. The damage to her public image when she was labelled 'box-office poison' didn't hurt her nearly so much as the humiliation she felt at being deserted by the people she had loved and trusted. During

30

all the years there was never enough success, never enough money or fame or love to fill the void. She seemed to carry the pain in a secret place where nothing ever really touched it, no amount of loving ever erased it. She never forgot a slight or an unkind word. She might not discuss how she felt, but she would carry the unpleasant image fresh in her mind for twenty or thirty years. She developed a belligerence about life, an assumption that people were destined to betray her, that her life was a battle against ever imminent defeat. It was during these years that she began to drink.

Finally, after seventeen years under contract to MGM, Joan Crawford left and signed with Warner Bros. studios for less money than she'd been making at Metro. Warner Bros. was an entirely new battle for her. She didn't have the secure niche that she'd had at Metro. She was not part of the family on this new lot, and she still had to do battle with the senior producers, the front office, and Jack Warner himself. In her opinion the scripts they submitted were worse than the ones she'd refused to do at MGM. What an irony that she had left one studio because of the poor quality of material she was offered, only to be given what she considered 'worse trash' at Warners. With the exception of *Hollywood Canteen*, a lavish war-effort propaganda movie featuring every star on the Warners payroll, she went on suspension and didn't work at all for nearly three years.

Phillip Terry was a handsome but relatively unknown actor. When she married him in 1942 I think my mother already knew her days at Metro were numbered.

She'd only been divorced for three years but she didn't like being alone. By her own admission she didn't love Phillip and said she should never have married him. He certainly wasn't powerful enough to do anything for her career. But she needed companionship and she needed an audience to reassure her that she was loved. She had an insatiable need for love.

Phillip was the second husband who came to live with her on Bristol Avenue. He had his separate suite consisting of a large bedroom and a dressing-room-bath. It always seemed as though he were more a guest than a part of the household. He was allowed little voice in how things were to be run. Had he known in advance how demoralizing it was going to be for him, I'm sure he never would have considered marrying Joan Crawford.

In 1943, Joan and Phillip together decided to adopt a baby boy, whom they called Phillip Terry, Jr. I do not remember their marriage, but I certainly do remember the night my baby brother arrived.

I was asleep in the big four-poster bed with the white organdy canopy. I heard voices and woke up slowly. There was a light on in the room and I could see the shadows of several people standing around a crib across the room from my bed. The people were whispering. I sat up. Everyone turned around. I scrambled out of bed and ran over to the crib to peer through the railing. I was about three and a half years old and not yet tall enough to see much in the semi-darkness. Someone picked me up so that I could see better. I looked down and there he was – a fat, smiling baby brother. I wanted to touch him. He looked like a big doll with his blue eyes and blond curls. From that night until we left home as teenagers, my brother and I shared a bedroom.

The door to our room was always left open and the hall light burned all night because I was afraid of the dark. Sometimes the dolls on the shelves in my room would dance in the shadows and I would be scared of them. Sometimes there were wolves under my bed and I'd have to lie very still so they wouldn't know I was there. Sometimes I lay so still it was as though I were frozen. I don't think I was so scared of the dark before I started sleeping in the big four-poster bed. At first I used to have nightmares and fall out of bed in the middle of the night. Mommie would come running from her room. I would be screaming. It was quite a distance from the top of my mattress to the floor. I had to use a step stool to get into bed.

When I was about four, I started having the same dream over and over. I'd been kidnapped by a band of men on horses. Mommie was trying to find me. The men and horses would stop to rest. I could hear Mommie: she was just around the bend in the road; she was coming to rescue me. But, just as I could actually see her, the men would scoop me up and ride off. Then I would be crying and fall out of bed.

I had not made up the entire kidnap terror. Only a few years before I was born, the Lindbergh kidnapping had been a national tragedy and I'd heard Mommie talk about it.

Then too, before this new baby brother arrived, there had been another one. His name was Christopher and he hadn't been with us very long before his real mother came to our house and wanted him back. It was a terrible scene with screaming and shouting and everyone running around. But the woman did get her son back and we were left without a Christopher.

Evidently through publicity stories on baby Christopher, which included his real birth date, the natural mother had been able to locate her son. After that episode, Joan Crawford wasn't taking any further chances.

From that time on, she changed the birth dates on our certificates. She didn't change mine, but on my brother's she changed the date to 15 October, and later, when she adopted two girls she called twins, she changed theirs to 15 January.

Although Mommie and Phillip Terry planned to adopt Phillip, Jr, together, my new daddy never formally adopted me, so I still belonged to my mother alone.

After they were married Phillip was given the job of disciplining me and administering my spankings. Up until that time Mommie had been using the hairbrush or her hand. She'd succeeded in breaking three hairbrushes across my bottom after complaining that she'd already worn out her hand. I was about four or five.

I don't remember exactly when regular spankings from Mommie started, but I do recall the first real disagreement between us.

Mommie insisted that each of us learn to swim in our pool at an early age and since I was the eldest, my swimming lessons started about age three. A year later, at four, I could swim quite well. Like all kids learning something new, I was eager to show off to my mother. She decided we would have a race. The first race was only the width of the pool and she let me win it. After that I wanted to race again, only this time it was to be the entire length of the pool. We raced several times. She beat me easily. I was furious with her. I swam over to the steps and climbed out of the pool. Dripping wet I stood looking down at her and said, 'You don't play fair. I'm never going to play with you again as long as I live.'

I remember that my mother laughed. She said, 'Christina, I

could have won all the time. I'm bigger than you are. I'm faster than you are. *I can win all the time.*'

That day she made me get back in the pool with her, but I refused to race her again. Years later, when both my brother and I became excellent competition swimmers, she never got in the pool with us.

I was only four when this brief clash of wills occurred but I know that neither one of us ever forgot it. Maybe she'd already succeeded in making me as much of a fighter as she was. Maybe this was the very first indication of independence and the baby mutiny that was to enrage her so during the following years. But there was probably no way for either of us to know in that particular moment that this brief exchange was actually setting the stage for our future relationship lasting more than thirty years.

About the discipline and the spankings, Phillip and I had a deal. We would go down to the building across from the pool, called the theatre, where they showed movies. The deal was that I would get one additional spank each time I had to be punished. The first was a breeze because I only got one spank, and it was all over. It was actually a nice time with Phillip in the theatre at the beginning of our deal. We would talk and he'd ask me what I thought I was being punished for and I'd tell him and then he'd give me his ideas on the subject. Of course I'd vow never to do it again. Then he'd pick me up and carry me back to the house. It was nice and I liked the feeling of being close to him. He had a kind face.

Then one day I got the shock of my life. He gave me a spanking that really hurt. I mean really hurt. His hands were bigger than my mother's and, of course, he had more strength. I cried. But not all of the crying was for the spanking; about half of it was for the betrayal. After that, all the spankings hurt, more and more. It had turned out to be a rotten deal. Now he didn't pick me up and carry me back to the big house. He just held my hand firmly as I walked beside him sniffling. We didn't even look at each other.

THREE

Our house stood in the middle of a quiet but very fashionable neighbourhood known as Brentwood. Our property covered nearly an acre, which began on Bristol and ended on Cliffwood. It was one of the few that went clear through from one street to the other. We had four next-door neighbours. In front, the Robert Prestons occupied one house and the Feddersons the other. For a while, Larry Olivier rented one of the Cliffwood houses and we became good friends with him and his son.

Across the street Frank Fay, who had been a big silent-screen star, owned the entire block. When my mother first moved into our house, Frank Fay was married to a young actress named Barbara Stanwyck, with whom Mommie became friends. They were about the same age, and when Barbara decided to end the marriage and escaped by climbing over the high wall entirely surrounding the Fay estate, my mother took her in until she could find another place to go. On Sundays Mr Fay often donated his estate to the Catholic church for fund-raising events. Mommie was always provoked by our street being filled with people and automobiles. The way she talked about the church people you would never have guessed that she'd once considered herself a Catholic. I never knew that she had been a Catholic until after her death.

Behind the Fay estate, Cole Porter had a beautiful house where Mommie often went for dinner parties. I visited it again years later when Mike Nichols was living in it. A few houses down the street Hal Roach and his family lived. I was friends with both daughters and we were always at one another's birthday parties.

Too far away for me to walk but still considered part of the neighbourhood lived Shirley Temple. Mommie took me to visit her once. Her parents greeted us at the door to a nice but not lavish house. The thing I remember most about the visit was our tour of Shirley Temple's closets! Her parents had saved all her clothes and all her movie costumes. Several entire rooms had been converted into closets that had big sliding doors that covered the length of the rooms on both sides. Inside the closets were two tiers of clothes racks filled with little dresses and every movie costume. The clothes seemed to be arranged chronologically because on the beginning of our tour we saw tiny little dresses which appeared to grow larger as the tour progressed. I never saw so many clothes; even my mother didn't have so many clothes, and she had closets filled to the brim. I actually did meet Shirley Temple that day, but my most vivid memory is of her incredible closets.

There were, of course, lots of other movie people who lived near us. Tyrone Power, the Henry Hathaways, whose son Danny was a favourite of mine, the Jaffes, whose son Andy was my very first boy-friend in elementary school, the Wheelwrights, and the McCauleys. Sharon and Linda McCauley were two of my closest friends, particularly Linda who was my age. We told each other all our secrets. She was just about the only person in the whole world that I totally trusted. She kept every confidence just as though she'd never heard it.

My early birthday parties have become a part of the Hollywood legend. In truth, there were only four years during which they resembled circus spectaculars.

My first birthday was celebrated quietly in New York City. It was my second birthday in Brentwood that initiated Mommie's extravaganzas for me. She invited fifteen children of varying ages to share the afternoon with me. She had a full merry-go-round set up on the badminton court in our back yard. In addition to the usual children's games, she provided a clown to entertain us. I remember vividly that I was absolutely terrified of that clown. When he came near me I screamed and ran to my

36

mother for protection. I guess everyone else just loved him.

The party on my third birthday was even more elaborate than the preceding year's party. Mommie invited twenty children who were sons and daughters of her friends in show business. We had the merry-go-round and the clown again but this year a complete puppet show was added and for some inexplicable reason she'd even found a *trained pig* ! The pig was dressed like a clown with a big ruffle around its neck and could sort of walk on just its hind legs. The pig was a big hit. After the merry-go-round and the puppet show and the clown and the pig, Mommie served all of us a supper in the main dining room.

But it was my fourth birthday party in June of 1943 that was the grandest spectacle of them all. It was a private circus, a miniature Disneyland before one ever existed for the public. There were balloons everywhere, and music filled the entire backyard. There were several brightly coloured clowns, an organ-grinder, and his monkey, who was in an adorable costume with a little red hat on his head. There were ponies to ride around the lawn, and I loved the pretty ponies best of all. There was also a magician who put on a wonderful magic show in a little portable theatre. There were all sorts of games to play. Group games like pin-the-tail-on-the-donkey and tug-of-war. All the little children were dressed up, even by Hollywood standards. The girls had fluffy dresses of pretty pastel fabrics and ribbons in their hair. The little boys wore short pants with velvet jackets and long socks and some had ties. All the children had a starched and polished look to their clothes and to their faces as well.

If this was a gathering of the progeny of Hollywood's royalty, then I was the crown princess. My dresses were of the finest hand-embroidered organdy. My petticoats and fancy panties were trimmed with lace and satin ribbons. My shoes and socks were so white they glistened. My pale golden hair fell in cascades of soft curls that were held away from my face with more satin ribbons. As closely as hours of devoted human effort could make me, I was perfectly beautiful. The perfect child in every respect : my clothes were certainly gorgeous, my manners irreproachable, my curtsey smooth, my hair softly golden. There was no doubt about it, I was the incarnation of the perfectly beautiful child.

37

Mommie had created me in the image of perfection and then created these birthday parties to celebrate another successful year of happiness with that creation.

The luncheon feast this year was held again in our formal dining room, which was nearly a separate wing in itself. The big dining room table was removed (heaven only knows where, since it could easily seat twenty-five people) and a rented table that could be lowered to 'kid size' was substituted. Then children's chairs were placed around the table in a scaled-down replica of adult formality. The table stretched nearly the length of the dining room and was decorated with wonderful fanciful figures and animals. Each child had a place card and party favours.

These little children sat at the long table without any smiles on their faces because they were on their best behaviour. We had little pointed hats on our heads like so many dunces. The mothers and servants hovered over us, ministering to our wants and passing around the food. The uniformed nannies in the background looked very stern in white starched uniforms and sensible shoes.

I sat at the head of that table presiding over a large group of four-, five-, and six-year-olds, but no one was paying much attention to me and I felt bewildered.

I didn't know most of the children who were invited to my parties very well. I only saw them a couple of times a year at other birthday parties. I often felt left out of the games and festivities because I was quite shy around large groups of people, even other children. Today, I cannot remember the names of most of the twenty or more children in the picture of my birthday party luncheon. I didn't know them then, and I don't know them now.

It was during those parties that I had my first memorable feelings of loneliness. It was my party and I was dressed up in organdy and lace and satin, feeling vaguely out of place.

Indeed, it was the year of my fourth birthday that I threw an absolute fit just as the children were scheduled to arrive. I was up in my room getting dressed with the nurse tying the bow of my pinafore and Mommie putting the finishing touches to the ribbons in my hair. I asked if my friend from two houses down

38

the street had arrived yet. She was supposed to come early. My mother said she'd forgotten to tell me, but that little girl would not be at the party. I looked directly into my mother's eyes and announced: 'In that case, I'm not going to the party either.' This was my special friend, she was my constant playmate during the week. She lived a few houses away from us and Mommie had told me that her mother was a housekeeper for the family who owned that house. My friend was black.

After my announcement, I sat down on the floor and refused to budge. There was much scurrying around, and in just a few minutes that little black face appeared in the doorway to my bathroom. She looked at me sitting in the middle of the floor and we both started to giggle. I got up and the two of us went hand in hand downstairs to my party.

Those legendary parties lasted until I was about six. After that there was just a group of school friends over for a swim, and many of my teenage birthdays were spent at boarding school.

During my growing-up years I came to depend rather heavily on the servants for some sense of continuity. A good deal of my happiness revolved around my nurse. She became the central person in my everyday life.

Several days before my fourth birthday, a Scottish lady named Mrs Howe came to take care of my infant brother and me. It was Mrs Howe who taught me to skip rope and ride a bicycle. She played tea party with me and I made dreadful concoctions out of sand and seeds and olive pits I found in the yard under the trees. I loved pretend games and could play them for hours, sometimes alternating between two and three characters at one time. Mrs Howe had a devil of a time teaching me to ride the bike because every time I fell off I'd get mad and cry and vow never to touch it again. But persistence paid off and eventually I learned. Mrs Howe was very firm with me but she was always honest and fair. It was this wonderfully tenacious woman who helped me through the first really serious punishment of my life.

I had to take a nap every day, but sometimes I just wasn't very sleepy. Often I would lie awake in my bed and tell myself stories I made up that had elaborate plots and running characters. I continued the stories from one day to another just like a serial. On this particular day I wasn't falling asleep, and I was bored with my current fantasy. I was about five and sharing a room with my brother, who was only two and still a baby. My bed was up against the wall on one side and as I daydreamed I ran my finger over a seam in the wallpaper, tracing the design.

Without much real thought on my part, I picked at the seam. Before I knew it, several little pieces of the wallpaper had fallen away, leaving a small but obvious blank spot on the wall. All of a sudden I realized what I had done and tried to retrieve the little pieces of paper and attempted to stick them back together. I spat on the torn pieces and tried to patch the spot. It didn't work. Where the wallpaper had got wet there were now smudge marks. The whole thing looked worse than if I'd left it alone.

At about this time, Mrs Howe came in to get me up. When she saw what I'd done she slapped my hands and scolded me. I knew she'd have to tell my mother about it.

When Mommie came home she went to my room to see the reported damage for herself. Right then and there she put me over her knee and spanked the daylights out of me. I really howled. Mommie's spankings hurt.

But that was not the end of it. She was determined to teach me a lesson that no amount of spanking could accomplish. That's what she said as she marched herself into my dressing room and opened the closet door. She reached inside and withdrew my favourite dress. It wasn't the fanciest dress nor the most expensive, but it was my favourite and she knew it. It was a yellow dress with white eyelet embroidery, and it looked like a spring daffodil.

Mommie held it up ominously. She took it off the hanger and went to a drawer where the scissors were kept. I looked at Mrs Howe, but she appeared to be as mystified as I was.

When my eyes returned to my mother, who was across the room, I was horrified. Mommie had taken the scissors and completely shredded my favourite yellow dress! It was hanging in tatters with just barely enough shape left to indicate it had been a dress and not just a rag. Tears sprang to my eyes and I started to cry.

Then my mother marched towards me holding the tattered dress in front of her. The sound of her voice stopped my tears. She told me that I was going to have to *wear* that shredded thing for *one week*! If anyone asked me why I was wearing a torn dress I was to reply only, 'I don't like pretty things.' With that pronouncement she dropped the dress at my feet and left.

Mrs Howe and I were both stunned. Finally it was Mrs Howe who made the first move. She helped me change into what was left of my poor yellow dress.

That next week seemed interminable. I cried most of the time and kept to myself. I was mortified at my appearance and tried to become invisible. Mercifully, none of the servants ever mentioned the dress and they tried to behave as though there was nothing wrong.

The one humiliating time that I had to go downstairs to see company on my mother's orders, I simply stared at the floor and tried to get through it as fast as possible. My mother's brief explanation regarding my shocking appearance was that she was teaching me a lesson. When I was dismissed, I ran for the safety of my own room.

Within a few days the dress was soiled. I thought maybe it would be washed but that did not happen. I wore that dress every day, all day, for one solid week. As the days went by it got dirtier and dirtier until it was nothing but a filthy rag. The material had unravelled and there wasn't much left to cover me except my underwear. You could hardly tell that it had once been yellow.

As I struggled through the disintegration of my most favourite yellow dress and the humiliation of looking like a street urchin, I wondered if I wouldn't have been better off left in an orphanage.

My mother seemed oblivious to my pain. No one comforted me. No one seemed to want to even talk to me. I felt like a social outcast, my sins too serious to be mentioned. By the end of the week, what I'd originally done was totally overshadowed in my mind by this hideous lingering, living punishment.

At the end of the seventh day, after I had taken my bath and got into my nightclothes, I marched myself down to the incinerator and threw the filthy ragged remains of what had been my favourite yellow dress into the coals and watched as it sank into the soft grey ashes.

I didn't find out until years later that Mrs Howe had told the rest of the help what had happened. They'd all agreed not to ask me about the dress so I wouldn't ever have to give the answer my mother had prepared for me.

While Mommie and Phillip were married there were times when they forced me to choose between them. I remember the last time. An argument occurred over which movie to show at home, his or hers. They turned to me to cast the deciding vote. I didn't want to see either one, I just wanted to get out of there. But I'd never seen a film of Phillip's so I thought I should choose his film. They were angry with each other for some reason, and at that point my mother walked out of the room. 'Call me when you've decided,' she snapped at me as she left.

I waited a moment feeling very uncomfortable with Phillip staring at me and knowing it was up to me to decide. We were standing in the kitchen, and when I figured that she'd had enough time to get upstairs, I called my mother on the house phone. I couldn't look Phillip in the face as I told Mommie which movie I wanted to see. That evening we screened a film starring Joan Crawford.

It wasn't long after that night that Phillip left. One day he just didn't come home again. I don't think much was said about it, except that he wouldn't be back. I never even had a chance to say goodbye to him. He was just gone.

Phillip had been a nice man and I did miss him. But Mommie did cruel things he couldn't seem to prevent. Like the time my nurse found me tied up in the shower with the door closed. And another time when Mommie locked me in the linen closet with the lights off as a punishment. Mommie knew I was scared of the dark. I thought rats might come down from the attic and eat me alive.

After Phillip left, an amazing thing happened. Within twenty-four hours there was not a trace of him left anywhere in the entire house. His room and bath were stripped of every single personal item. All the pictures of him in my mother's room and the library downstairs were gone. And in our baby scrapbooks where all the photographs of my brother and me were neatly mounted on page after page, Phillip's image was ripped out of every picture in each of our books! Sometimes only his head was ripped off. Other pictures were torn down the middle to remove him completely. One or two of the photos were left with just a severed male hand sticking out beyond the torn part. Except for those mutilated photographs it was as if he had never existed at all, that he had just been a figment of my imagination. I remember feeling it was so scary to think of someone just disappearing all of a sudden that I couldn't think about it much. We never dared mention his name again after we found the torn pictures. It was years before we ever saw him again.

The lesson indelibly etched on me was that when Mommie dearest got mad enough she ripped people to shreds and made them disappear. Somehow my Mommie dearest could make grown people like Phillip disappear. That thought scared me so much it was like falling into eternal darkness.

I spent more than twenty-five years trying to make sure my Mommie dearest loved me, trying to win her acceptance and approval so she wouldn't get that mad and make me disappear too.

FOUR

We used to spend part of each summer up north in Carmel. At first we went as a family but beginning when I was eight, I spent six weeks each summer at Douglas Camp.

It was a long drive up the coast in those days. We left home in the afternoon and spent the first night in Santa Maria. The next day we would complete the journey to Carmel. We always stayed at the Del Monte Lodge in a private cottage. At lunch in the big dining room we looked out over the green lawns and to the sea beyond. Mommie was always happier here. She seemed to relax and enjoy us more than she did in Los Angeles.

There were many years when my mother never left California. The longest trip she took would be to Carmel with my brother and me. Douglas Fairbanks, Jr, had taken her to Europe on their honeymoon in the 1920s and she'd been to New York on the train numerous times, but for nearly thirty years, mostly she lived and worked in Los Angeles. She just didn't take long vacations. She'd spend a week with us in Palm Springs, La Quinta, or Carmel, but that was the extent of it. Instead of a vacation she'd create busy work at home, cleaning out basements and answering an endless stream of correspondence. Carmel, then, was a super treat for all of us.

My mother would knit and read and take walks while we went horseback riding or swimming. She loved the country. We used to go for long walks picking wildflowers and watching the dog jumping through the long grass. She didn't play golf but

44

she liked tennis. She would always have stacks of scripts and weeks of trade papers to read and the comic-strip section from the Sunday papers, which she called the funnies. The comic strips and gossip columns were cut out of the daily newspapers for her to read when she had time and the rest of the paper went into the trash.

After a few days in Carmel, she'd be telling jokes and playing tricks on us. Mother valued a sense of humour and insisted that we develop one. More often than not, it was at our own expense.

At first she'd point out some foolishness in our behaviour and we'd be required to laugh, although I usually felt more like crying from embarrassment. By the time I was just eight or nine, I learned to laugh whether I felt like it or not because our mother could get quite provoked if you didn't see the humour as she saw it.

It was a curious sort of training, as I look back on it. She was preparing us for the world outside as she knew it. It was something you had to practise, this sense-of-humour business, and she gave each of us ample opportunity. There was something about the specifics of what she found so funny that made me feel naked and unprotected, as though she could see through my skin and into the secret vulnerabilities of my soul. Her wit could be brutal. She said she knew those unspoken secrets because she had eyes in the back of her head. I believed her.

She also loved dirty jokes. She loved to tell them, and she equally enjoyed hearing them from others. I usually tried to escape quietly during one of these sessions because I learned quickly that they were not winning situations for me. I knew that if I laughed she'd turn to me and ask me to explain the punch line and if I didn't laugh she'd get a kick out of making sure everyone knew I didn't understand enough about sex yet to get the point of the joke. There was something mortifying about having to laugh at your own expense under such scrutiny. It was something she didn't do when we were alone, but she found it irresistible with an audience.

Mother particularly loved walking along the ocean and each visit must have walked miles before we left Carmel. One night she was restless and asked me to go for a walk with her. It was dark, and we didn't have a flashlight. But the sky was relatively

45

clear and the moon was bright. I followed her across the lawns
to the seawall. We walked along the seawall with only the sound
of the waves pounding and the dampness of the sea spray for
company. It was a lonely place.

We sat down on some flat rocks and looked out towards the
open sea. We sat there in silence a long time. She took my hand
and held it firmly. Very softly she starting talking to me. I had
to lean towards her to hear above the sound of the surf crashing
against the rocks. She looked so beautiful in the moonlight that
I had a hard time listening to what she was saying. The wind
blew her hair gently away from her face and her profile was
illuminated by the moon and reflections from the clouds. She
was talking to me about life, about herself and what she wanted
and how hard it was to get ... how hard it was to be happy.
She said that I made her happy, but all of life wasn't that easy.
She told me how poor she'd been and how lonely as a child, how
hard it had been for her. She talked for a long time, and I tried
with all my might to understand what she was saying to me. But
some things I couldn't understand. I was only about seven and I
just didn't know what she was talking about. So I held on to
her hand with all my strength and concentrated on her face. I
never took my eyes off her for an instant. I was trying so hard to
understand, to help her. She started to cry. She said she wasn't
really sad but that it was so beautiful here. I put my arms
around her neck, hugging and kissing her. I wished with all my
heart that I could make it all right for her. 'I love you, Mommie
dearest' was all I could say. She turned and looked at me
through tears. She smiled at me. Then she ran her finger across
my forehead as though to smooth away a frown. She rumpled
my hair and gave me a hug. 'Let's go, it's getting cold.'

She held my hand the whole way back. At one point she stopped and looked at me. 'You don't understand very much of what
I've said, do you?' In despair I shook my head no. She almost
sighed as she said, 'It's all right, Tina ... You'll understand
more when you're a little older.'

When we got back to the cottage she made me some hot
chocolate and we sat in front of the fire until I fell asleep with
my head in her lap.

I've wondered if I hadn't been seven and if I'd understood all

46

the things she said to me that night – I've wondered many times if my life with her would have been any different.

The first starring role my mother did for Warners under her new contract was a picture for Jerry Wald called *Mildred Pierce*. Jerry had to fight the front office to get her the part and after nearly three years without any work at all, she was very nervous when the picture started shooting. She left for the studio about 5 A.M. while it was still dark and wouldn't return until well after dinner. Sometimes she didn't get home until after we were asleep. She worked on the picture six days a week, and on Sunday she slept until almost noon. Sunday afternoons were taken up with the hairdresser, the manicurist, and finally the masseuse, who came to the house in succession to prepare her for the coming week's work. We rarely saw her during those days, but since we had a nice nurse at the time, our lives went fairly smoothly. Mother was so glad to be working again in a good film with a really good part that she hardly had time to think about anything else. During the three years she hadn't worked most of our house had been closed up, the furniture covered, and the doors closed to any rooms not necessary for everyday life. Despite the display she put on with the occasional lavish parties, those were the days of no extra servants, and she did some of the housework. For a while even our big kitchen was closed down and we cooked over a Sterno stove in the basement. We had to help in any way we could, but my brother and I were still too young to be of much real use. Because of the war, our entire front lawn was turned into a Victory garden, and after our Japanese gardener was taken off to a relocation camp quite suddenly, we had to tend the vegetables ourselves.

But now, in 1945, even though the house seemed emptier without Mr Terry, life was going better for my mother. Unfortunately, the picture couldn't last indefinitely and the day eventually came when it was finished.

So, Mother spent more time at home and our lives changed drastically. I went to Gretna Green public school and left every morning long before she got up. Jenny, the cook, would wake me, and after breakfast off to school I went with my lunch box. When I came home my mother was usually out and I went to play with my brother.

At first only weekends were difficult. We lived according to a rigid and unchanging schedule. We got up every day at the same time whether it was Monday or Saturday. We ate breakfast at the same time and did the dishes and made our beds right on schedule. The older we got, the more inflexible the schedule became.

Since our lives were run like the army, we had a half hour to eat each meal, the next half hour to wash the dishes and the rest of the day was fully programmed too. We were not allowed in the kitchen except to get things necessary to set the table.

The cook was a crucial factor in my life. If we happened to have a cook who had not only talent but also some compassion, I fared rather well. If not, my life became miserable. There weren't many foods I absolutely hated, thank God, but there was one : blood-rare meat.

During and right after the war, meat was scarce and my mother bought it on the black market. She lost no time in telling us how expensive it was and how lucky we were. We were to remember 'the starving children of Europe' and eat every single scrap of food on our plates. That was no idle threat, either. Nothing easy, like no dessert if we failed to heed her warning. The punishment for not eating had a number of different phases to it. First, if I didn't finish the quivering piece of reddish-blue meat in the time allotted for meals, I indeed received no dessert, but that was only the beginning. I didn't really care about the dessert part very much, but when it was evident that we were going to have beef of any kind for dinner, I would beg the cook to give me a well-done piece. My pleading was done in whispers, of course, so the nurse couldn't hear me. Even if my mother wasn't home she left strict orders for everyone in the house to report any infringement of the rules to her. If there were no broken rules reported for more than a few days, Mommie figured someone was holding out and the household inquisition began. Most of the time, I guess it was less trouble for the people who worked there just to follow the rules, even if they didn't agree with them.

Anyway, sometimes my pleading went for naught and I ended up with the blood-rare food on my plate. Mommie had an idea that at those black market prices, it was more nutritious for us

48

rare. We'd all heard the story of how Mother had rickets as a child, suffering from malnutrition. She said we should be grateful that she cared about us enough to provide such good food.

I wished I could have sent all of my portion of that meat to those starving children for the duration of the war. But when the war was over I could not understand : if meat was still so expensive and I hated it so much, why did I have to eat it?

One night when we were served black market steak, I tried to eat the nearly raw meat in teeny bites covered up with whatever else was on the plate. I wasn't allowed to drink my milk with my food, so I couldn't just put a little piece in my mouth and wash it down. Try as I might, the food never came out even. I would eat all the cooked edges of the meat and be left staring at the blood-rare centre. I could not swallow those pieces because every time I tried to, I gagged.

So, at the end of the half-hour mealtime, my plate was removed to the refrigerator to await breakfast. The next morning, I got a glass of milk and that cold plate which by now was greasy and yukky. I was not allowed to sit down at the table, but had to stand at my place for the entire half hour. I did drink my milk, and that was all.

Very well, back to the refrigerator with my plate. Lunch progressed the same.

So far, since lunch yesterday I'd had two glasses of milk and lots of water. I could hear my stomach gurgle and I didn't feel very well. I didn't think it was funny or cute and I honestly wasn't trying to be impossible.

For dinner I had the same plate cold from the refrigerator but now I was not allowed at the table. I had to stand and stare at this horrible grungy plate placed on top of the chest freezer on the back porch. I guess my plate was becoming an unpleasant sight for the rest of the table. I tried to eat a couple of pieces of the wretched meat and ended up vomiting in the servants' toilet.

The next morning I didn't even want to get up. I knew that awful plate was down in the refrigerator waiting for me. And the worst of it was that now I was really getting hungry. Three glasses of milk were not enough to keep a nine-year-old going for very long. I was beginning to think of ways to hide pieces of the meat so it would look like I was eating it. But there was no place to hide it, and our dog was not allowed near us during meals.

Breakfast smelled delicious. Bacon and eggs were cooking and the aroma reached up to my bedroom. My stomach was not gurgling now, it was growling. I went downstairs thinking that the ordeal just might be over. After all, I was just a kid and it was two full days since I'd been allowed a meal. I set the table with a place for myself as usual. When the nurse came downstairs, she told me I would not be allowed breakfast until I finished my plate of old food at the freezer. I couldn't believe it.

I marched myself out to the freezer and there it was: the same plate from two days ago. How I hated the sight of it. I felt completely helpless. Why did everybody hate me? It's just unfair. What did I do that was so bad? I hate bloody meat; so what? Everybody hates something. Even Mother – she told me so herself. When she was a little girl, she took a big helping of what she thought were mashed potatoes. Her mother told her if she took that much on her plate she'd have to eat all of it. Mother laughed and said she'd be happy to. It turned out to be mashed turnips on her plate, not mashed potatoes. She hated turnips, but Grandmother made her eat every mouthful.

I looked down at my plate and cried. I just stood there getting madder by the minute, smelling the bacon and eggs for everyone else. When my half hour was up I marched in without a word, put the plate in the refrigerator and did the dishes. I'd been doing dishes since I was four years old and had to stand on a step stool to reach the sink. For some peculiar reason it pleased my mother to tell people that I'd been doing dishes since I was four.

Someone telephoned Mother at the studio to tell her that I wouldn't eat, and I had to talk to her that afternoon. When I called her at the studio she yelled at me for being a selfish, ungrateful child. How could I be so ungrateful with all the starving children in the world? Didn't I realize how hard she worked to pay for all the things we had? How much better off we were than other children? I was to go to bed early without any dinner and she'd take care of the spanking tomorrow. She hung up without saying goodbye.

I lay in my bed crying. I wasn't even hungry any more. I

didn't understand why she got so mad at me, why everything I did seemed to make her angry. I thought about the starving children. I thought about running away from home, but I had nowhere to go.

FIVE

There were now four children in the Crawford house. When I was eight years old my brother, whose name had been changed to Christopher, and I moved into Mr Terry's old room and our former bedroom was redecorated as a nursery. We awaited the arrival of what we were told were twins. Several times we thought they were being delivered and the entire household quivered with expectation. And several times we were disappointed because the new babies did not arrive. The long-awaited moment came without fanfare one day at lunch when a baby broker brought two infant girls to our back door. They looked adorable and we were very excited but they did not look like twins to any of us. Mommie explained all that away by saying they were fraternal rather than identical twins. She had ordered twins from the broker and twins they were going to be. She named one girl Cathy and one girl Cynthia. The two babies were taken up to their nursery and gradually took their place in the family.

On Saturday mornings from the time we got up, through breakfast, through all our regular chores, and even when we went out into the back yard to play, if Mommie was home and asleep we were not allowed to speak above a whisper. The nurse had to whisper and the rest of the servants had to whisper. The entire household had to whisper until Mommie was ready to get up, even though it was a twenty-two-room house and her bedroom was totally secluded.

Whispering inside the house was difficult at best, but whispering out in the back yard past the pool was impossible. Our property covered nearly an acre so it never made sense to me, but that was the rule.

It was very hard to think up games that didn't require talking. The easiest was hide-and-seek but a silent version of cowboys and Indians came in second. It must have been quite funny to watch us 'galloping' around the yard with our toy six-shooters, whispering 'Bang, bang' and the victim falling to the ground silently. Badminton was also easy to play without any noise but we didn't have enough people. In the summertime we could go swimming, but we were forbidden to splash or dive or make any noise. So Chris and I became adept at underwater swimming and played all our games under the surface. We even learned to talk to each other underwater, which was hilarious.

If the weather was bad and we had to stay indoors, whispering was a torture because we weren't allowed to play the radio or any of our records. We played only silent games.

In addition to the whispering rule, we also had to walk on tiptoe as long as Mommie slept. It may sound ludicrous, but it wasn't in the least bit funny. The whole house whispered and tiptoed around until Mommie decided to get up. More often than not she arose just before lunch. If we were out in the yard we could see the venetian blinds at her bedroom windows open and that was the signal that she was up. Usually she would call out to us and say good morning. But even if she didn't, we would know that the open blinds meant she was awake. Then we would go into the house to check and make sure that the cook had received the call for her breakfast. If she had, it was safe to talk in a normal tone of voice. If she hadn't, it was still whispers. And if Mommie didn't get up before our regular lunchtime, we had to continue to whisper through that meal and into the afternoon.

This was not a special-occasion procedure; it was not connected in my mother's mind to any kind of punishment, either. It was standard, everyday procedure, one of the many household rules that were fully enforced all the years I lived at home. It was made clear to all of us that this was Mommie's house, to be run entirely on her orders, for her personal convenience. No one else had any rights, no one else had any say in what went on or how things were to be done. Since she paid all the bills, she pointed out to us that it was her privilege to have things done exactly as she wanted them and that was that. There was no further discussion, there was never any negotiation on that or any other subject once she'd given her opinion. And about the whispering she was adamant. If we ever made a sound that should have the awful misfortune to be blamed for waking her before she was ready to arise, the entire house heard her wrath. If we were outside playing, those venetian blinds would fly open and her voice would bellow across the garden: 'Goddammit ... how many times do I have to tell you to keep your voices down!' All movement would come to a halt in the yard. The nurse, Chris, and I would literally freeze in our places. 'Christina, you come in this house this instant.' With that, the bedroom window would slam shut.

Slowly I trod towards the house, knowing that one of those vile spankings that hurt for days was in store for me. Mommie was always in a terrible mood if anyone accidentally woke her up and the spankings for this infringement of the rules conveyed the full force of her anger. She spanked so hard she broke hairbrushes, wooden hangers, and yardsticks across my bottom. The spankings left large painful blisters and the long red welts would be visible for days.

In the fortuitous event that nothing roused Mommie prematurely from her bed, one of us would take her breakfast tray upstairs to her dressing table. Many mornings when I arrived to set the tray carefully on the large glasstop table, she was across the room at the sink, washing her face in a bucket of ice water and then taking two aspirin. It wasn't until later years that I understood the significance of the aspirin. No one looks terrific when she first gets up, but my mother looked about as far away from being a movie star at this time of day as anyone could imagine. Even in the summertime she wore white pyjamas that were tailored like men's pyjamas. She had dozens of sets of them exactly alike except that they had different-coloured piping around the edges and matching coloured monograms. Under the pyjama top she wore a white T-shirt and on her feet she wore white socks. Sometimes she even wore white gloves to keep the cream on her hands during the night. She had short red hair, which she kept away from the cream on her face with an elasticized headband. When she got up in the morning her hair, somehow, was always standing straight up, looking like a firecracker explosion. To top off this outfit, she had her face tied up with something called a chin strap. Before she had breakfast she unravelled all this paraphernalia and put on a robe. I would stay a minute or two and then scurry down to lunch.

On Sunday if she got up in time we had to go to church. We got dressed up and drove to the Christian Science church in Beverly Hills. Most of the time I went to Sunday school, which I hated. Not the school itself, but the whole process. Because we didn't go often enough, I had to go to the office each time and be reassigned to a class. I seldom knew either the teacher or any of the other children and usually was behind in the lessons. I liked the singing but used to wish that the rest of it would just be over quickly. I was given a quarter for the donation, which I had securely tucked inside my white glove. We didn't necessarily have to wear a hat, but I always had to wear white gloves whenever we went anywhere. Once in a while, I was allowed to go inside the big church and sit with my mother. I would try to sit very still and be a good girl. Even though I liked the big church better than Sunday school, it was hard to sit still that long, especially since I didn't really understand most of the words in Mary Baker Eddy's book. The singing was nice and I knew most of the words to the hymns, so I enjoyed that part, and looked out the window or daydreamed through the rest of it.

The problem came on the way home when Mother asked me the inevitable question: 'What did you learn today in church?' Try as I might, I never quite got the whole thing straight. I could remember some of the Bible stories but not much from Mrs Eddy. Mother would sigh and explain the parts I'd left out, and I would sit in silence the rest of the way home.

If we didn't go to church on Sunday, Mommie would call me into her sitting room after lunch while Chris took his nap. She sat on the couch and I sat on the floor. Together we did the lesson. Christian Science had each Sunday worked out so that you could do the lesson at home. I thought that was very clever. There was a small pamphlet that told you which chapters and verses of the Bible to read, followed by which pages from *Science and Health* by Mary Baker Eddy. By now I could read adequately and my mother regularly gave me some of the Bible parts to read aloud. When we had finished with that, she would read Mrs Eddy's words because I couldn't pronounce most of them. What I remember most is the part about God is good and there is no evil, sickness, or death. But again, I daydreamed through most of it.

After the lesson was over in about an hour and a half, and I'd had a few moments to stretch, my mother would place her regular call to Sorkie in New York. I met Sorkie only once when I was a very small child, but until her death in 1959, I know that she was the most influential person in Mommie's life. Sorkie was a Christian Science practitioner who lived by herself in a small New York City apartment. My mother had met her when she was younger and was devoted to her. Sorkie was a rotund woman, and to the best of my knowledge she is the only fat person my mother ever tolerated.

Mommie called Sorkie on Sundays and almost every other day of the week for a least twenty-five years. Sorkie knew everything there was to know about my mother, her children, her friends and every event in our lives. On Sunday we called Sorkie to tell her we loved her and had done our lessons. We always had to report to Sorkie after church as well. She had a kind voice with a slight accent and was always pleasant to talk with. After I dutifully told her I loved her, she would speak to my mother for a while. At those times I was not allowed in the room.

Mother depended on being able to call Sorkie at any time of the day or night. Sorkie was somehow *always* home and would talk for as long as needed. Mommie trusted her absolutely and as I look back I think she was the only person in the whole world that my mother did trust. Year after year, my mother poured out her troubles and her triumphs to Sorkie. Sorkie was there, just as close as the telephone.

Whenever there was trouble in the house, which became progressively more frequent, my mother would be on the phone to Sorkie for advice, solace, and absolution. I think Sorkie was the sustaining influence in an unpredictable existence. Sorkie was a combined surrogate mother, spiritual leader, and emotional counsellor. Although my mother categorically refused to consider any form of psychological guidance in later years, I think in many ways Sorkie provided a kind of therapy as well.

But for my brother and me it was infuriating to have a voice on the phone be so overwhelmingly influential in our lives. When we got in serious fights with our mother or some equally disastrous event had taken place, we either had to speak to Sorkie, who usually made us apologize to Mother, or Mother herself would call Sorkie and transmit to us whatever advice she had received. One way or the other, the result was that Mother was right and we were wrong and nothing much had changed except that Mother felt vindicated and morally justified in meting out the punishment that always followed.

I don't know if Sorkie ever really knew the true story of the way we were treated at home, given that our mother was prone to exaggeration about everything. But I do know that among her friends no one had the influence over my mother that Sorkie did. Most people didn't even know about the relationship except that Mommie had a Christian Science practitioner in New York. But for me, Sorkie's voice over the phone was often the court of last resort. Though she was supposed to be a kind woman, her decision was rarely in my favour.

The religion did not preclude our being sent to doctors nor prevent Mother from drinking and smoking. Those were ideals, she explained, goals towards which one worked. We had regular checkups by old Dr Fish, and when we were sick he came to the house.

Mother also had her doctors upon whom she relied increasingly as the years went by. It might be an oversimplification to say that later on she became a hypochondriac, but it was something very close to that. There were times, however, when her fetish for cleanliness took possession of her. It was then that she took three and four showers a day and brushed her teeth every few hours. She could not stand to have her hands dirty and would wash them repeatedly. She had one closet with shelves full of cleansing potions for every part of her body and used them all with religious fervor. No matter how often she bathed and scrubbed, it never seemed sufficient; it just managed to keep the worst of the scourges at arm's length.

My mother's preoccupation with cleanliness permeated the house we lived in. When Mommie wasn't working she organized regular cleaning forays into every nook and cranny of the house and yard. No sergeant in charge of latrine duty could have done better. It was at these times when frustration or anxiety or sheer insanity overtook her that she mustered every able-bodied creature within shouting distance and pressed them into service. We were an unlikely crew, always falling far short of her expectations. We were never fast enough or diligent enough or tenacious enough to please her. She fired commands faster than any number of us could carry them out and that sent her into a frenzy. She was surrounded by dolts and nincompoops, dunces and malingerers. Was no one besides herself even remotely competent in this world? Was it so much to ask that literate human beings obey a simple order? Why was she chosen out of the multitude to suffer the indignities of inferior servants and simpleminded children? Through these exhortations and the added threat of permanent, total banishment from her presence for ever, she prodded her troops ever onward. Under her command, three female fans, a nurse, a secretary, and two small children accomplished miracles. Together we moved tons of books, boxes, furniture, and clothing. In teams we cleaned out closets, scrubbed down and repainted lawn furniture. We moved trunks from one storage basement to another. We hauled and swept and pushed and pulled and mopped and rearranged until she was satisfied or until her own craziness subsided, whichever came first.

But the worst of these voyages into cleanomania were what later became known between my brother and myself as the night raids.

What was so terrifying about the night raids was that they could not be predicted. They sprang full blown without warning. We were always asleep and it was always dark outside when they started. Months would go by without a night raid and then there it would be, startling you out of a sound sleep, running full speed ahead and already out of control.

What mysterious combination of external and internal events led up to my mother's volcanic behaviour? I still do not know. What I know is that they were the most dreaded of all the journeys she took us through.

Three night raids are still vividly clear in my mind and they are typical of the others.

Chris and I had already moved into Mr Terry's former room, which had been redecorated for us with twin beds, new wallpaper, and new furniture. There were sliding-door closets in the bathroom that Chris used and a large walk-in closet for me right across from my bed near the door.

I was awakened out of a sound sleep one night by a crashing sound. I opened my eyes, sitting bolt upright in bed. I saw that my closet door was open, the light was on, and various pieces of clothing were flying out into the room. Inside the closet my mother was in a rage. She was swearing a blue streak and muttering to herself. I dared not move out of my bed for fear of her wrath being taken out on me directly. After the closet was totally demolished and everything in it spewed out onto my bed and the floor, Mommie emerged breathless and triumphant. She had a wild look in her eyes, and as she descended upon me I was terrified.

She grabbed me by the hair and dragged me into the closet. There before me I saw total devastation. The closet was in complete shambles. It looked as if she'd taken her arms and pushed everything off the shelves. Then she'd ripped the clothes off their hangers and thrown both clothes and hangers out into the room, where they lay sprawled over half the floor. Last to go were the shoes, which she'd thrown hard enough to hit the far wall of the bedroom. They clattered against the venetian blinds as they fell.

Shaking me by the hair of my head she screamed in my ear, 'No wire hangers! No wire hangers!' With one hand she pulled me by the hair and with the other she pounded my ears until they rang and I could hardly hear her screaming. When she finished hitting me she released my hair and dumped me on the floor. Then she ripped my bed apart down to the mattress cover, throwing the sheets and blankets across the room. When she had totally destroyed my entire part of the bedroom she stood in the doorway with her hands on her hips. 'Clean up your mess,' she growled, turning on her heel. The only other sound I heard was the double doors to her room slamming shut.

Had I bothered to look at the clock I would have seen it was

59

well past midnight. I didn't make the effort because it was a useless waste of my strength. I did look to see if Chris was still alive in the next bed. Once he was sure that she was gone and not coming back, he turned his body slowly to face me. It was probably the first time he'd dared to stir since the beginning of the night raid. He couldn't get up because he was tied down to the bed. Mother had a barbaric device she called a 'sleep safe' with which she made sure Chris could not get out of bed. It was like a harness made of heavy canvas straps, and it fastened at the back. It was orignally designed to keep babies from falling out of bed, but she had the thing modified to accommodate a growing boy. The way it worked was that the person lay face down upon the sheet and the straps that came from underneath the mattress went around his waist and across his shoulders. All four pieces were fastened together with a huge steel safety pin like the kind they use for horse blankets. From the time I can remember, we were forbidden to get out of bed at night to go to the bathroom or to get a drink of water without specific permission. Sometimes we would yell our lungs out and no one would come. There were times when my brother simply had to go to the bathroom, and I would undo the wretched sleep safe and stand guard while he raced to the bathroom and then jumped back into bed. We had it timed just like an Indianapolis pit stop because both our lives depended on expert teamwork. I would have got in more trouble than Chris if we'd ever been caught, and we both knew it. He would get beaten for getting out of bed but I would have been nearly killed for letting him out of the sleep safe.

When I was small Mommie had tried the sleep safe on me. I hated the contraption so much that I begged her to let me sleep without it, promising never to get out of bed without permission. But my brother was a very active boy and my mother got out the sleep safe once again. From the time he was a baby, she kept him tied down to the bed. As Chris grew, so did the sleep safe. Eventually it became a source of continual punishment for my brother. Every night he was pinned into this harness, even though he was way past the baby stage. There were many times he railed against the insult, against the physical evidence of mistrust his mother was bestowing upon him by forcing him to be tied down every night of his life, but he was just helpless to do anything about it. The sleep safe conspiracy my brother and I formed was just one example of how we managed to survive.

This particular night raid my brother had escaped scot-free and I didn't begrudge him that. He couldn't get up to comfort me and didn't even dare whisper for fear she would hear us and return. He looked at me sadly, and through my tears I stared back at him. My head hurt where she had grabbed my hair, and, as I gingerly rubbed the place, a few snatches of hair fell out. But the frightful ringing in my ears was beginning to subside. I was grateful the beating was over.

Slowly I pulled myself to my feet and surveyed the damage. All this, I thought, for a couple of lousy wire hangers. Something had come back from the cleaner's or the laundry downstairs on wire hangers. Mother forbade us to use them in our closets. I hadn't changed to the proper hangers right away. I guess it hadn't seemed so terribly important at the time, which I now regretted.

It took me hours to redo the closet with everything neatly folded and put back on the shelves, all the clothes returned to their proper covered hangers. I blearily mated the shoes and lined them neatly on their rack. Just as I turned out the closet light I remembered that my bed still had to be remade and seriously thought about just sleeping on the floor. But there was always the possibility that she might return, and I dared not chance a repeat performance. As I struggled to remake my bed in near exhaustion I realized that it was beginning to get light outside.

The day after one of the night raids, all was ominously silent. I don't know if the servants knew about the raids and simply kept their doors locked or if our room was far enough away that the sound didn't carry to the other side of the house. Generally Mother didn't speak a word to me for several days after a night raid, and, in fact, I rarely saw her. I was sort of silently banished for a period of time, and then, as mysteriously as it had materialized, the situation disappeared and life returned to near normal.

There was one night raid the whole house heard because it

61

took place in my mother's dressing room with all the doors wide open and lasted for a long time.

As punishment for some infringement of the rules, my mother had decreed that while she was out for the day I had to clean her dressing room. It was a large room with mirrored walls over the sink at one end of the room and the glass-top dressing table at the other. The floor was blue linoleum and there were two white fluffy throw rugs. During the better part of the afternoon I had cleaned the mirrors, polished the dressing table, and scoured the sink. Then I scrubbed the floor with a mop and dried it on my hands and knees with a towel so it wouldn't streak. Both the nurse and I were satisfied that I'd done a good job even though I wasn't more than nine years old. It had been one of the hardest jobs I'd been given to do all alone and I was glad it was over. I didn't get to play outside at all that day, but at least the punishment was over.

Mother didn't come home until after I was asleep and in the middle of that night one of the most vicious night raids took place.

I was sound asleep in my bed when Mother burst into my room. She was already yelling as she hauled me out of bed. Before I was fully awake she had dragged me by one arm down the hallway that connected her suite of rooms with ours. Through the open double doors I stumbled as she shoved me ahead of her. I had no idea what was wrong or where we were going, but I was now wide awake. When we arrived in her dressing room it began to dawn on me what was happening.

Something was evidently wrong with the way I'd cleaned the room earlier in the day, even though the nurse had inspected all my work. The best I could gather from my mother's ranting and raving was that the floor had soap streaks in it. I couldn't see anything wrong with it, but then neither I nor anyone else seemed to have the same set of standards she did. Then I made one of my classic mistakes and said that I didn't see anything wrong with the floor. That sent her into a renewed fit of anger. With lightning speed she backhanded me squarely across the face, which caught me off balance and sent me to the floor. She threw open the door under the sink and grabbed a large can of Bon Ami scouring powder. Just as I got to my feet she flew at me in a frenzy, wielding the can of Bon Ami like a baseball bat. She beat me over the head with the Bon Ami until the can burst open with a small explosion. A cloud of white scouring powder filled the entire room, settling over every square inch of mirror and glass and linoleum. I had that powder in my hair and all over my nightgown. It was getting into my mouth and I spluttered and spat it out for fear it would poison me. She was still screaming and beating me with the now mutilated can. By this time I was yelling back at her to stop hitting me and the noise must have awakened everyone.

Finally she threw the useless container across the room in total disgust. It looked as though it had been snowing inside these four walls.

'Clean it up,' she said. 'How?' I moaned. 'You figure it out,' she stormed at me, and left.

I sat down and a puff of white scouring powder billowed up around me. I couldn't believe the terrible mess that faced me. I couldn't use a vacuum cleaner because we had one of those old-fashioned uprights good only for carpets. All I had to work with was a broom, a bucket, a couple of big towels, and a mop.

I had to go over every inch of that room four or five times because the scouring powder made a white paste as soon as it got wet and there was an entire can of it scattered around the room. It was tedious and torturous work. Before I could even begin, I had to wash my own face and neck. The powder stuck to the rest of my body and as I sweated with the hard work, little rivulets of perspiration coagulated with the powder in white patches that began to itch. There was no time to go and take a shower, so I just continued to try and clean up the unbelievable mess.

Through the whole night I worked and sobbed. I didn't even care if anyone heard me as I trudged through the process again and again, trying to get the damnable white powder cleaned up. I prayed to God to punish my mother and told anyone who would listen how much I hated her.

Somewhere around four thirty in the morning I decided that I could work no longer. I didn't care if she punished me again, I just couldn't do any better. If it wasn't perfect, I couldn't help it. I was only nine years old and I couldn't do any more. I truly wished that the earth would open and just swallow me up and take me out of this eternal misery and punishment. I sobbed as I wrung out the mop for the hundredth time and I sobbed as I emptied the dirty water in the bucket. I sobbed as I walked to my room and I was still crying in the warm shower.

It was nearly five o'clock in the morning when I wearily climbed back into bed and still the tears were streaming down. Finally I just gave up fighting and cried myself to sleep.

There was one night raid that was not directed at me personally and was not intended as a specific punishment for any of us. This particular night raid was my mother's alone, although we all participated.

It was summertime and the evenings were cool in Brentwood. That night the moon was nearly full and shone brightly over the garden. Sometime near midnight I was roused out of my bed by the nurse. She whispered for me to put on my robe and slippers immediately and come downstairs. I peered at her face trying to discern what was going on but she just looked tired and agitated. Quickly I followed her instructions and together we hurried down the stairs and she led me out into the yard. Once outside I heard some noise over by the rose garden and could see a couple of people scurrying around.

We had a most wonderful rose garden. It was one of those old-fashioned formal gardens with stepping-stones through it and each plant labelled carefully. The roses it produced filled our house with lovely fragrant bouquets most of the year. It covered an area approximately fifteen by fifteen feet and had dozens of different varieties. Since it was summer, the entire garden was in bloom and even in the darkness the fragrance filled that part of the yard.

Nurse and I proceeded in the direction of the rose garden. As we came closer I saw Mother and the cook already in the middle of the rose garden. I didn't see particularly well in the dark and even with the extra light from the moon it wasn't until I was standing right at the hedge that separated the rose garden from the lawn that I fully realized what was going on.

Mother had a pair of large pruning shears with which she was systematically cutting each and every rosebush right to the ground! Because the garden was in full bloom, many of the bushes were nearly four feet tall. Most of them had great big flowers on them and as the branches fell to the ground, the lovely roses were getting trampled underfoot. I was horrified. I started to say something but the nurse quickly clamped her hand over my mouth. Since my mother's back was to us, she didn't see what had happened. She was finishing with one of the bushes, which was now not more than a stubby knob sticking a few inches out of the ground. She straightened up in preparation for a fresh assault on a neighbouring bush and saw me. As the moon lit up part of her face I could see that look in her eyes again. It was a haunted, excited look and there was no use trying to talk to her or stop her from completing her current course of destruction.

'I want all these branches cleared out of here,' she commanded with a sweeping gesture.

We had no gloves, no wheelbarrows or tools with which to work. I was grateful that my thin summer robe at least had long sleeves because there were large thorns on most of the branches. I don't know how long the poor cook had been out here, but the woman looked to be on the verge of tears. She was a plump, middle-aged woman who kept to herself and usually got along with Mother. The only trouble she'd had was when my mother threw out everything in the entire refrigerator during the cook's day off. When the cook returned, Mother informed her that the refrigerator had been a mess and she didn't want to find it that way again. Cook later told me that Mother had thrown out half a roast beef, a new ham, and all the fruit and vegetables as well as the leftovers which cook usually saved for the cleaning woman's lunch. Cook was furious with the waste and what she considered an unwarranted invasion of her domain. She was a fine cook and she took great pride in running an efficient kitchen. But, as usual, it was Mother's house and she could do whatever she wanted.

So, plump little cook trudged back and forth with armloads of prickly rose branches as did the nurse and I. We worked in silence punctuated only by mother's muttering to herself and by an occasional order from her to speed things up.

After about an hour of this thorny work, we were all scratched and bleeding. Mother wouldn't let us stop until we were finished so I licked the wounds on my arms and wiped my hands on my robe. We were all a bloody mess, but the job wasn't finished.

When Mother had finally succeeded in cutting every last rose-bush right down to the ground and the last branch had been hauled away, I thought we would be able to go back to bed. But there was one last surprise in store for us.

Mother told me to go down into the gardener's tool room by the incinerator and get the big saw. Totally mystified, I simply did what I was told and returned in a few minutes with the largest saw I could find. I handed it to her without saying a word. Talking to her when she was in these moods was equivalent to asking for a beating, and I had learned to keep my mouth shut and to just try to get through the ordeals as quietly and unobtrusively as humanly possible.

Mother took the big saw from me and walked over to the orange tree which stood at one end of the totally mutilated rose garden. It was a mature tree standing maybe eight feet tall, producing lots of oranges. It was covered with fruit.

The nurse, the cook, and I stood at a kind of breathless attention watching her as she began to saw the trunk of the orange tree! Finally we heard a cracking, splintering sound and the orange tree toppled over into the stubby remains of the rose garden.

When all was quiet again, my mother stood back to survey her night's destruction. Apparently satisfied, she ordered us all back to bed. The look on her face indicated a sort of jubilance.

Without a word we dispersed like shadows in the night. I climbed back into my bed without even bothering to wash. The blood had dried by now and wouldn't dirty my sheets so I could wait until morning for the clean-up.

The next day after breakfast I took Chris and we went to look at what had happened the night before. In the bright sunlight it really looked hideous. The beautiful rose garden was totally destroyed. I didn't know enough about plants to know if it would ever grow back, but it looked ugly and sad this morning. The fallen orange tree was not completely severed and dangled by its partly sawed-off trunk.

When the gardener showed up for work he went past the kitchen window as usual with his cheery 'Good morning'. It was only a moment later that the devastated rose garden came into his view. We waited with bated breath for his reaction since no one had the heart to tell him in advance because no one knew what to say. Mother was still asleep and the whispering rule was in effect. But Les didn't whisper when he saw the rose garden and the orange tree. He let out a graphic string of swear words that rang out loud and clear in the early morning air. As he stomped past the kitchen window again on his way out to his truck, he shouted so the entire neighbourhood could hear. 'You tell that crazy woman I quit!' That, unfortunately, was the last we ever saw of Les the gardener.

SIX

I don't have any pictures of Grandmother but I can remember her vividly. Her name was Anna and she was a small woman with brown hair, sparkly eyes, and a soft voice. She spoke with only a hint of a Southwest accent. She wore simple dark cotton dresses and plain black shoes. Mother didn't like the way she dressed. She said it was depressing to see those dark dresses with the little flowers and polka dots.

Grandmother could do everything. She made pickles and relish, jams and jellies. She made delicious pies and cakes and whenever she came to visit us she always brought our favourites: chocolate pie for my brother and banana cake for me. She always seemed so pleased with our squeals of delight each time the shower of our hugs and kisses fell upon her.

Twice I remember my mother taking us to visit her. She lived in a small house on a quiet street in Hollywood. She had a small garden with flower beds and a vegetable patch where she grew the cucumbers and tomatoes for the pickles and relishes she brought us so faithfully.

I liked Grandmother's house. It was warm and old-fashioned. I used to wish I could stay overnight with her some time but I was not allowed to spend that much time with her.

Mother and Grandmother didn't get along very well. Grandmother was not included in any holiday festivities, she was not invited to our birthday parties, she never stayed to have lunch or dinner with us, and there were no photographs of her anywhere in the house. Mother was always very sketchy about the details of her own childhood, her relationship with her own family. What few stories she did tell about her early years tended to change with each recounting. They were coloured with bitterness and passed over briefly.

My mother was born Lucille LeSueur in San Antonio, Texas, in 1904, although when she came to Hollywood she lied about her age and changed the year to 1908. When she was still a baby her father deserted, leaving his wife, young son Hal, and an infant daughter to fend for themselves. Mother never saw her real father again. She hinted once that she might have been illegitimate, that her mother was not really married the first time, but that may have been more a feeling than a fact. When Grandmother married for the second time, it was to a vaudeville theatre manager named Harry Cassin, who moved the family to Lawton, Oklahoma. Young Lucille was devoted to this man, who became the only real father she'd known. She called him Daddy Cassin and changed her own name to Billie Cassin by the time she was just nine. She spent hours sitting backstage with him while he worked, and it was during these days that she decided to become a dancer and go into the theatre herself.

She was not specific about what happened, but in 1915, when Billie was about eleven years old, her beloved Daddy Cassin also deserted the family and the marriage ended in divorce. This time the family ended up in a Kansas City, Missouri, hotel and was plunged into total poverty. The only work Anna Cassin could find was in a laundry. Since she had no money, she made arrangements for herself and the two children to live in one unused room behind the laundry. My mother said it was hot in the summer, freezing in winter. There was no cooking stove, no proper bathroom, and there were three people living in just one room. Both children had to help with the work in order to make ends meet, and young Billie had to give up all thoughts of dancing lessons. But at night Billie would sneak out behind the laundry after her work was finished and practise her dancing in the dirt, in the darkness. It was during one of these surreptitious rehearsals that she accidentally got a piece of glass lodged in the sole of her foot. The doctors said that she'd be lucky to ever walk again without a limp. Even after they removed the glass fragment they said she could forget about becoming a professional dancer. My mother said that as soon as her foot healed, she started practising again. It took her months and months of painful, frustrating failure before she was able to walk without a limp and then she went right back to dancing. It was a feat of pride, determination, and honour for her. It was the first indication of the incredible willpower that later became synonymous with the story of her success.

Anna Cassin made arrangements with the sisters of St Agnes Convent for her daughter to attend the school on scholarship. Billie was to work a prescribed number of hours a week in return for her room and board. Years later, when Mother told us the story of her years at St Agnes, it was tinged with a steely anger. She said that she had to scrub floors and wash dishes in addition to performing other chores around the school, which took so much time that she missed most of her classes. She said that the school lied to her mother when they sent home passing grades and kept promoting her. She said she hated that school and the next one she was sent to under similar conditions. She also hated her mother for sending her away while keeping her brother Hal at home.

Her mother married for a third time just as Billie was finishing high school. Mother later implied that this man was only her mother's boyfriend, not her husband, and that he tried to seduce her. She was never very clear about exactly what the situation at home was during these few years, but when she finished high school she went to Stephens College for women in Missouri. Mother herself said that because of her time-consuming chores at the schools she'd never got more than an eighth-grade education. There was no way she could bluff her way through college. She said that despite the kindness of the administration, she only lasted a few months.

After that fiasco, Billie took various department store jobs and entered any dance contest she could find. She eventually landed a brief chorus job in a Kansas City hotel. From there she went to Chicago and on to Detroit where she danced in various clubs. She had changed her professional name back to Lucille LeSueur before J. J. Shubert saw her and offered her a job in New York in the chorus line of *Innocent Eyes*. During her few years in

New York she lived in a small walk-up apartment near Broadway and augmented her income by being a Roseland dance-hall girl. It was during these years that the persistent rumour began of her being a prostitute.

Between 1921 and 1924 Lucille LeSueur and her mother didn't see much of each other. Her mother didn't want her to go into the theatre and had done what little she could to prevent it. However, by 1925, when MGM decided to run a movie magazine contest to change their promising starlet's name, Lucille gave a newspaper interview in which she said that she'd reconciled her differences with her mother, who was now in Hollywood with her.

By the time Joan Crawford became a star in 1928 the difficulties she had with the mother and brother she supported were well known. Once she became a big star her mother and brother wanted not only monetary support but also a share of the limelight. Although not the typical stage mother, Anna made her presence felt by making what her daughter felt were difficult demands. Uncle Hal was by all accounts extraordinarily good-looking, charming, and quite the ladies' man. He did bit parts in pictures but his career never went far. Mostly he seemed to be in constant trouble with women, with drugs and drinking, and finally with ill health. My mother bailed him out, then had to get the studio to help her with the more serious charges so that his escapades wouldn't become public knowledge and hurt her own career. She told numerous people that her brother was a good-for-nothing drunk and that he had contracted venereal disease.

The sad part was that Grandmother had placed her early hopes entirely on her son, Hal. She believed that he would fulfil the promise of getting the family out of their dismal circumstances. My mother told me that Grandmother favoured Hal during their growing-up years, giving him the best and her the leftovers. According to one story she told, Grandmother used to divide the bread between the two children, giving Hal the inside soft portion and my mother the crust.

By the time I was growing up Grandmother and Uncle Hal were relegated firmly to the background and exerted no influence in our lives.

But there was a terrible scene one night in the dining room when Mother was having a small dinner party. Uncle Hal arrived in what appeared to be a desperate frame of mind. When I walked into the room I heard Mother calling him a drunk and telling him to leave immediately or she'd call the police.

Evidently Hal had come to ask for money and they'd had a fight about it. She said she'd given him all the help she was going to and that all he ever wanted was more money. Uncle Hal was crying now and pleading with her. He called her Lucille.

Mother ordered us out of the room. We were scared by the name-calling, the shouting, and the sight of Uncle Hal crying. I don't know if he was drunk, but I remember that he looked terribly upset and kept saying that she'd ruined his life.

In a little while the police did come and forcibly took him away. I never saw Uncle Hal again after that night. I heard Mother say to someone on the phone that Hal was in a sanatorium. She'd had him committed for three years. That was it. He was just gone and there was no mention of him ever again.

He was another of those people in my childhood who made my mother mad and then disappeared for ever.

Shortly after the incident with Uncle Hal, Grandmother was no longer allowed inside the house at all. The last time I saw her was through the back screen door. She handed the chocolate pie and banana cake to us as usual and my brother and I tried to be cheerful but all three of us had tears in our eyes. Grandmother didn't stay very long but we did sneak the screen door open quietly so it wouldn't squeak and we each hugged her. Both of us gave her a big kiss and whispered, 'Goodbye, Grandmama.' We closed the screen door very carefully without making a sound. After that Grandmother didn't come to visit us any more. We asked if she was sick but Mother didn't want to talk about it. She seemed angry and said Grandmother was ungrateful for everything Mother did for her. After all, she supported her and gave her a car, what more did she want? There was no pleasing Grandmother, she said. All she knew how to do was take and take.

In the years that followed, I tried to keep in touch with my grandmother. I wrote her cards and called her from boarding school. When I moved East she'd send me hangers with the small sachets and crocheted covers just like the ones she'd made for us at home. I'd heard that Uncle Hal had a job in a sporting-goods store and had been sober for some time. In fact, the last letter I received from Grandmother included regards from him.

I had a friend in Los Angeles who visited Grandmother at least once a month. It was she who sent me the telegram that my grandmother had died.

When Anna B. LeSueur, or Crawford, as she later called her-self, was dying, her doctors called my mother, who was now living in New York, to tell her that Grandmother was very ill and was calling for her daughter. The doctors put Grandmother in a hospital in Los Angeles and a few days later called Mother again to tell her they did not expect Grandmother to live very much longer and that she kept asking for 'Lucille'.

Grandmother died in August 1958, without ever seeing her Lucille again. Mother had been too busy to leave New York while her mother was alive but she did fly to Los Angeles to make the funeral arrangements at Forest Lawn.

It was after I'd moved back to California in the early sixties that I heard Uncle Hal had died. He was all alone then, living in a downtown hotel and working as a night clerk.

Grandmother and Uncle Hal . . . I've often thought they paid a terrible price for the early years they shared with my mother. Some people say that Grandmother died of a broken heart. I know that Mother was ashamed to be seen with her. Uncle Hal was a different story. He became the focus of my mother's lethal sibling rivalry. In the end, Mother rid her life of both of them. They represented only pain for her.

SEVEN

The first steady boyfriend Mother had after Phillip Terry left was Uncle Greg. He was a boisterous, fun-loving man, and I thought he was the most handsome, dashing man alive. He was very good to us. At Christmas and on birthdays his gifts were always perfect. I was between eight and nine years old when he and Mother had been going together for some time. I asked him privately once if he was going to be our next daddy. Though somewhat taken aback, he leaned down next to me and said he didn't know about that but he was deeply touched that I had asked. I noticed that he had tears in his eyes but I didn't understand why. I grew to love Uncle Greg and looked forward to the days when he came to take my mother out.

There was one aspect of their relationship that scared the daylights out of me. They used to have terrible fights late at night.

My bedroom door was always left open, and more than once I woke up to the sound of loud voices downstairs. Mother would come running upstairs slamming her bedroom doors shut behind her. Peeking out from under the covers on my bed I could see Uncle Greg pounding on the double doors and hear them swearing at each other. Finally she'd open one door and they'd continue the fight in her room.

I was frightened because I hated the screaming and yelling and kicking and pounding. But I wasn't afraid for my mother, I was afraid for myself. She never seemed to be hurt the next day and she kept on seeing this man. A couple of times during these fights I thought about hiding under my bed but then I remembered how much trouble I'd be in if my mother ever found out, so I pulled the covers over my head and waited, hoping no one would think about me.

One time during the height of the yelling and swearing I heard Mother climb out onto the balcony that connected her suite of rooms with mine. She was yelling something about calling the police and he was calling her dirty names. The whole neighbourhood must have heard them. Uncle Greg followed her out onto the balcony, whereupon Mother climbed up to the roof! At this point Uncle Greg must have had second thoughts because he called her a few choice names and left through my bedroom door!

Mother eventually managed to get down off the roof but I heard lots of clattering and swearing in the process.

I heard her telling close friends some unkind things about this most eligible bachelor. She said she was damn sorry she'd bought him all those presents and mentioned some suits and jewellery. But after a while he returned and in front of me they acted just as though nothing had ever happened.

I dared not mention to my mother that I heard all those fights, and she never acted as though I knew, which I thought was very strange. How could I help but hear them when they took place right outside my open door and he used my room as an exit?

Mother had other dates as well. When they graduated from being casual dates to being her lovers, she made me call these men 'uncle'.

No matter what time they were to pick her up for a date she was never ready. She would be up in her dressing room with just her underwear on, putting the finishing touches to her makeup when the doorbell rang. It was my job to go downstairs and greet the date, fix him a drink, and then, depending on my instructions from her, either bring him upstairs or sit in the room we called the bar and talk to him.

Even though I was not yet ten years old, I'd had a good deal of practice being bartender and could make most of the ordinary mixed drinks. In fact, I took secret delight in making drinks just a little too strong so I could see what effect they'd have on the adults. Usually they got drunk.

So, when I asked the date of the evening what he'd like to drink, if he was new he seemed surprised, but if he was one of the regular 'uncles' he told me not to make it as strong as the last time. I never paid any attention to his instructions, even though I smiled charmingly and vowed to follow his wishes.

One night the doorbell rang and Mother told me to answer it as usual. She said the man's name was Brenner and that I'd never met him before.

I skipped down the stairs, knowing the entire routine by heart. I opened the front door and gasped. A bald-headed gypsy man wearing yellow pantaloons, sandals, a necklace, and nothing else was standing at our front door. Except for the necklace he was naked from the waist up. I slammed the door in his face, locked it, and dashed upstairs in a panic insisting that Mother call the police immediately! Instead of being upset, she asked me to calm down and tried to explain. The man at the door was an actor name Yul Brynner. He was making a picture called *The King and I*, and he must have come from the studio in his costume. I stared at her and thought: the fights with Uncle Greg are one thing but a half-naked, bald-headed gypsy man at the front door that *I'm* supposed to entertain is something else altogether.

Against all my protestations, I found myself headed back downstairs to the front door again. I tried to be polite to this Mr Brynner but it was very embarrassing. I fixed him a whopper of a drink and left the room immediately.

I didn't mind so much that Mother wasn't ready when friends like Uncle Willie and Uncle Jimmy came over. I called them uncle as well but they were more like family and not considered dates at all. Uncle Willie had been a movie star in the silent-screen days and Mother had done several pictures with him when she was starting out at Metro. The studio had given Uncle Willie an ultimatum, however, and Uncle Willie had to choose between his career and his relationship with Uncle Jimmy. Uncle Willie left pictures and became a successful interior decorator. Mother once said he and Jimmy had the best marriage in town. Uncle Willie and Mother were great buddies. He called her 'Cranberry' or 'Sarah' and took delight in teasing her about her tendency to dramatize and exaggerate every story. Uncle Willie had a cutting sense of humour and I enjoyed sitting with him, listening to the local gossip.

Uncle Butch was also like family. He would take Mother to parties and they'd go dancing together. He was an actor, a handsome man my mother originally met in New York at a party Walter Chrysler gave for her and Franchot in 1935. We all adored Uncle Butch.

Somehow it was all right for these men to see my mother getting dressed because they were such old friends. But the others, the dates we didn't know very well, made the situation uncomfortable. I thought it was rude of my mother to be dressed only in her underwear and a robe when dates arrived. As she and her date sat and talked up in her dressing room over their drinks, she'd put on the rest of her clothes right in front of him. I usually tried to find other things to do then.

I began to tire of the constant parade of uncles. Everywhere we went we'd find another uncle appearing out of nowhere. When we went on vacation to Carmel or Alisal Ranch ... surprise! There was an uncle waiting for us.

Once Mother left my two five-year-old sisters and me to fend off reporters in a San Jose motel while she drove to San Francisco to secretly meet one of her lovers we called uncle. I didn't know what to say to the reporters so I just said that we were on our way to meet friends in Portland, Oregon, and that my mother was off shopping. This particular trip was a zoo because we met one uncle in Carmel and quite a different uncle in San Francisco and neither knew about the other. I felt as though my sisters and I were just a camouflage for all the other activity. During the entire trip I was like the maid or the secretary as I took messages, washed clothes, packed suitcases, and tried to fool the press.

Finally I put my foot down. I refused to call any more of these latter-day Don Juans uncle. It would be just plain 'Mr' from here on unless I particularly liked them or they lasted more than a couple of months. There was something about looking into the eyes of a stranger, having to smile, and say 'uncle' that I could no longer bear. It was such a sham. Mother was furious

77

with me, but nothing she said or did made me change my mind and finally she gave up. As long as I was polite, she never said another word about the uncle business.

The worst part was that my mother didn't even like these men. She said dreadful things about them behind their backs even though she always kept the jewellery they gave her. Some of the men didn't even speak proper English, which I found offensive. After a series of dark-haired Eastern types vanished from the scene Mother seemed to stick to her directors for the next few years.

Mother said that receiving the Academy Award in 1946 for her performance in *Mildred Pierce* marked the end of her Hollywood. I thought that was a strange statement. But the more I thought about it, some of what she may have meant took shape.

The seventeen years she spent at Metro were not only the Golden Age of Hollywood but also the great years of her own career. She rode the crest of fame with a joy and a dedication unmatched by most other stars. She loved being 'the Star' and devoted her considerable energies to the perpetuation and nurture of her career. Then with the departure of her mentor, Louis B. Mayer, and the beginning of the war, major changes began to take place over which she had no control.

Signing her contract with Warners, she not only took less money because her last pictures had not been successful at the box office, she also felt that she was taking second best. Metro was 'the' studio and everyone knew it. Warners' roster of stars couldn't compare with MGM's. It was the beginning of a long descent she battled for the rest of her life.

In the early 1940s, she found herself out of work, labelled box-office poison, and in the position of having to make a comeback. That implied having already failed. For my mother, failure was the worst sin of all.

Her big house in Brentwood was mortgaged to the hilt and practically shut down to four rooms. Still she held out for a picture that would be worthy of her stardom again. She won that battle in the eyes of the world, the press, and the studio by capturing the Academy Award, but privately she knew it was a victory of irony.

Mother told me that the awards started out as more of a dole and a reward to the studios rather than a fair vote of the members on the basis of true merit. During the 1930s she'd had a fight with the Academy board over this policy and renounced her own membership. Their policy had been to rotate the awards from year to year so that no studio could win in the same category two years in succession. It didn't matter how brilliant an actor's performance was: if a star had won the award the year before, no one at the same studio had a chance this year. She lost her fight with the Academy but when she walked out she vowed that if she was ever nominated and won the Oscar she wouldn't be there to accept it.

In 1946, when Joan Crawford won the Oscar for Best Actress in the picture *Mildred Pierce*, she was *not* present to accept. She was at home in bed with pneumonia.

I remember the night. Mother had been in bed all day. Friends called periodically to see if she was going to be well enough to attend that night, but she told everyone she was too ill.

Late that night the all-important call came through: she had won the Oscar! Her health seemed to improve dramatically. She bounded out of bed and took a shower. She put on some makeup and her prettiest negligee with a satin bed jacket. She brushed her hair and waited for the photographer to arrive. Her director, Michael Curtiz, brought the Oscar to her and the photographer snapped pictures from all angles. They shared champagne and congratulations.

After everyone else left I stayed with her for a while. I knew this was a big moment. She sat holding her Oscar, turning him around to view from every angle. She let me hold the statue for a few minutes. He was surprisingly heavy. Then we walked down the stairs together and she placed him all alone in a special little niche at the bottom of the staircase. Mother stepped back to admire him. Turning to me, she said with a note of sarcasm, 'I said I wouldn't be there, but I never thought it would turn out like this!'

I was seven and my brother was four when we spent the winter of 1946–47 back East in New York for reasons that were never explained. Mother still had her apartment on East End Avenue, but we didn't stay there with her. She rented a big house in Bedford Village, New York, and that's where Chris and I lived with three servants while Mother stayed in the city.

Before we left for the house in the country, Mommie took us to lunch at the '21' Club, after which we were going to see a matinee performance of the Broadway musical *Annie Get Your Gun* starring Ethel Merman. Mommie had just won the Academy Award a few months earlier, and she was a big star again. We'd heard rumours that there was public unrest in New York City that winter, but she didn't pay much attention to it even though in Los Angeles Mommie had a bodyguard named Lou Bennett who accompanied her on all public appearances.

We were just finished with lunch at '21' when Uncle Bob Kriendler came to the table to talk with Mommie. It seemed that there was a sizable crowd gathered outside the restaurant waiting to see Joan Crawford. It was not the usual small, faithful band of fans who followed Mommie wherever she went. We knew all those women by their first names. This crowd was different. They were getting tired of waiting to see a famous movie star. They were restless, even beginning to push and shove. Uncle Bob looked very concerned and told Mommie that he was going to have the waiters line the short walk between the restaurant and the street where our limousine was parked.

Mommie hurried us into our coats and hats. Our nurse, Miss Brown, was stationed between us. Mommie told us to hold on to her hand tightly when we left the restaurant and head straight for the limousine, no matter what happened. I looked at my mother, wondering what it was all about. Outside I could see a big crowd of people pressing against the iron grillwork at the top of the stairs. I could hear what sounded like angry voices filtering through the restaurant's heavy glass and iron front doors. Uncle Bob was now on the phone calling the police. He wanted Mommie to wait inside until the police arrived.

Mommie said that she'd never had any trouble with fans before and that they were probably just cold and tired of waiting. She thought that as soon as she went out to see them they'd calm down. Uncle Bob emphatically disagreed with her and pleaded with her not to try to leave just yet. Mommie said we'd be late for the matinee she'd promised us if we waited any longer, and decided to take matters into her own hands.

Bob Kriendler made all his waiters form a living wall around Mommie, Miss Brown, little Christopher, and myself as we left the restaurant.

The moment those big heavy doors opened, I could feel a rush of cold air and hear the angry shouts of the huge crowd. The strange, angry people were everywhere! They were down the stairs in a flash, surrounding our little family and knocking down some of the waiters. They were hanging from the roof that covered the stairway to the street. It couldn't have been more than fifteen or twenty feet from the front door of the restaurant to the door of our limousine, but we couldn't get there!

Literally hundreds of people were shoving pens, pencils, and autograph books at my mother. We were separated from her by this horde of shouting fans who pushed and shoved and jabbed at her. Miss Brown had been knocked down and nearly trampled by the mob. I was terrified. I clung to my brother and tried to protect him from the mob with my own body. But the big people pushing and shoving and falling all over simply swept the two of us up in their own momentum. Chris and I were clinging together, crying.

Mommie realized that she'd lost us somewhere in the crowd and she began screaming for her babies. I heard her voice over the others begging the crowd not to hurt her babies! Everybody was yelling, the people in the mob were yelling, Mommie was screaming, 'My babies ... don't hurt my babies!' The waiters from '21' were shouting for the crowd to calm down, and finally the police arrived with their nightsticks.

By that time Mommie was nearly hysterical with terror. Chris and I were sobbing as we tried desperately to keep from being trampled underfoot by the big people. I couldn't see anything except dark coats and flying autograph books. Even in this bitter-cold weather there was the rancid smell of wet wool and sweat. I barely managed to keep my brother and myself standing upright in the stampede.

A policeman grabbed us and carried the two of us still clinging to each other, taking us to the merciful safety of the limousine. The police pulled Mommie away from the crowd and, once she was inside the car, the police beat people away and slammed the door. Our driver couldn't move the limousine even one inch. There were crazed people all around us, beating on the car, climbing on top of it, and peering upside down into all the windows.

More police arrived and forced the crowd off the car and back onto the sidewalk. When the policemen and their cars finally cleared a path for us, the chauffeur slowly began moving the long black limousine away from the crowd.

Miss Brown was not with us. She'd been stabbed in the head with a ball-point pen and had to be taken to the doctor.

Mommie calmed us down and wiped our tears. She looked us over very carefully to see if we'd been hurt. Since we appeared only to be shaken up, she decided that the best thing for us was to go to the matinee as planned. It would take our minds off what had just happened.

We arrived at the theatre just as the orchestra had started the overture. In the darkness, an usherette led us to our aisle seats in about the tenth row. Mommie sat with us until the play started and then left. Poor Mommie spent the first act in the ladies' room, throwing up. She had to go back to the apartment and go to bed.

My brother and I had a wonderful time. Miss Brown was back from the doctor's by the beginning of the second act. For years after seeing that musical, I wanted to be just like Annie in *Annie Get Your Gun*. I wanted to be a cowboy. But after that day, I didn't care much for either fans or large crowds.

The next afternoon we drove up to the country. Mommie spent the weekend with us and then returned to New York City.

I had my regular schoolwork to do every day since I'd been taken out of public school in California to come on this trip. Chris wasn't in school yet, so he got off easy. But after a few weeks with no other children to play with, we both got lonely. Sometimes Mother came up on the weekends and sometimes she didn't.

Once, a man we knew as Uncle Charlie came to visit us. He brought us some beautiful pheasants he'd shot. He was disappointed that Mother wasn't at the house with us, but he and I sat and talked for an hour or so. Years before when Mommie was young, Uncle Charlie and she were in love. He had taken her on trips to the Pocono Mountains, where they went for long walks in the woods and he taught her how to shoot a gun. I remember the stories she told about hunting with Uncle Charlie. She still had the beautiful rifle he'd given her, which had a hand-carved stock. I had come across it once when we were cleaning out the basement. She said she didn't want to shoot the gun any more but she couldn't give it away. It was from Uncle Charlie and Mommie was very sentimental about him. She loved Uncle Charlie, I knew that by the way she looked when she told me the stories about the Pocono Mountains and walking in the woods with him. But, she said, Uncle Charlie was married and would never be able to get a divorce from his wife. She had tears in her eyes when she got to that part of the story. Poor Mommie, the two men she'd really, really loved were both married when she fell in love with them. The first was Uncle Charlie and the other was Clark Gable.

Although my mother received two additional Academy Award nominations in 1947 and 1952, she viewed the rest of her career as an uphill battle. Some of the joy had gone out of it. She had reached the peak too soon, too young. Now she felt she was backsliding – a slow, painful descent brought on by forces she couldn't see and circumstances she couldn't control.

So she dug in deeper and became more entrenched in her own preconceived notions about the world, all the while clinging desperately to the maintenance of her image as a star. It was the image itself she nurtured and with it she tried to turn back the clock. She began to drink more than just socially.

It was then that the fan mail began to take on more importance. It was the last measure of her old glory and she devoted herself to answering every last piece of it, autographing every single photograph personally. This was something she could control. The fans became the source and the wellspring of her feeling of stardom. As her films steadily declined, the fan mail was an infusion of her life's blood, the last vestiges of hope she had to hold on to.

Our house became a veritable production line geared to servicing the prodigious amount of letters and requests for photos. She spent thousands of dollars on the eight-by-ten glossy pictures and mailing envelopes. She had two secretaries. One worked at the house and the other did only fan mail.

Half the downstairs was turned over to this production line on weekends. Several female fans were asked to volunteer and I worked alongside them addressing envelopes and stuffing pictures into them. Hundreds of pounds of those completed photo mailers left our house each Sunday night.

Part of Mother's personal publicity campaign was the secretary's job of noting every birthday and anniversary celebrated by others of importance, whether my mother knew them personally or not. Sometimes she just read about a date in the trade papers and sent that person a birthday greeting. The top of each page on her calendar was filled with these notations. At the end of each year the secretary dutifully typed them onto the new calendar, omitting the divorced and the deceased. What started out as a memory jogger turned into part of the stardom hype and finally became a trademark that gave Mother special recognition and something to do long after the work and the public life ended. It became the very last shred of the image, the career. Towards the end of her life it was like an old friend that sustained her sense of purpose.

But in the years following her Academy Award in 1946, my mother was doing battle with the world. She was fighting for her professional life and it took a heavy toll on all of us.

EIGHT

When I was a very little girl, Christmas was like having a department store wrapped up and delivered under our tree. Santa Claus came down the chimney in the living room and filled the house with toys and music. We always had a huge tree. It touched the ceiling and filled half the room. I used to sit for hours looking at the lights dancing their way merrily across the shiny red, blue, green, and silver balls. The radio played hours of Christmas carols, cook made special holiday treats, and it was a gloriously exciting time.

Friends would come to visit bringing armloads of presents. The mailman made two deliveries a day to unload cards and packages by the dozen. People I never met sent us beautiful gifts, many of them handmade. Each year there would be another little pearl for my add-a-pearl necklace and there were always savings bonds which my mother put away in the bank for me.

Christmas Eve was when Mommie opened her presents. Until I was five or six, she would open them after I had put out the cookies and milk for Santa Claus and had been tucked into bed. As I grew older she allowed me to stay up and spend Christmas Eve with her.

Her presents were placed in the formal blue-and-white living room, not under the Christmas tree. They were beautiful packages and there were so many they filled nearly the entire room. We were hardly ever allowed to go into the formal living room because it had a white carpet that got dirty very easily and there were miniature antiques on the shelves which we were not allowed to touch.

I used to stand in front of those shelves with my hands tightly clasped behind my back and be fascinated by the tiny pieces of furniture on display. There were also small porcelain boxes with old-fashioned pictures painted on them. I looked at the pastoral paintings of ladies in long, full skirts and gentlemen with satin pants and lace cuffs and wondered what story they were telling.

It wasn't until years later as a teenager that I had the courage to sneak into the living room by myself and actually pick up one of the little boxes. I could hear my heart beating and kept a wary ear tuned to catch the sound of approaching footsteps. I felt almost like a criminal and my hands were shaking. Very carefully I picked up my favourite porcelain box, noting exactly where it had been placed on the shelf. I wanted to put it back precisely so that no one would ever know. Slowly I turned it around to look at all sides of it, then upside down to look at the bottom. There was painting on all sides and some French words I couldn't understand.

Then I opened it. I must have done it wrong because I got a terrible fright when the top seemed to come apart. I was sure I'd somehow broken it. But, to my enormous relief, it was just a double top with a secret compartment.

This secret place was painted too, only at first I couldn't figure out what the picture was about. As I looked closer, it began to dawn on me what it was. It was like a page from a dirty book! The lovely lady and gentleman painted on the outside top of the little box were naked from the waist down and her legs were spread apart. I couldn't believe my eyes! Then I started to laugh. Quickly I closed the box and replaced it exactly. Then I went through the entire collection of porcelain boxes. Almost every one had a secret top and a different scene painted inside. One that was particularly memorable showed a marketplace. One stall was hung with an array of male sexual organs in all shapes and sizes. A woman with a long ruffled dress was making her selection and she had a large basket with her. She also had a sly smile painted on her face. I was horrified and laughing at the same time. In fact I was laughing so hard that tears were rolling down my face.

When each box had been thoroughly examined and replaced, I left the living room. I couldn't wait to tell Chris. This was the best thing that had ever happened. The funniest secret in the whole house.

When we were supposed to be taking our naps and the nurse was safely on the other side of the house, Chris and I tiptoed down the stairs and into the living room.

I showed him the inside hidden compartment in each of the porcelain boxes. He was just as shocked and giggled just as much as I had. We laughed ourselves stupid over the years of not being allowed to touch these porcelain boxes. We always thought it was because Mother was afraid we'd break them. What she was really afraid of was that we'd open them!

Anyway, on Christmas Eve after dinner, Mother would begin to open her presents. There were boxes of perfume and lace things. And usually she received jewellery and silver pieces for the table. If she had a steady date, he often had already given her the present and she would wear it. It was usually jewellery.

Mother preferred things that matched and were monogrammed, so almost everything she received was monogrammed and matched.

When I was old enough to write legibly, she would hand me the card from the present and I would write on the back of it a brief description of the gift, including colour. There were so many presents that she'd otherwise be unable to remember exactly what was from whom. She wrote all the thank-you notes many days later. When she was about half through opening her gifts, she stopped and we'd go into the library where the tree was. We'd put out all the special gifts that weren't wrapped. That was, of course, long after she was sure that I didn't believe in Santa Claus any more.

Then I would go to bed and she'd finish opening her gifts by herself in the living room. Sometimes she'd be there till after midnight.

One Christmas Eve when I was about six, I lay in my big four-poster bed and listened with all my might to hear Santa Claus. The next morning I announced that I had really heard Santa arrive and that I had even heard his sleigh and the reindeer on our roof!

Christmas morning followed the same pattern for five or six years. Chris and I would wake up and run downstairs. The library door would be closed and locked. Behind that library door would be Christmas ... waiting for us. We would try to peek through the keyhole but we couldn't see much. Anyway, we had to have breakfast first. I never knew exactly why, but the regular schedule had to be followed on Christmas morning like any other day. So we ate breakfast, did the dishes, and made our beds, then got dressed. By that time Mother was usually up and our Christmas could begin.

Like wild Indians we dashed into the library the minute she opened the door. Magically, the Christmas tree lights were on and the gifts piled high everywhere you looked. It was unbelievably beautiful. The special presents from Santa were placed around the tree. They were the first ones we got. They were things like bicycles, big stuffed animals, or outfits of clothing.

After that we had to take turns opening presents. Each one had to have a thank-you note written for it, so we had to write on the back of each card just as Mother did. There were a number of Christmas mornings that lasted until it was time for lunch. The opened presents were replaced under the tree neatly in their boxes and the papers and ribbon taken to the incinerator. Some of the satin ribbon was saved, and we rolled that up and put it in a separate box.

We had brunch with Mother. Then in the afternoon we could go out and play with our new toys just like millions of other children.

As the years progressed, our Christmases became less a family holiday and more a public spectacle. The presents were put on display for the many guests who came over on Christmas day for open house. The tree was moved from the library to the front entrance hall directly opposite the front door. Many times we weren't allowed to open all of the gifts until there were other people to watch. Then each of us could take one package and open it in front of the small audience of guests.

The process of Christmas also changed after Mr Terry left. A few weeks before Christmas our house became a production line again with hundreds of packages to be wrapped for other people. The whole thing turned into tedious hard work on behalf of people I didn't know and would probably never meet. It was geared to impress strangers with my mother's generosity.

By the time I was nine, our family Christmas was mostly for show. There were still lots of presents under the tree but we were not allowed to keep the majority of the ones that were given to us by Mother's friends. We never saw most of the gifts once Christmas was over. Mother didn't explain exactly why but they were put back in their boxes and later given away to other people, even though Mother could afford to buy new gifts.

At first we were allowed to choose which gifts we'd like to have, and if she agreed, we kept them. But that didn't last long. What happened from the time I was about nine until we didn't have Christmas celebrations at home any more was that Mother chose a few gifts for us, mostly inexpensive remembrances from fans plus whatever she'd given us.

The rest of the Christmas presents were stored in closets and carefully labelled. We had to take them, rewrapped, to birthday parties during the remainder of the year. Of course, it was usually the best of the presents that we couldn't have because Mother didn't want to be embarrassed by giving children of other movie people cheap presents for their birthdays. Towards the fall of each year, Mother would figure out how many more presents were needed, adding a couple more for insurance, and the rest would be given to a hospital or children's home. That way the closet shelves were cleaned out in preparation for the next holiday.

As if it weren't hard enough to open all those presents knowing full well that we'd never see most of them again until we gave them away, we were required to smile dutifully when visitors and guests expressed awe and admiration, even envy, over the number of beautiful gifts and asked us if we knew what lucky children we were. There were times when I just wanted to scream that it was all a fake. There really was no Christmas and this was all a scene from another movie starring Joan Crawford and her four lovely children. The epitome of the glamorous movie star in the make-believe world of happiness for ever. But I didn't scream, I didn't say anything. I didn't even try to tell them the truth because nobody would have believed me anyway. What they saw on the surface was what everyone wanted to believe. A real-life Land of Oz. I'm sure it all looked perfect. A few people probably saw through it, but although they may have registered a sense of discomfort when I was paraded out to smile and shake hands and curtsey while Chris bowed like an English gentleman, they said nothing. Our manners were impeccable and archaic, well executed and mechanical. We lived by 'Do not speak unless spoken to', and I often drifted off into daydreams while smiling politely and appearing to pay attention to what was going on around me.

I guess I started tuning out about age nine, not so much because I was bored but because it was less embarrassing that way. Mother seemed to take delight in finding ways to make us look foolish or to accuse us of doing something wrong in front of everyone. She was at her best with an audience.

But, categorically, the worst thing about the entire holiday was thank-you notes. I took boxes of stationery and the gift cards up to the desk in my room and the ordeal would begin. Each gift had to have a note and I was not allowed to simply compose one standard reply and copy it. I didn't have a huge repertoire of phrases but I did the best I could. At first I used to have to line the paper faintly in pencil. Later on I was able to write fairly straight without the lines. There could be no error on any note, so that if I made a serious mistake, I had to start all over again. Mother insisted that the notes be written in ink.

I started in the morning after breakfast and my chores were done and would work until time to set the table for lunch. After lunch dishes were done and we'd taken our rest, I sat back down at the desk and had to fight with myself to get started. I stared out the window past the giant oak tree and down into the garden below. I longed to go out and play but I wasn't allowed to do anything except my housework until those thank-you notes were finished. So I plodded on, hour after hour, trying to write pleasant notes without any mistakes for presents I was never going to enjoy.

It was tedious beyond words. My hand would get stiff and my back would begin to ache. I wasn't allowed to listen to the radio or play any records. The silence was broken only by sounds of

90

my own paper and pen. Every once in a while I would have to get up and stretch but it would be done furtively just in case someone might catch me not doing the notes.

The worst part was being alone. I could hear people talking in other parts of the house and in the yard. After a couple of days of this solitary confinement the task was nearly finished. I took the stacks of notes to my mother and she would look them over. To my horror she started making marks through them with her pen. She said with a tone of contempt that my writing wasn't clear enough or this line was slightly crooked. She became angry as she told me she didn't think I'd said nearly enough about how wonderful the present was or I hadn't described it fully.

With a sinking heart and a hatred of her I could barely conceal, I took the majority of the notes she'd thrown at me back upstairs to write over again. It became a never-ending process. No matter how hard I tried to make them perfect the first time, she found something wrong and I had to write them over two and three times. As Christmas vacation dragged on, my other privileges were gradually taken away because I hadn't finished the thank-you notes. If I dared complain, I had more work given to me as a punishment. Mother bawled me out for being the most ungrateful child she'd ever known and then I got into more trouble for my sour face and bad attitude.

In truth, I was grim. I hated those notes so much that some days I had to force myself to pick up the pen. I ruined many of them with my own tears, which fell over the stationery, making big splotches. I ached from the hours of sitting at the desk, and I hated Christmas. I started daydreaming about the day when I'd be free to leave home. I did my work and wrote those hateful notes until school started again.

When the time came to take down the tree, I was ordered to put all the presents I wasn't going to be allowed to have back in their boxes, each labelled in pencil, and stack them neatly on the closet shelf. There they would lie in untouched repose until someone else's birthday party months later.

It was with some astonishment that I recently heard a radio recording made in 1949 about our family Christmas. The following is a direct transcript of that recording. (The italics are added by the author.)

GEORGE FISHER (*announcer*): I know this report wouldn't be complete without a thorough description of exactly how one Hollywood family spends Christmas Eve and Christmas Day. So a few hours ago I took my tape recorder out to the Brentwood home of Joan Crawford. Miss Crawford and her four children have graciously consented to tell all of us exactly the way in which they'll spend this holiday weekend. The broadcast marks the radio debut for Miss Crawford's eldest children. They are as excited about it as any youngsters would be. So now, let's hop into an imaginary sleigh and whisk out to the home of one of the foremost actresses in America today, Miss Joan Crawford.

Now we are settled in the living room of Miss Joan Crawford's tastefully decorated home. A colourful Christmas tree at one edge of the room is almost snowed under with packages. Across the white carpet on the other wall is a stately colonial fireplace prepared for the flames that will be warming the room before long, and the mantel is waiting for the Christmas stockings. Miss Crawford and her children are seated on one davenport facing me.

Miss Crawford, my listeners and I are so pleased that you have invited us in to share a few moments of this Christmas Eve with you.

JOAN CRAWFORD: We are very happy to have you with us, George.

GEORGE: Suppose you start, Miss Crawford, by introducing your children to our radio audience.

JOAN CRAWFORD: This is my eldest daughter, Christina.

CHRISTINA: Hello, everyone.

JOAN CRAWFORD: And my son Christopher.

CHRISTOPHER: Hi, everybody.

JOAN CRAWFORD: My twins Cynthia and Cathy, who will content themselves with smiling for your listeners since they are not quite three.

GEORGE: Hello, Cynthia and Cathy. And how old are you, Christina?

CHRISTINA: I'm ten, Mr Fisher.

GEORGE: Christopher, you're certainly growing up fast. How old are you?

CHRISTOPHER: I'm just seven, Mr Fisher.

GEORGE: Will there be four stockings, one for each child, or does your mother have to hang up a stocking too?

CHRISTINA: Oh, we insist that Mother hang up her stocking right beside ours.

GEORGE: Christopher, are the stockings always full when you wake up?

CHRISTOPHER: Sure, Santa Claus fills them up while we're asleep.

GEORGE: Have you ever tried to sneak downstairs and catch St Nick at work?

CHRISTOPHER: No. He won't come to our house if we're awake.

GEORGE: That's a fancy tree in the corner of the room. Who decorated it?

CHRISTOPHER and CHRISTINA: We all did!

CHRISTINA: Except Mommie had to put the decorations on the top where we couldn't reach.

GEORGE: Miss Crawford, here is a question that will interest every parent in America. At what hour do you suppose the youngsters will awaken tomorrow morning?

JOAN CRAWFORD: I am afraid they are likely to be awake and up by six thirty at the latest.

GEORGE: Will they come straight into your room and awaken you?

JOAN CRAWFORD: I'd be disappointed if they didn't. Christmas morning is the favourite day of the year for all of us.

GEORGE: Well, do you try to get your children to eat breakfast before they start opening their presents?

JOAN CRAWFORD: Yes. I've always insisted they eat before coming in to the Christmas tree. Every other morning of the year they dawdle over their food, but Christmas morning, breakfast is the quickest meal on record.

GEORGE: Christina, do you and your brother and sisters send presents to lots of people at Christmas time?

CHRISTINA: Yes, we do. But besides giving to our friends, we like to send presents every year to boys and girls from other countries across the ocean.

GEORGE: And I suppose you receive all sorts of gifts from people you don't even know.

CHRISTINA: Oh, yes! People who see Mommie in the movies send us lots of lovely things.

JOAN CRAWFORD: It's so nice, George, remembering the children every year.

GEORGE: It's easy to see looking over the gigantic group of packages under the tree now that the youngsters will have enough presents to keep them busy for months.

JOAN CRAWFORD: *Yes. You see, I don't let them have all their presents at one time. They'll get to play with them all, you know, all day tomorrow, and then we put a large group of them aside. From tomorrow on they earn their gifts.*

GEORGE: How do you mean they earn them?

JOAN CRAWFORD: *Well, if they stay on their good behaviour, they are given their choice of what present they want next. Christopher had his birthday in October and he still hasn't received all of his presents.*

GEORGE: I suppose you give away a good many things.

JOAN CRAWFORD: *We don't give away any of the Christmas presents. I don't think that would be fair to the people who send them. What we do do is to have a complete housecleaning three times a year, every plaything, every article of clothing, is carefully gone over and large bundles go to the children's homes and hospitals.*

GEORGE: Do the children help you with this?

JOAN CRAWFORD: *Oh, yes. I think it's excellent training for them. I always see to it that they give up something they really love. Otherwise, they don't really learn the value of giving.*

GEORGE: Christopher, what one thing do you want more than anything else to be in one of your packages tomorrow?

CHRISTOPHER: A pair of Hopalong Cassidy guns.

GEORGE: And Christina, what do you hope St Nick leaves for you?

CHRISTINA: More than anything else in the world, I'd like a collie dog like Lassie.

GEORGE: Miss Crawford. Could you tell us what you would call your most exciting Christmas?

JOAN CRAWFORD: I think the happiest moment of my life was the Christmas the children came into our home. I don't see how any home can be complete without children or how any Christmas can be really enjoyed without youngsters around.

GEORGE: Now, suppose you tell us what's going to happen for the rest of the evening after I leave you?

JOAN CRAWFORD: Well, Cynthia and Cathy will be off to bed pretty quickly, but I've discovered that there's no point in trying to get Christina and Christopher to bed for hours. So they'll help me with the last-minute things and we'll talk about tomorrow and watch the Christmas tree lights. Then in a little while we'll welcome some of the children's friends, who'll be in to help us sing Christmas carols. I imagine we'll sing 'Jingle Bells' even before Cynthia and Cathy go to sleep.

GEORGE: Christina, what's your favourite Christmas-time song, dear?

CHRISTINA: My favourite Christmas song is 'Little Town of Bethlehem'.

GEORGE: And Christopher, what's yours?

CHRISTOPHER: 'Away in a Manger'.

GEORGE: And we'll want to know your favourite too, Miss Crawford.

JOAN CRAWFORD: I think I've always loved 'Silent Night' best, George.

GEORGE: Then when your friends leave, Christopher, what happens?

CHRISTOPHER: Mother reads to us.

CHRISTINA: Yes, we're reading *A Christmas Carol* this year.

JOAN CRAWFORD: Helen Hayes sent us about four years ago a beautiful illustrated copy of Dickens' *Christmas Carol* and it is one of our most prized possessions. I started to read it to them last year but Christopher couldn't take it, it was too scary for him. He's a bigger boy this year, though, so we started it several weeks ago and we'll finish it tonight.

GEORGE: And then surely you finish up by reading ' 'Twas the Night Before Christmas'?

JOAN CRAWFORD: Oh, no Christmas Eve would be complete without that.

GEORGE: Do you remember the last two lines?

CHRISTINA: I do.

CHRISTOPHER: So do I.

GEORGE: Well, then, as a Christmas present to all of us, do

you suppose you could say those lines for us?

ALL TOGETHER:

'And I heard him exclaim as he drove out of sight,
Merry Christmas to all, and to all a good night.'

GEORGE: And a Merry Christmas to you, Cathy, Cynthia, Christopher, and Christina, and of course, to you, Miss Joan Crawford. Thanks again for allowing all of us to share a part of your Christmas Eve.

JOAN CRAWFORD: Thank you so much, George. Merry Christmas to you and to all of your listeners.

And so the millions of fans across America were given a capsule glimpse into the glamorous world of Hollywood with the nearly perfect picture of one happy, lucky family. We had everything, so the story went. We had the gifts and the money and the beautiful famous movie-star mother.

I remember being dressed up and paraded out in front of interviewers and photographers with my little rehearsed responses and photo-perfect smile. We were like echoes of Mother's constant drive for perfection and gentility. Out of the cauldrons of Hollywood's melting pot she had clawed her way to the top, and now we were the final stars in the crown, proving her not only successful but also morally superior. Her generosity in taking not one, not two, but *four* orphaned children into her home was extolled in numerous movie-magazine stories.

When the reporters and photographers left, we returned to our rooms and changed our clothes. It was a case of extremes. One minute we were treated like privileged royalty with reporters paying careful attention to our every word, and a few minutes later we were little more than extra servants doing Mother's bidding.

NINE

At times when there was no man around, my mother often wanted to go out anyway. On those evenings she told me that I was going to be her date and we were going out to dinner. The two of us would get dressed up and get into her black Cadillac.

In no time at all we'd pull up in front of one of her favourite restaurants. Sometimes it would be the old La Rue on Sunset Boulevard, other times it would be Jack's at the Beach or maybe Romanoff's, where her friend 'Prince' Mike Romanoff would greet her warmly and show us to one of the best tables. For lunch we often went to the Cock 'n Bull, but my favourite place for dinner was Don the Beachcomber's in Hollywood. I loved the Polynesian food, the waterfalls, and the booth we always sat in which looked like a grass hut. Wherever we went the owners fawned over us and my mother smiled happily. She told them that she was taking her big girl out to dinner, and they'd tell me what a pretty young lady I was. No matter what restaurant it was, people would come by the table to sit and talk with us. Mostly my mother would talk business with them while I sat quietly and ate my food. She told her friends that *I'd* wanted to come to this restaurant and I'd been such a good girl that she couldn't refuse me. I was used to the routine and I'd just smile politely. I already knew that unless Mother and I were alone I was not supposed to join the conversation, and by now I really didn't mind.

One night at the Beachcomber's a tall, strange-looking man

came to our table. Mother greeted him warmly and introduced him to me as Howard Hughes. He stayed with us most of the meal and was obviously trying to get Mother to be more than just cordial towards him. When he finally realized that he wasn't getting anywhere, he kissed her on the cheek and left.

'He's weird!' I whispered to her, not entirely sure he was out of earshot. Mother laughed.

'He's Howard Hughes, Tina, and he's *very* rich!'

It was while we were waiting for the bill that she told me that years ago, when Howard Hughes was starting in the film business as a producer, he'd wanted to put her under contract. She had refused him a number of times, even though he was offering her a tremendous amount of money. She said she didn't want to ruin her reputation. She said that Howard wanted to buy people, that he wanted to own people. More than once he'd put an unsuspecting, ambitious young actress 'under contract' and she'd never do one movie. She might not see him for months at a time but she had to be at his beck and call twenty-four hours a day. Mother said that other women were used for exploitation and she didn't want any part of that.

When Howard Hughes failed to entice her into signing a contract with his studio he tried to get Mother to go out with him. She finally accepted, and they went out a couple of times but all he wanted to talk about was machinery and she wasn't much interested. He was also deaf in one ear and wore a hearing aid about which he was vain and didn't want anyone to mention. Mother also said that he had a mania about washing his hands and was deathly afraid of germs. Coming from my mother who was the most cleanliness-minded person I could imagine, I thought this poor Howard Hughes must really have problems!

I thought about him for a while as my mother was paying the bill and felt sorry for him. He was a strange, tall, rumpled man who seemed ill at ease with us and with himself.

Mother and I usually had a good time on our 'dates'. She would chatter away about the people who came to our table for one reason or another. It was funny that she hated to have her own dates 'table hop' and talk to other people in the restaurant but was delighted when she benefited from the same practice. If it hadn't been for all the men that did table hop, we would have been left talking to ourselves all evening, which was certainly not the purpose of these outings. Since my mother never got up and went to visit anyone else's table, because she said it was bad manners, everyone else got up and came over to ours.

When we got home, having discussed the entire evening in detail during the drive, Mother would often ask if I wanted to sleep with her. It wasn't exactly an open question, it was more like a request. I always felt bad about saying no for fear it would hurt her feelings. She had two giant beds in her room, one at either end of what we called her sleeping porch. Sometimes I would sleep in the other big bed but sometimes she would want me to sleep in the same bed with her.

She divided her bed into two parts down the middle using great big pillows. She said it was so that we wouldn't bump into one another during the night. Then she got into her half and I crawled into my half and she went to sleep.

I would lie awake for ages. There were two things I didn't like about sleeping with my mother. One was that her blankets were so heavy that I felt like I was being buried alive. The other was that I couldn't move. She claimed that I wiggled incessantly in my sleep and said it woke her up. So I would try to remember not to wiggle, which meant not moving all night long. I was so worried I'd wiggle and she'd wake up mad at me that I tried not to even go to sleep. Finally, of course, I'd doze off but I woke up in the morning stiff as a board from trying not to wiggle.

I was a very good student even in the elementary grades and enjoyed school. Because the work became increasingly easy for me, my teachers decided to skip me ahead one half grade.

So, over a weekend in February, I went from the top of the third grade to the top of the fourth grade. The transition wasn't particularly difficult except for one subject: maths. Somehow in the moving process I had missed a significant part. I had to have Mrs Howe tutor me after school for the rest of that year.

There were new friends to be made and I was now a little younger than most of my classmates. We were all still near enough in age, though, and making friends wasn't that difficult.

That same year, in a burst of civic-mindedness, my mother directed our Brownie troop production of *Hansel and Gretel*.

She held rehearsals on the small stage in our own theatre and managed her little troupers very patiently.

We were very excited the day of the performance as we put on our costumes and Mother helped each of us with our makeup. Unfortunately, I got a classic case of stage fright during my inauspicious acting debut and forgot half my lines, which shortened the play by about ten minutes.

Mother was very strict about where she let me go, so most of my friends had to come to my house to play. My two best friends from school were named Judy and Cynthia. Their families were not in show business and they were different from my own neighbourhood friends.

Judy and I started out as archrivals. She was the tetherball champ and no matter how hard I tried I couldn't beat her. After school one day we met behind the fence and had a fistfight just like the boys. I didn't have any more success winning our fight than I had at tetherball, and after Judy landed a solid punch that gave me a whopping black eye, we called a truce.

With my school friends, Mother had a peculiar habit that I found downright embarrassing. She insisted that they call her something other than Miss Crawford. At first she suggested they call her Aunt Joan but that didn't work very well because most of them didn't feel comfortable with our family aunt-and-uncle convention. It was then, to my total horror, that Mother suggested the nickname of Stinky!

The girls were as taken aback as I was. But Mother repeated it: 'Stinky.' She wanted my friends to call her *Stinky*.

It was humiliating for me to hear the girls call her Stinky to her face and even worse when they made a big joke of it at school behind her back. When the other kids teased me about it, I just told them to go to hell.

But that wasn't nearly as bad as some other things the kids said. First there was the whole business about my not having a father. I tried to explain that I was adopted and Mother said that made me specially wanted, more than other people wanted their own kids. What I got in return for my explanation was snickers and pointed remarks about being a bastard.

It was so unusual for someone to admit being adopted in the

1940s that I didn't even meet any other adopted children outside my own family until many years later. The common practice then was for parents not to tell children they were adopted until the children were nearly grown up, if indeed they ever divulged the truth.

But Mother told us even before we were fully able to understand all the details. At first she said that she chose us from a pink cloud. I used to look up in the sky and think that the different-coloured clouds were where different-coloured people came from. It seemed very logical.

Some of the kids at school also told me about the nasty rumours they'd heard about how my mother had got to be a big movie star by first being a prostitute. I cried all the way home that day, but I never told my mother about it. I thought I'd probably just punch the next kid who said that right in the mouth.

In contrast with the cruel teasing at school, there was the business about being a 'movie star's daughter'. Most of the other kids at this public school were from middle-class families, few had anything to do with the film industry, and some were poor.

In fact it was a shock for me when I was invited to some of the birthday parties of my classmates. Because of the kidnapping business, Mother felt uncomfortable when I was with people she didn't know very well. Unfortunately, this overprotectiveness was taken as an insult by some of my friends' parents, as though Mother were implying they weren't good enough.

Nevertheless, I was eventually allowed to go to a school friend's birthday party. I knew everyone at this party because we were all classmates. But I was conspicuously overdressed compared with the other girls and I felt uncomfortable. What I always wanted to do was fit in and be accepted. But my expensive party dress immediately set me apart. Then, too, I had to be so careful of my clothes and not scuff my shoes that I knew I couldn't play most of the games. I had taken off my white gloves the minute I got into the house but it wasn't quick enough to escape the eyes of my friends, who had never seen anyone their own age dressed so formally. Nobody said anything, but I could see them exchange glances.

My present was, of course, one of last year's Christmas gifts that I wasn't allowed to have. It was bigger than any of the other packages. It was wrapped in beautiful paper, tied with an elaborate satin bow, and stood out like a spotlight in the midst of the more ordinary presents.

The girl's mother was beside herself. She tried her best to act normal, but she was lost in the excitement of introducing me to all the neighbour friends who 'just happened' to drop by. She introduced me as 'Joan Crawford's daughter'. Several times she actually forgot my first name or else didn't consider it necessary to add. I shook hands, smiled, and curtseyed as I'd been taught to do. But I sensed that everyone was staring at me. After the first few introductions I just said hello and left it at that.

When we went out into the small back yard no bigger than the space we used at home to hang laundry in, I felt sorry for my friend. Her family must be very poor, I thought, and tried harder to be polite about this sort of sad situation.

It wasn't until several more of these schoolmates' birthday parties that a monumental truth began to dawn on me. Little by little I realized that most people didn't live the way we did.

The houses of my public-school friends weren't like our house or the homes of my mother's friends. And it wasn't even the houses that surprised me as much as the yards. I was well into the eighth year of my life before I realized that not everyone in the world had swimming pools! There was an entirely different world out there beyond the one I knew.

At first I didn't realize exactly what was going on with some of the kids I met during the fourth grade. It was a confusing time because they teased me about dressing funny, about not having a father, and then, for no good reason, they'd be very nice to me.

It was a bit of a paradox that Mother would overdress me for the birthday parties, which was embarrassing, and then make me wear overalls to school, which was also embarrassing. It was unusual for little girls to wear overalls to school in those days. I guess Mother thought it was more practical, but it made me feel funny not being dressed like the other kids. After a while I begged and pleaded and she gave me some cotton dresses. At least part of the time I didn't stick out like a sore thumb.

When the same kids that teased me about my funny clothes

and high-topped shoes suddenly did a turnaround and were nice to me, I was so pleased to have the teasing subside that I interpreted their change of behaviour as an indication of friendship. Since it was well known that I was hardly ever allowed to go anywhere, the only way to pursue their friendship was for me to invite them over to my house.

Usually after a couple of hints from them about our swimming pool, I would ask my mother if I could invite school friends on Saturday and she usually said yes.

Sure enough, the children would arrive right on time to go swimming. Afterwards Mother let us have a Good Humor bar as a treat. Sometime soon after that, one or another of the kids would bring up the subject of my mother being a movie star. Then someone else asked if my mother would give them an autographed picture. If Mother was home, I'd go into the house and ask her if my friends could have pictures and her autograph. She was always happy to oblige, coming down to the pool with a stack of the latest eight-by-ten glamour portraits and sign each one individually with the child's name on it.

In a short while the afternoon would be over and the kids left with their movie-star pictures tucked under their arms.

Up until that time I'd seen only one of Mother's movies, *Humoresque* with John Garfield. I was in love with John Garfield. I adored him. He was my hero. I was just eight when I saw that movie. To my horror, at the end of the picture my mother walked into the ocean and died! I'd been sitting next to her during the film but she'd got a phone call and left before the movie ended. I was so engrossed that I didn't realize she was gone. Even though we were seeing the movie at home in our own theatre, I forgot where I was as I became riveted to seeing Mommie on the screen for the first time. The movie was very sad. At the end she walked into the sea. I was crying. When the lights went on again I turned to hug her. But she wasn't there! For an awful moment I thought the movie was real and that my Mommie was really dead! I screamed and ran out of the theatre like a crazy person. I ran everywhere looking for her, screaming 'Mommie . . . Mommie' until finally I found her in the house, still talking on the phone. I threw myself across her, sobbing in agonized relief.

Anyway, Monday at school when I'd bounce up to the same kids who had just been at my house swimming on Saturday, the reception was entirely different. They didn't act like my friends at all. I was very hurt and didn't understand what could have happened.

One day I was nearly in tears over the situation. After school my friend Judy and I sat down to talk about it. It was Judy who finally told me the truth. All those kids wanted was to see a movie star's house and get the autograph to prove it.

I was so mad at Judy that we nearly had one of our old fights. I called her a liar and rode off on my bike in a total fury.

I didn't talk much at home that night. When it was time to go to sleep, I lay awake in my bed going over and over the past few months. I knew that Judy had told me the truth. After those kids saw the house and got their autographed photo, they weren't my friends any more.

It was inescapably clear to me that those kids didn't care a bit about me. They didn't even really care about Mother. All they wanted was to see some movie star in person. Some of the kids at school didn't even bother with the invitation part. They just asked me point blank for the picture and continued to pester me about it until I either had to tell them to just forget it or go through the whole process of asking Mother and then taking the pictures to school. I felt like a pawn, constantly being used by all sides of my small world.

I already knew that Mother used us for all those publicity stories in the movie magazines. It wasn't hard to tell the difference between our regular routine and the make-believe life the photographers always wanted. Everything changed when publicity people were coming to the house. I had to get dressed in one of the matching mother-and-daughter outfits we were always photographed in and didn't wear at any other time. Then Mother and I went through the whole day doing things for the camera and changing from one matching outfit to another. The publicity people had all these fake scenes they wanted us to act out as if it were part of our normal day. There was always a writer asking silly, set-up questions and noting down all the rehearsed answers. Mother told me beforehand what she thought the questions would be and told me what to answer in reply.

We would practise that a few times until she was satisfied that I had it right. She made me pronounce my words carefully and stand properly. She said that if they asked any questions other than the ones we'd just rehearsed I was to keep quiet and let her answer. She always said that you couldn't be too careful with the press and it was better to say nothing than to risk being misquoted. So I was to smile and look pretty and be polite and speak *only* when spoken to and do as I was told. I was to be her *very good girl*.

My world was full of contradictions. When the publicity people and photographers were around, I was treated like the golden-haired princess. But at school the kids were mean to me because I wore overalls and didn't have a father. They pretended to be my friends just to get one lousy picture and see a movie star. It was beginning to be confusing as to who I was. Was I a princess or a bastard? None of these images of myself rang exactly true.

Once I decided to run away from home. I found myself standing alone, eating off the back-porch freezer for an infraction of some household rule. I was going to school that morning anyway and decided to just leave early.

Before I got very far down Sunset Boulevard I heard the sound of screeching brakes and looked behind me to see Mother's black Cadillac coming to a dusty halt. She jumped out of the car and hauled me off the street. She was furious with me and demanded to know just what in the world I thought I was doing and where I was going. Scared to death, I mumbled something about Cynthia's house.

Driving like a maniac, she took me to my friend's house, where she told the entire family about my 'runaway' plans. They were sympathetic but clearly wanted nothing to do with the situation.

Going home in the car, Mother asked me how come I always seemed to like everybody else's house better than my own. She said, 'Every time you go over to someone else's house they always have such glowing reports about how helpful you are, which is odd, because you never want to lift a goddamned finger in your own house.'

As I sat there listening to her I wanted to run away all over again. Somehow she turned the report of my good behaviour into a condemnation of me. I didn't know how she did it, but I knew I couldn't win. No matter whether I was good or bad it got me into the same amount of trouble. If I tried to be a good girl, she said I was only being good to show off or that I was only being good because I wanted something.

It seemed that it was getting harder to trust anyone. I waited longer before I made friends. And if it looked as though Mother was paying special attention to one of my friends I would decide to keep my secrets to myself and not tell them anything personal. They could still come over and play from time to time, but they wouldn't know how I felt or what I thought.

Mother was just as strict about school as she was about our home. She had always demanded good grades from me and I got into trouble if I didn't get all A's on my report cards. If my grades dipped below A, my privileges at home were taken away and I had extra work to do.

Fortunately for me, I liked school. It was fairly easy for me, and, except for maths, I didn't have to work too hard. Ironically, that's why the school kept double-promoting me. I guess the point was that if you didn't have to struggle, something was wrong.

It didn't matter too much, though, because my scholastic 'holiday' was about to come to an end.

PART
TWO

TEN

Over one weekend in February I skipped another half grade at school and went from the middle of fifth grade to the middle of sixth grade, leaving all my friends behind. Before I'd had a chance to make any new friends, Mother transferred me to the Chadwick School in Palos Verdes.

In keeping with all the other major changes of my life, there wasn't a long discussion about this transfer. On a Friday my mother asked me what I'd think of going away to boarding school. Two days later, on Sunday, she packed me up and drove me there.

I didn't have a chance to think about whether or not I'd like boarding school, and I didn't have a chance to say goodbye to my teachers or classmates. The whole thing just sprang out of thin air. It wasn't even a punishment, because things had been going unusually well for me at home.

I hadn't the vaguest idea where we were going, but we seemed to drive for a long time. After about an hour, Mother started looking for the school sign along a country road lined with pepper trees. Finally the blue-and-white sign appeared. We drove up a long hill with fields on either side of the road. When we stopped it was in front of a small house on the school campus known as the Cottage.

The housemother came out to greet us with a friendly smile. The Cottage was really a dormitory for elementary-school girls. The housemother showed us to the room I was to share with three other girls and introduced me to my future roommates.

This was such a totally new experience for me that I became very shy and hardly said a word. At ten and a half years old, with the changes happening so rapidly, I didn't seem to have time to adjust to one change before another was upon me. I was beginning to be unsure of myself.

Then it was time for Mother to leave. I was overcome with a sense of panic. I burst into tears and clung to her as though to keep her from leaving. She held me for a moment and then very firmly made me let go of her. She tried to reassure me that I'd make new friends here and that I'd like the school. Nothing seemed to stop the waterfall of my tears. I couldn't believe that she was really going to make me stay in this strange place where everybody else already knew one another. I wanted to go home with her and forget about boarding school. She said no. That was impossible. All the arrangements had been made and I was to stay and try to make the best of it. I'd be coming home in two weeks. My mind sort of wandered away from her at this point. *Two weeks!* That sounded like an eternity to me. I wondered if I'd make it. I was still crying when she drove away.

I didn't particularly like this new school and was continually homesick. On weekends, when I went home, I would cry all the way back to school. Even Mother cried sometimes and said she'd miss me. I began to notice that my brother and sisters had developed relationships that didn't include me so much any more because I was away most of the time. Sometimes when I went home there were new servants I didn't know and often Mother had a new boyfriend. Many weekends there were parties and I had to help with the work. Sometimes Mother got in extra help, but when she didn't, I played bartender.

By and large, though, the end of my sixth grade went smoothly. I finished with decent grades, but I didn't want to return to boarding school the following year.

That summer I turned eleven. In many ways I was still just a child, but because I was tall for my age, Mother took some precautions and tried to tell me about the physical changes my body would soon be going through. She wouldn't let me wear a bra yet because she said it wasn't good for you to be all bound up. Then she tried to explain about menstruation. I listened atten-

erits. After a certain number of demerits, you had to
ork or, at worst, couldn't go home weekends.
d difference that set Chadwick apart from the world
before was the other students. Most of them, I dis-
were from backgrounds similar to mine. They came
on-picture-industry families and many of them were
used to be called 'broken homes'.
d to have a joke about divorce:
1: 'How do you like your new father?'
2: 'I like him a lot.'
1: 'Yeah, I liked him too. We had him last year.'
e thing about being at Chadwick was that you didn't
the inevitable 'What's it like to be a movie star's
' routine. I felt a sense of companionship and under-
hat I hadn't experienced at public school.
der and Mrs Chadwick were remarkable people who
chool with love, dedication, and hard work.
Chadwick was a co-educational country boarding
h a working farm on the property. The fields grew
heat and the farm raised chickens, pigs, and rabbits for
room. The school also had a stable and some horses.
of the Palos Verdes area had been developed yet, so
wide-open spaces to ride. As the months went by, my
l continually to improve. I was only in trouble once
hat wasn't serious.
of us had the idea that it would be funny to spike the
our seventh-grade Christmas party. One of the girls
student, and we managed to sneak some whiskey from
's liquor cabinet, pour it into Coke bottles, and
eseal them. We even figured out a way to mark
an' bottles for our teacher, but during the excite-
party someone muddled them and we were caught.
terrible moment when we were called into Mrs
s office. She had a way of looking at you that made
orse than whatever the punishment was going to be.
you felt that you'd betrayed the ultimate trust she
ach child under her care.
'd told our version of the story and promised never to
in anything similar again, we were each given de-

tively and nodded my head, although I didn't really comprehend the full meaning of our conversation.

The majority of the summer was peaceful because Mother went to Lake Louise in Canada with Uncle Vincent, one of her directors. I liked Uncle Vincent even though we'd had one awful incident with each other.

One night many months before, I'd been at home, sitting downstairs watching television by myself, when I heard a noise coming from the office, two rooms away. At first it was just some loud voices, but in a few minutes I heard what sounded like screaming and my heart leaped into my throat. It sounded like my mother who was screaming!

I dashed through the door and towards the office. When I ran into the room all I saw was Uncle Vincent hitting my mother. She was sprawled across a chair and was trying to defend herself.

Without stopping to think, I flew at Uncle Vincent and started pounding on him with my fists, trying to kick him and screaming at him to let go of my mother. She was crying and I was crying too, but out of shock and fear. I'd heard other fights my mother had with men, but I'd never actually seen one of them before. Until Uncle Vincent managed to get a grip on both my arms and hold me away from him, I continued to beat at him while Mother cowered in the chair. I was yelling, he was yelling, Mother was crying.

But in a matter of minutes it was over. Mother was still sniffling as she told Uncle Vincent he'd better leave. I walked over to the door and imperiously told him to get out immediately. Of course, I was scared, but I was trying to be brave.

After he'd left and the door was securely locked, I went to Mother and tried to find out if she'd been hurt. I wanted to call the doctor, but she refused. I helped her upstairs.

A few days later my piano recital was being held at our house. I didn't like the piano much, but the recital was a yearly event. Mother had prepared a lovely party for the occasion.

The reason I didn't like piano was that I knew I didn't play very well. I had no real talent or flair for music and each step forward was a struggle.

I was four years old when I started piano lessons. Mother was very much the proud parent and she invited Helen Hayes to listen to one of my little memorized pieces. Dutifully, I went to the grand piano and played. Aunt Helen said something to me like 'Very nice, dear', but to my mother she shook her head and whispered, 'Joan, I'm afraid she plays like an iron butterfly.' Mother was undaunted by her friend's evaluation, however, and insisted that I continue to take lessons for many more years.

By the time of this recital, I was competent but not talented. Since I was to be the hostess, the timing was unfortunate. Mother informed me the morning of the recital that she had invited Uncle Vincent. She said it would be rude not to let him come because of the minor incident a few days ago.

I stared at her, appalled. It was unthinkable to me that she should invite him to my recital. I thought it showed very little concern for my feelings, but I didn't say so. Then she landed the final blow. She said that no matter how I felt, I had to be polite and she'd appreciate it if I apologized to him.

Apologize? ! I said no : flat out *no*. I wouldn't apologize because I hadn't done anything wrong. She looked at me with those icy blue eyes and said that it would be necessary for me to say I was sorry.

I was sorry, all right. I was sorry she'd invited him, I was sorry I had to have this stupid piano recital, I was sorry I had to play hostess, and I was very sorry I hadn't just let him beat her up or do whatever it was that happened during these fights she'd been having with men since I was seven years old.

Then and there I decided that was the last time I'd try to intervene, even if it sounded to me as if someone was trying to murder her. I wasn't going to be humiliated any more. There was something about these situations I just didn't understand, so it was better for me to stay out of them.

After I apologized, the subject was not mentioned again. But, nearly twenty years later, when I was an actress myself, Uncle Vincent was one of the few people from my childhood who actually helped me. He hired me to do a part on one of the television shows he was then directing.

Near the end of August that summer I turned eleven, I was in my bathroom changing clothes one afternoon. I noticed a spot on my pants, and when I took them off I saw blood. I let out a

shriek sounding like a wounded
down the hall into the nursery, wh
ing my sister's bath.

After Mrs Howe calmed me dow
take care of my new condition, sh
bathroom. I burst into a renewed fit
on the floor, where I kicked my feet
had an old-fashioned temper tantrum

I couldn't understand why my mot
out. I couldn't see anything so wor
woman'. I wanted to be a cowboy a
hard to make my feelings understood
bed; I got terrible cramps and took t
and took to my bed. I was convinced
remedied the situation, but no matter
one would do anything except get th
face.

I hated not being allowed to go swim
to play kickball or climb trees. I hated
with trying to cope with this new stage
my feet and pounded my fists and sob
avail, because puberty and my 'period'

The most embarrassing part of all
sisted on telling anybody who would lis
of it as an accomplishment. I would blu
story about 'becoming a lady' started.

During the next year at Chadwick I b
was in a different and rather special s
class was larger and I was no longer th
friends and liked my classes. But tho
differences.

The first thing that dawned on me aft
girls' dorm was that the rules were no
ones I lived with at home. We were giv
ments in the dorm or dining room, bu
we worked in teams. Compared with t
to do at home, it was easy.

The disciplinary system was also more
For a serious infraction of the school re

merits and a sound lecture on the responsible behaviour expected from each student at Chadwick School.

In the early spring of 1951, when I was eleven and a half years old, an event occurred that would change my life for ever – a definitive experience that tore the fabric of my emotional life into shreds so small I wondered if I'd ever be able to piece it all together again. It became a reference point in my life, and I thought of things in terms of before and afterwards. For me it was like dying and fighting my way back out of the grave. The memories are of pain and the events still so crystal-clear that they stand alone like Dali figures on an otherwise empty canvas.

I had been listening to the stories of some of the older girls at night in the dorm. In between the whispers and the giggles and the long silences, I had begun to put together the excitedly romantic story of one girl's adventures with the boy who was in charge of running the stables. He was a student on scholarship and spent most of his time outside classes at the stables taking care of the horses. I vaguely knew who he was, but I'm sure the stories were more exciting than the boy himself. As the weeks wore on I became totally captivated by veiled references to what went on at the stables. It was like one of those romantic magazine stories.

Though not yet twelve, I looked more mature. During art class when the boys used the workshop next door, through a series of secret notes, I arranged to meet that boy on a Friday night. He was older than I, about sixteen and not in my group of friends. But he was nice-looking and very close to my idea of a cowboy.

Ever since I had seen that play in New York, cowboys had been my heroes. I wanted to be a cowboy myself until I discovered that girls weren't supposed to want to be cowboys, so I changed my goal. Now I wanted to be an actress when I grew up, but I loved cowboy movies and I loved to ride horses.

Before the Friday-night basketball game I took particular care with my shower, my hair, my jeans and shirt. I had to be careful not to look like I was getting specially dressed so no one would suspect my plans. I borrowed a bra from one of the older girls so I wouldn't look like such a kid to him.

With my heart beating a mile a minute, I signed out after

dinner for the basketball game. I could hardly act natural during the first half of the game. I tried to cheer for the boys I knew but it sounded hollow and false. I thought that any minute someone would ask me what was the matter with me and the whole adventure would be over before it started.

In fact, no one paid much attention to the cleanly scrubbed eleven-year-old girl sitting on one of the back benches. At half time, when everyone else went to the bathroom, I left the court and disappeared into the darkness at one turn in the path. From there it was just a matter of making my way carefully through the bushes around to the back of the stables. Since no one rode at night, there was only one light on in the tack room at the far end of the row of stalls. The rest of the stable area was in darkness.

There was only a small sliver of a moon and I could barely see where I was going. Finally, after what seemed like an hour but was probably only five minutes, I found my way along the back of the stalls to the corner of the tack room. The night sounds were all around me and crickets interspersed with the sound of horses moving in their stalls.

Carefully I crept around the protective edge of the board walls and past the big stack of hay bales. I stood in silence for a moment looking at the tall dark-haired boy I had planned to meet here.

Though I didn't say anything, he must have sensed me standing there in the half light that spilled past the door of the tack room, because he turned to face me. I could still hear the sound of my own heart beating, half in anticipation and half in fear. I thought that he was better-looking than I'd remembered him in the workshop, and he seemed taller, almost six feet. He walked towards me and smiled. I didn't move.

When he was standing next to me in the semi-darkness, he took my hand. He wasn't exactly handsome but I sort of quivered when he touched me. 'Let's go over here,' he said, leading me quietly to one of the clean, empty stalls.

Inside the stall it was even darker than in the pale moonlight. There was the smell of fresh hay and old wood, of leather and horses. These were all happy smells for me, familiar smells of days spent riding with my braids flapping behind me and a sense of freedom as my horse galloped through the countryside.

He kneeled down on the hay and drew me to him. I was glad it was so dark because I felt very awkward. He was gentle and easy and I started to relax when he kissed me. I lay back on the soft, crinkly hay and heard it rustle beneath me as we moved.

He was so warm and the sensation of his hand on my body so comforting that I didn't even realize that he'd unbuttoned my shirt and unfastened my borrowed bra until it was already done. I struggled a little bit but as he continued to kiss me, I felt like I was melting. He put his jacket underneath me and I never felt the hay as my jeans slipped down below my knees. I'd never had any experiences with a boy before, I'd only been hurriedly kissed maybe twice. I had no real idea what adult sex was all about because no one ever talked about it. I wasn't really thinking about anything. I was just sort of floating in the sensation of his touch and the sound of his soft voice.

All of a sudden a stab of pain shot through me like a rocket, nearly making me scream. My whole body contracted with that pain and involuntarily I started crying. He slapped his hand over my mouth so that no sounds actually escaped and the pain disappeared as quickly as it had occurred. I didn't know what had happened. He lay on top of me now and held me very tightly.

I was scared. I felt I'd been hurt somehow but I wasn't sure. He dried my few tears and continued to kiss me gently. 'You've never done this before, have you?' he asked. I shook my head, no. 'How old are you?' he whispered. 'Almost twelve,' I replied. He let out a low whistle between his teeth and said, 'I thought you were closer to fourteen.' I didn't know exactly what he meant by that, but I did have a strange sense that somehow I was a disappointment to him, although he was being very kind about it. Then he said, 'Let me tell you something and try to remember this as you're growing up. Don't let just anybody do it . . . you choose who you want and be careful.' I nodded my head in agreement and then he helped me get dressed.

He kissed me once more when we were standing in the doorway to the stall. Without saying any more, I walked away into the darkness.

That would have been the end of it, I guess, except I told one of the girls and he must have told a couple of his friends and by

Sunday afternoon I was summoned into Mrs Chadwick's office. Later that same day they had a doctor examine me. The verdict was that I was still a virgin.

No matter what the doctor had said, the rumour was that I'd either been raped or had an affair with this boy at the stables. Neither part of the rumour was true, but it spread so fast that the school was faced with a potential scandal. Finally my mother was called. She was horrified. After a tear-stained meeting between the three of us – Mrs Chadwick, my mother, and myself – during which Mother called me a common whore, Mrs Chadwick told me to go back to the dorm and take a long, hot bath. They would decide what was to be done with me and Mrs Chadwick would speak to me later.

Walking despondently back to the dorm, I tried to sort out all the conflicting thoughts that kept bumping into one another in my head. I was scared. I was embarrassed by the personal questions I didn't really know how to answer. I relived every detail of Friday night and tried to understand what I had done that was so awful in the minds of the adults. Except for one brief minute of pain, it had been a nice experience for me. I felt a closeness, a moment of belonging, a sense someone cared about me. I didn't want to be a bad girl; I never started out to do anything terrible.

My mother's reaction hurt me very much. Of all people, I thought she'd understand. She'd had so many boyfriends, told so many dirty jokes about sex, got dressed in front of half the world. I didn't understand why she was so mean to me, calling me a whore and refusing to even listen when I tried to explain.

Up until now I guess everyone had just thought of me as a little girl. I guess it shocked them. What I couldn't figure out was why I was getting into such trouble for something they knew never happened. The doctor told them in front of me that I was a virgin. I heard him tell both my mother and Mrs Chadwick while I waited outside the door to the office, but the door was open.

The next afternoon I was back in the office. This time there was just Mrs Chadwick and myself. I sat with my hands clenched in my lap and felt a stinging lump in my throat.

She told me that I was going to face a very difficult time in the days ahead. They would let me stay in school because I was so young and could not be blamed for the entire thing. The boy was going to be expelled and I was going to be punished. Mother didn't want me at home for a while, she said. I was not allowed to go on the midsemester ski trip. The final punishment was to be one hundred hours of hard work. During the time that I was working off my punishment I was to be allowed no privileges.

As the litany of my punishment droned on, I sat dully staring at the middle-aged woman across from me. I couldn't believe my ears. Until that very moment I had not realized the full impact of what had happened. In its own way, this was as bad as the night raids at home, only I wasn't being physically beaten.

I left the office and walked like a ghost back to the dorm. The bleakness of my future had been graphically spelled out for me. I fleetingly wondered if it wouldn't have been easier just to be expelled and get the agony over with, but I forgot about that when the image of my mother's wrath appeared before me. She was so furious with me that she never asked if I was all right.

Somehow I got through the next week. I saw people staring at me but if I looked back they'd quickly turn away. Mostly I was just left alone.

During the vacation, I worked at school six hours a day, every day but Sunday. I pulled weeds and washed windows. I cleaned out classrooms and washed cars. I dusted every book in the library and scrubbed down all the tables and chairs in the dining room. At first I hated the work but gradually I got used to it. No one bothered me and I was alone most of the time.

But when school started again after the semester break it was a different story. By then the rumour had turned into a full-fledged story and it seemed that everyone had heard it.

For the next few weeks I was constantly on the verge of tears. At night I cried silently into my pillow so my roommates wouldn't be able to add to the rumour. During the day I did my best to get through classes and began to pour all my energy into my schoolwork. It was the only source of reward left.

Mother was still angry with me after several months, so she didn't come to visit me and I didn't go home until the end of the school year.

It was nice to see my brother and sisters again, but it didn't take me long to discover that we now had a horrible new nurse. Mrs Howe wasn't working full time for us any more, and the woman we had was a young, athletic brute who had her own ideas about how to treat us when no one else was around. She wasn't just strict, she was downright mean. She spanked us with a hanger or a belt, landing the blows wherever she wanted and not just across our bottoms. She had a miserable habit of twisting our ears to get us to do something, and we hated her.

One night Mother was dressed up to go out on a date, and she left instructions that I could watch television until the Spade Cooley programme was over. My brother and I used to scream with laughter over the live car commercials done by a man who called himself 'Leather-britches'. He'd bang his hand down on the hood of the car, telling you what a great deal it was while the whole vehicle rattled and shook. As he slammed doors and pounded away, my brother and I rolled on the floor with laughter. It was our favourite part of the programme.

Without saying one word to us, the nurse turned off the television during one of those commercials. 'Mother said we could watch to the end of Spade Cooley,' I told her.

'This show is nothing but silly trash,' she replied with a note of disgust in her voice.

'It doesn't matter what *you* think ... Mother said we could watch it!' I snapped back. With amazing speed, she slapped me across the face. I hated being slapped in the face. I hated it when my mother did it to me and I wasn't going to take it from any nurse. I raised my hand to hit her back but she grabbed me by the hair. She was considerably stronger than I was and she managed to pull me by the hair all the way upstairs and into my room. Once inside the room she released me by throwing me down on the bed. Then it looked as though she was coming after me again. I pulled my knees up to my chest and just as she leaned over to hit me I kicked her in the stomach with both my feet as hard as I could. To my astonishment, she went flying across the room and landed in a heap under the window. I had effectively knocked the wind out of her but she was not unconscious.

I sat on my bed staring at her, wondering what would happen next. After a minute or so she muttered something to me and then staggered out of the room holding on to her stomach.

The next morning I didn't say one word to the nurse, and when Mother asked me what had happened, I told her exactly. She asked me where I had got the idea to kick the nurse in the stomach. With a look of total innocence I replied, 'That's the way they do it in the cowboy movies.'

The nurse was promptly fired, but I didn't get to watch my cowboy movies for a week. I thought it was a fair price to pay if it got rid of that woman we all hated.

We were generally having trouble keeping any servants. Cooks, nurses, secretaries, and the rest came and went with regularity. Many of the nurses couldn't tolerate what one referred to as the 'reform-school discipline' we had to live under. If they were ever caught trying to bend those rules even a little bit, they were fired. After a while it was hard to keep their names straight as one blended into another. For a period of time we hadn't been able to keep anyone longer than a couple of months. Just as we got used to one, she packed up and left, and we never saw her again. It seemed to me that the nicer they were, the faster they left.

We did have one terrific nurse, who was English. She was neither young nor old and she knew wonderful games which she taught all of us. She was strict enough to satisfy Mother and kind enough to be tolerable to us, but she didn't last long, either.

It was in the middle of 1951 that Mother did one of her last pictures for Warner Bros. It was not a very good film and she knew it. She also probably knew that she wasn't going to be under contract to that studio much longer either.

Since Mother didn't share her problems with anyone in the house, we were only aware that she seemed angry and edgy much of the time. Mother had a 'wounded animal' attitude towards adversity. She tended to go off by herself to brood and suffer alone rather than let anyone know she was hurt. That may have spared her ego to some extent, but it kept things bottled up inside her and left little room for discussion or sharing in her relationships. She thought other people should behave in the same stalwart, solitary manner and saw it as a mark of weakness if they didn't. What her attitude really did was confine her behind a mask of strength, and it kept people, including her children, at a distance. It contributed in great measure to her loneliness and to her feeling of having to fight every inch of the way alone. She had a terrible time trusting anyone or letting others see that she was human with the failings and frailties that usually implies. She made mistakes but she wouldn't admit them. Things that went wrong in the household were said to be someone else's fault, even if the blame was hers alone. She lied to herself about life as it went on around her until she could no longer tell the difference between reality and her personal version of it.

She had set her course. Any deviation from that prescribed routine was interpreted as failure, lack of willpower. She put great store in personal willpower and attributed her own success to it. That willpower guided her through the rough waters of each day. It was translated into rules governing all facets of household management, the children's discipline, and her own career. Nothing was left to chance or experiment or interpretation by others. She had set the rules without consultation and enforced them without deviation. By virtue of having been created, those rules carried with them the weight of moral rightness. They were absolutely right in her mind. Everything and everyone else was simply wrong. Her way was *the* way and she would not listen to any contrary opinion. She believed that enough rules, rigidly enforced, would keep the world in order. It was a way of holding back total chaos and with it any spontaneous, chance infringement on her territory.

There is no creature more perverse than the human being. If there is chaos in a life, no amount of regulation and willpower holds it in abeyance for ever. The inner turbulence will find the weakest link in the armour of each personality. For my mother that weak link was alcohol.

One night during that summer vacation, I was watching television until my usual bedtime. When I went upstairs I noticed that one of the doors to Mother's suite of rooms was open. I knew she was home but I didn't hear any sounds of movement or talking on the phone. I went into my own room and got ready for bed. By then it was about nine thirty and I knocked on Mother's door intending to say goodnight. There was no answer to either my knocking or my calling, which I thought was strange.

I went downstairs to check if she was anywhere else in the house but she wasn't. When I went back to her doorway I thought I heard a small noise like a moan but I wasn't sure. I walked into the upstairs sitting room and through the main door into her dressing room. There were a few lights on but I didn't see her anywhere. I made a circular tour of the dressing room and bath area and started down the narrow hallway on the opposite side of the room. When I went through the first door I nearly stumbled over Mother's body lying on the floor.

Seeing her lying so still sent a surge of panic through me. I kneeled beside her and tried to rouse her, thinking maybe she'd just fainted. I couldn't get any response, though I did see she was still breathing. Since I was unable to move her by myself, I rushed to get some help.

The first person I found was our English nurse. Half babbling my story, I pulled her back to where Mother was lying unconscious. I was afraid that she was sick. I had to fight to remain even relatively calm. We leaned over the body and turned Mother face up.

'Should I call the doctor?' I whispered. The nurse shook her head negatively. 'What's wrong with her?' I whispered again. The nurse looked me straight in the eyes and said, 'She's drunk.' 'Drunk? Are you sure?' I asked her. She just nodded her head affirmatively and said, 'It's not the first time,' and indicated that I should help her carry Mother to bed. I was surprised how difficult it was for the two of us to manoeuvre the limp body safely across one room and into bed. Once there, we covered her and I arranged the pillows under her head.

We turned out the lights and closed the sliding doors behind us. I said goodnight and the nurse went back to her room on the other side of the house.

I lay in bed thinking about what had happened, trying to piece it all together. I thought about the times Mother seemed to be different and I never knew why. Then I realized that it was usually in the evening after she'd had a few drinks. Then I thought about the aspirin in the morning, which had been going on for several years now. But a hangover would explain why she was so mean in the morning even if she'd slept until nearly noon and we'd had to whisper and tiptoe around. I'd heard other kids talk about their parents' drinking problems. I tried to think back over those conversations and sort this out for myself, since I was certain there wasn't anyone I could trust to discuss it with me.

Nothing was ever mentioned about the incident. I don't know if my mother ever wondered how she got into bed that night, but I never said a word to her.

Before I left for camp that summer there were several more times when the English nurse and I carried Mother to bed. Her passing out drunk didn't scare me any more. I just found myself listening for the significant noises at night and then getting the nurse to help me. There was a dreamlike quality about the whole thing, since in the light of day, no one mentioned either the specific incident or the overall problem. It was as though none of it ever happened. But when I came home from camp, our nice English nurse had quit.

The rest of the help we were now getting from the employment agencies were next to useless. The cooks were incompetent. One woman was so nervous she actually burned a pot of green beans so badly that the entire mess, including the pot, had to be thrown out. She lasted one day.

The replacements were no better. They turned out frizzled, rubbery fried eggs, burnt toast, soggy vegetables, and watery sauces. They couldn't be trusted to do the shopping properly, broke things, and generally lived in a state of chronic nervous collapse. Mother's screaming didn't improve matters. She had a way of giving people a long string of orders all at once, expecting them to remember all the instructions and do them in the exact order she'd given them. For all of these people, that was an impossible feat. They couldn't seem to do the job they were hired for, let alone anything creative or complex. Mother was in a state of rage that never let up between the firing of one unfortunate and the hiring of the next. An atmosphere of extreme agitation permeated the entire household. After a while, the most qualified person in the world who would have come into that kitchen would never have had a chance. The only good thing from my point of view was that these incompetents couldn't cook meat rare!

Word of Mother's rampages filtered back to the employment agencies. The turnover at our house became common knowledge, and eventually the agencies wouldn't send us any applicants. So Mother hired one of the fans as a secretary and another fan as a nurse.

Fortunately I spent six weeks of that summer at camp in Carmel. Unfortunately, most of those six weeks was spent in the infirmary with a miserable combination of boils and poison oak. I was the original calamine kid that year.

When I returned from camp looking much improved but still dreadful, Mother said that Mrs Chadwick wanted to speak with me. There was some question about whether or not I would return to school. My heart was in my throat as I dialled the phone. In the last year and a half I'd grown to really like the school. I had assumed I would be going back in the fall, now I didn't know what to expect.

Mrs Chadwick told me she realized that I still had a struggle on my hands and she wanted to give me the opportunity to decide whether I wanted to stay or if I thought it would be easier for me to start over fresh somewhere else. I hadn't anticipated that I'd have a chance to make this decision about my own life, and I had to think for a moment. My considerable difficulties with the previous school year paraded across my memory. I thought about what progress I'd been able to make and knew that she was right about still having to struggle. But I also thought about my friends, particularly the ones like Hoagy and Jane who had stood by me. If I left now it would be an admission of defeat. If I left, I wouldn't be around to defend myself. I was determined to fight for full acceptance. I said I wanted to stay at Chadwick. She said she was proud to hear I had the courage to see it through.

I had no way of knowing that the eighth grade was going to be the worst year yet.

ELEVEN

At home I had been living under a permanent 'second chance' status ever since that fateful Friday night six months before. I was given no leeway for minor infractions of the rules under this 'second chance'. I had the feeling that whatever I did was suspect and it began to make me nervous. I was never sure whether this would be the day when I did something that would wipe out even the tenuous status of my existence and I'd find myself in serious trouble again. I lived those days certain that I was standing on the brink of an unseen disaster.

There were only four eighth-grade girls who were boarding students that year, so it was decided we would all live at the Chadwicks' house and not at the dorm on campus.

At the beginning of school there was nothing to indicate that this was going to be such a difficult year for me except perhaps the 'second chance' attitude at home.

So many of the students lived in the West Los Angeles and Beverly Hills areas that a private bus service was arranged to take us to and from school twice a month. At first I went home every other weekend like everyone else. But those weekends with Mother were not going well and I knew it. There seemed to be an endless list of things I was supposed to do when I got home. We were chronically short of help, and many times I spent most of the weekend doing laundry and cleaning house. If my mother was having company there was all the silver to polish, and the dining room table to set. And in the evening when guests arrived I often tended bar and served them dinner. Mother was trying to keep up appearances.

When I got home on Friday I'd be just fine. By Saturday I'd be tired, and on Sunday I was nervous all over again. It was not unusual for me to lose weight during those weekends because Mother was for ever after me. Either I hadn't done something properly or I moved too slowly. She kept me running from the time I got up until long after dinner.

Chris was about eight now and beginning to feel the brunt of the work, too. More than once she kept him up until after midnight scrubbing the floor of the dining room in which we ate. She made him do that floor on his hands and knees time after time as she found one flaw after another, first in his work and then in his attitude. It was, by now, a familiar pattern. I couldn't do anything to help him. If I opened my mouth, both of us got in trouble.

Mother's strategy with the family was divide and conquer. One of us kids had to be in trouble all the time. Now it was my brother's turn to be the family scapegoat. I was at school most of the time, so he was next in line. Mother whipped him at the slightest provocation. She hadn't changed any of her strict rules of conduct to accommodate a boy. Chris was at the age when he wanted to ride bikes and play ball and go swimming all day, but he was held captive in a houseful of women. My brother was forced into playing catch with the nurse, riding his bike only around the back yard, and when he did have a friend over, they had to be careful about the flower beds or making too much noise. He had no father to play with or learn from. There was no man around who might understand from his own childhood what a young boy growing up goes through. Most of the whippings and the trouble he got into for simply being a boy seemed cruel. Chris began to change from a happy, charming little prankster with a mischievous twinkle in his eyes to a highly-strung young boy.

As I watched the hateful way Mother treated my brother, I realized for the first time that she really didn't like men. The real reason Chris was being punished was that he'd ceased being the adorable little baby Mother could dress up and cuddle. He was turning into a boy who would soon grow into a man. Look-

127

ing back over those years, I also realized that part of Mother's hostility to her son was a spillover from her childhood battle with her own brother. She had never in her life experienced a positive relationship with a man. When she was a child herself, three fathers deserted her, later she annihilated her older brother, and in her adult life, all three of her marriages had ended in divorce.

In later years Mother professed to be mortally afraid of her son. If so, her fear was the result of her own guilty conscience. Better than anyone else, she knew those years of abuse, whippings, and tying the boy down in bed every night. All Chris ever tried to do in his early years was to get away from her and survive.

But if my brother was having problems, mine seemed to double. By the end of these weekends I was worn out, not so much by the work but by the constant strain. I was on the verge of tears half the time, and the other half I was sullen and quiet, withdrawing into myself as a means of protection.

Mother had several long talks with Mrs Chadwick. She said I was a bad influence on my brother and sisters. She said it would be better if I didn't come home for a while.

I knew why she didn't want me at home any more. I was old enough now at twelve to understand, to see what was going on in the madhouse. I was a witness to the beatings she gave my brother, the revolving boyfriends who came and went at all hours of the night, her increasingly serious problem with alcoholism, the homosexuals she surrounded herself with, and her inability to control that violent temper she unleashed periodically. I wasn't old enough to intervene, I couldn't do anything to stop her, but when I looked her square in the face she *knew* I understood all of it and she found my knowledge intolerable. So she turned the turmoil at home into a reason for banishing me.

I didn't particularly want to stay at school every weekend, but in a way it was a relief. At least I knew what to expect from life there and things went smoothly.

What I didn't anticipate was that since I was no longer going home on weekends, Mother would call Mrs Chadwick at least once a week in the evening to check up on me. She just couldn't leave me alone or allow my life to go peacefully. I dreaded those phone calls. No matter how calmly the week at school had gone, there was always something Mother magnified out of proportion. Then I'd have to take a verbal beating while she bawled me out for whatever this week's trumped-up charge happened to be. After the phone calls, I'd be in tears again.

It took me months to figure out that Mother was drinking when she made these phone calls. I couldn't convince Mrs Chadwick, though, because Mother was deceptive. She didn't sound drunk. She didn't slur her words or wander off in her train of thought. She seemed to be even sharper and quicker than normal. But she was always angry and always irrational. She made up stories about things that had *never* happened. She became fanatical about rules and regulations. She'd badger Mrs Chadwick to relate every minor detail of my behaviour until she found something to be angry about. Then she made her accusations with such authority and conviction that no one dreamed of challenging the truth of them. It would be her word against mine and she won. Then she insisted on a severe punishment for me.

But finally Mrs Chadwick, who believed in the intrinsic good of every human being, began to sense that I couldn't always be the one who was lying. She lived with me every day and I didn't lie about anything else. She knew I was doing very well at school, getting good reports and making friends.

But the better I did the harder Mother tried to find something wrong with me. She insisted on perpetuating her image of me as a bad girl who lied and was not to be trusted for an instant. She found ways to have me punished whether she was present or not.

Because I lived with this perpetual threat of doom and was under fire from my mother, I was set apart from the other kids and their normal routine. The faculty had been told to watch me carefully and I felt it. It was uncomfortable and there were times when I was honestly tempted to do something wrong just to warrant the suspicion.

My Christmas vacation at home this year was a total disaster. I spent most of the two weeks in my room being punished or writing those never-ending thank-you notes. What time remained I spent with the three female fans working on the assembly line in our dining room turning out stacks of completed photo mailers. Mother was now short of one secretary. The autographed photos to her fans all over the world had been backlogged for months.

I was so glad to get back to school I couldn't believe it. Naturally, Mother told Mrs Chadwick that I didn't deserve to go home again in the near future because of my insolent attitude. She said that I made the entire household unhappy. It was a nightmare. Mother took everything she did and put the blame for it on me. It was enough to make you believe you were losing your mind.

Mrs Chadwick sighed and shook her head. I had the awful feeling I'd disappointed her after our long talk just before the vacation when I'd promised to be good and to try to get along.

I was *always* promising to be good, but it never quite worked out. When Mother yelled at me I rarely talked back. When Mother was drinking I'd try to stay out of her way. It was the look on my face that got me into most of the trouble.

At school I had already learned not to call her after five o'clock in the afternoon. Even earlier in the day she might still be nasty, but any later than five she was definitely drunk and impossible.

I had no control, however, over what time she called Mrs Chadwick. One night in February around nine o'clock, just such an unwanted call occurred. Mrs Chadwick was on the phone with her for some time and then came downstairs to tell me to get on the extension. Mother wanted to talk to both of us. I knew instantly that something was wrong. I picked up the phone with trepidation, but though my mind was racing through the past few days, I could find nothing that might have caused trouble.

Mother's voice had that icy edge to it and I knew that she was already off and running in her rage. She asked why I insisted on wearing my coat to classes.

I couldn't believe that was the issue, or that Mrs Chadwick had even mentioned it to her. One day during the past week, I'd kept my coat on during one class because it was colder than usual. Mrs Chadwick had told me to bring a sweater that morning but I didn't think I'd need it. That evening she told me not to be so shortsighted again and that was the end of it. A simple miscalculation on my part that no one considered particularly important.

But here it was, blown totally out of proportion. I really couldn't believe it. As I listened to Mother spew her anger over the phone I realized it didn't matter what the reason was. Now it was just another excuse for one of her rampages against me. She was screaming on the other end of the phone and I had to hold the receiver away from my ear. She was shouting, 'Why the hell do you disobey everybody?' and 'Who the hell do you think you are to know it all?' I had no chance to explain; I just kept my mouth closed, hoping that if I didn't add anything she'd calm down after a while. I was wrong.

My silence just infuriated her more. I couldn't win. If I said anything, she told me I was being insolent. If I didn't say anything, she became enraged. I knew from experience that the conversation was getting worse. But I also knew I hadn't done anything wrong.

She had got herself into such a state that she believed I was simply bad, and if she didn't get bad reports about me then it could only mean that someone was covering up for me. She was convinced that I duped people into thinking that I was someone she knew I wasn't. She considered herself the only keeper of the truth. Again and again she glued herself to her own imaginings and refused to hear any opinion to the contrary.

Then she said that if I was so determined to wear my goddamned coat to class, I could wear it and nothing else! She said all my clothes would be picked up the next day. 'Mother,' I interrupted, 'the coat has only *one* button. I can't wear just that to school!'

'You should have thought of that *before* you disobeyed,' she snapped, and without another word she slammed the phone down, hanging up on us.

I couldn't move. I was riveted to the spot with fury. What the hell was going on around here that no one seemed to have the guts or the nerve to tell that insane bitch to knock it off? Everyone turned to Jell-O the minute she started raising her voice, which was also her favourite tactic. She bullied people into subservience.

Mrs Chadwick was ashen. She put her arms around me and I

burst into tears. 'Mrs Chadwick . . . what am I going to do? That coat only has *one* button!'

She sat me down and we started to talk. She thought that maybe in the light of day, Mother would reconsider. I told her she was wrong, that my mother *would* send someone to pick up all my clothes.

'Mrs Chadwick . . . *why* did you tell Mother that?'

She looked down at the floor and then straight at me. 'She simply wouldn't accept the fact that you are doing well. She insisted I go over each day in detail until I came to the business about the coat . . .' Her voice trailed off and the two of us sat in silence.

'Mrs Chadwick, I am *not* going to school in just my underwear and that coat! I don't care *what* Mother said or didn't say, I am not going out of this house in my underwear and a coat. Someone will have to forcibly drag me out and I'll fight every inch of the way. *I will not do it.*' I was surprised at the forcefulness with which I'd told her how I felt. It was the first time I'd ever done that.

She was in complete agreement. It was unthinkable to send me to school like that. She might as well be considering sending me naked.

The next day, just as I predicted, Mother sent someone to get all my clothes while I was at school. They cleaned me out. They took everything but one short-sleeved cotton dress.

Since it was only February, that left me with two dresses to wear for the next four months. I was so mad I couldn't talk. I was also mad at Mrs Chadwick for telling Mother in the first place. I'd told her that when Mother was drinking she became totally irrational, but up till now I don't think she really believed me.

Even though some of the girls offered to lend me clothes because they felt so bad about what had happened, I wasn't allowed to wear anything except those two dresses. Everyone was afraid Mother would find out that her orders weren't being followed and the situation would get worse.

That made me madder still. *How* was she going to find out if no one told her? Why was everyone in the world so chickenshit?

As days turned into weeks of having to wear those same two dresses, my anger sank into depression. Most of the other students were from wealthy homes and some of the kids were very clothes-conscious. A number of my girl-friends even had special clothing allowances. And then there was me, looking like a goddamned orphan.

After a month of this idiocy, my one pair of shoes wore out. At first it was just the stitching around the top and a hole in the sole. Then the entire sole of the right shoe began flapping. I'd asked Mrs Chadwick to tell Mother I needed another pair of shoes weeks before, but nothing happened. Finally, one morning I was so mad I threw the shoes in the trash and appeared barefoot. That did it. That afternoon Mrs Chadwick bought shoes for me with her own money.

I didn't go to most of the school dances because I was too embarrassed to appear in either one of my two dresses when all the other girls had special outfits. Anyway, none of the boys asked me because they didn't want to be embarrassed, either.

As the months progressed, my punishment had some unexpected side effects. Everyone knew what had happened to me. Some people felt sorry for me and would look at me with pity and I didn't like it. But having to wear my punishment week after week in full view began to make other people mad too. I sensed an invisible turning of the tide in my favour. I was too proud to ever complain, but people started going out of their way to give me encouragement, extra credit, little additional privileges; whatever was within their direct responsibility and didn't break any existing rules.

When the heat of summer began, I cut the sleeves off one of the two dresses. The trouble was that the two dresses were exactly alike except for the colour. One was blue plaid and the other was green plaid. I was so sick of looking at those two dresses! They'd been washed and ironed twice a week for over four months now and they'd begun to fade. The only change of clothes I had was my bathing suit and gym outfit. Four months turns into an eternity when you're twelve years old. I felt as if I'd been wearing those same two dresses half my life.

When school was finally over in June, I went home for a few weeks. I was more aware of the rules at home now that I'd been away from them for a while and learned to live differently. Not that the Chadwicks weren't strict, because they were. It was just that you could talk to them and the rules they set were reasonable, workable, easier to live with even if you didn't like them. At home it seemed that the rules existed for their own sake. The timetable was set primarily to keep everyone under control.

I tried to get to know my sisters again. They were about five and cute little girls. I realized they were growing up without knowing me very well because I'd been away at school most of the last two years.

Mother took all of us to Alisal Ranch in the Santa Ynez valley for a week. We liked Alisal because of its casual atmosphere. We were free to go riding and swimming all day and didn't have to check in with Mother every few hours.

When we arrived at the ranch, I had to laugh. There, by total coincidence, of course, was one of the current uncles waiting for us. I should have known. The uncles had a habit of turning up in the most unlikely places. I should have got used to it by now. This time it didn't matter so much because Uncle David was very nice and I genuinely liked him. He was married, but he brought his kids with him while his wife visited relatives, or some such story. In the dining room we all ate at the same table just like one big happy family.

Mother didn't mention one word about the dresses or my coat or the months of humiliation I'd just been through. It was as though it had never happened. Because she hadn't seen me day after day, she appeared to have forgotten all about it. It was bizarre how quickly she changed. Of course, the two dresses were unusable by the time I'd come home and they'd been thrown away immediately.

There was a new student back at Chadwick in my summer school class. His name was Jim Fadiman and at first I didn't like him because he was a 'know-it-all'. Then I found out that he really was brilliant, and I decided that if we didn't become friends we were so competitive that we'd be enemies. That was the beginning of a wonderful friendship.

After summer school was over I didn't go home again for the end of that summer. It had nothing to do with punishment. Mother was going to be in Texas with friends. She said she didn't have time to see my brother and me, that the nurse could only manage to take care of my sisters at home, so Chris and I would have to stay at school. All the other students went home, of course. Technically, the school was closed except for a few faculty members who lived on campus. Mother didn't write us or call us. It was peaceful but it was lonely and very boring.

I was allowed to spend one week with a girl-friend at her family beach house. I felt like Rip Van Winkle, waking up in a strange world. This was the first time I'd experienced what was considered a fairly typical teenage romp through summertime, complete with beach parties, drive-ins, and blind dates. In contrast with the previous dreary weeks, it was like paradise for me.

TWELVE

As I began ninth grade in the fall of 1952, Hollywood was in a state of enormous change if not chaos. The major studios were losing control over the film industry and their stables of stars, producers, directors, and writers. The McCarthy hearings in Washington, D.C., had the result of blacklisting talented men and women in every facet of the motion-picture industry, forcing them to find work in the New York theatre if they were lucky or migrating to Europe if they had no other alternative. MCA was on the brink of being forced to divest itself of either its agency or its production branches, and television was beginning to be a serious threat to the entire industry establishment.

Changes were happening quickly. The power structure altered rapidly. Nothing was going to be quite the same again. Very few of the new breed of independent films found their way into national release or distribution, but some of the most courageous were beginning to find a small measure of success. It was a very risky business.

My mother called me at school one night extremely upset. She said she had very bad news for me. From the tone of her voice and her choice of words, I thought someone had died. Then she told me that she'd left Warner Bros. She said that she no longer had a contract, she didn't have a job, and she was almost totally broke. For the first time in my life I heard the faint glimmer of humility in my mother's voice. She was not her angry self, she sounded embarrassed, frightened, and even apologetic. She'd been in Hollywood more than twenty-seven years and this was the first time in her career that she didn't have a studio contract, the first time she was without the backing, the security and the paycheck of a major studio. She was totally on her own for the first time since she was twenty-one years old. My mother was scared and I could hear it in her voice. The trauma was still too new, too immediate, for her usual defences to surface and cover up the hurt, the insecurity, and the panic. There was nothing I could do to help but listen. I sensed that she had no one else to turn to and that she needed to talk.

When our conversation was over she thanked me, asked me to be brave, and told me that she loved me.

A few months later, Mother began work on her first independent film, *Sudden Fear*. It was an excellent film, well written, excitingly directed, and interestingly cast. For her performance, Mother received a third Academy Award nomination as Best Actress. She did not win another Oscar, but her career accelerated again.

But when the picture finished filming, Mother was right back in the position of having to find another job. She did the only things she knew to do. She set up the fan-mail production lines in our house again, she read every line of the trade papers, seeking out producers with good projects, and she read mountains of scripts. She even enlisted my aid. I wrote script synopses for her on one-page, typed sheets. When I was home I read the trades aloud to her when she was having her massage and read scripts to her while she was having her hair dyed and her nails done. She worked nonstop trying to find ideas for films and even suggested television ideas to anyone who would listen. She made it her personal business to know all the gossip in town. She'd laugh sometimes about how far from the truth some of the items in the trade papers were and then proceeded to tell me her version of the incident. Hearing her change the entire colouration of the printed story from her own storehouse of information was a fascinating education. She had an uncanny sense of how things worked in her special world. She never tired of the innuendos, the inferences, and she put the pieces of the puzzle together in masterful fashion. I thought she'd have made a superlative spy.

There were two subjects, however, that she would never discuss. One was religion and the other was politics. Religion was a purely personal matter in her opinion. Politics was just totally off limits in her house. Unless it had something to do with the film industry, she didn't even allow any discussion of current events. We never knew how she voted, if she voted, or anything about her view of the rest of the world. The very mention of politics made her visibly uncomfortable. If anyone asked her opinion, she simply said that she never discussed religion or politics and left it at that.

Mother's 'comeback' with *Mildred Pierce* had got her a professional reprieve, which was followed two years later by a second Academy Award nomination for *Possessed*. But with the demise of her Warner Bros. contract and then the finish of her independent film she was having to struggle for each and every job. Even with a third Academy Award nomination for *Sudden Fear*, one picture no longer automatically led to another. She was in her late forties and fighting for every inch of her career.

In 1953 she tried to remedy part of her predicament by marrying Milton Rachmil, a Decca Records executive who had come to Hollywood to take over as head of Universal Studios. On the very day they were to be married in Las Vegas, Nevada, they had an argument and the whole thing was called off. That morning they left her house together in the limousine because they both had studios to report to before leaving for Las Vegas. On the way to work they had a fight about who was going to be dropped off first. That was the end of the marriage plans. Guests were called and the party in Las Vegas cancelled. I learned the story years later because at the time, Mother never mentioned her plans to us. She remained single for another two years.

Perhaps because she was so busy taking care of her personal life, Mother didn't have time to pay much attention to us. My brother and I both lived at Chadwick School and didn't go home very often. We didn't get into the trouble that usually followed one of those weekends at home, either, so it wasn't such a bad trade-off.

I continued to have difficulty convincing Mother that I needed clothes or that I wanted to fit in with the other students. What quirk it was that made my requests impossible for Mother to fulfil was beyond me. She had been such an integral part of her own generation as a young woman, rising to stardom as the epitome of the jazz age, that it seemed unlikely she didn't understand my feelings. But somehow she had become stuck in her ideas about clothes and fashion. She still clung to her 1940s image with the ankle-strap shoes and the big shoulder pads. Ten years later, in 1953, it seemed out of date. But, since she was inflexible, the solution of my problem with school clothes was left to my own ingenuity. I eventually found ways to supplement the clothes she provided with others more in keeping with current teenage fads. The only problem was that I couldn't take my other clothes home. But arguing over clothes with my mother was a minor part of my other concerns at school that year.

One night before dinner, I was part of a group standing around the outside patio waiting for the dining room doors to open. Next to me were three or four boys from the eleventh grade who were new students that fall. It was impossible for me not to hear what they were saying. I was the topic of their conversation. One boy was telling another that old, tired story about my seventh-grade mishap, only over the years the story had been considerably embellished.

I was so tired of fighting this battle time after time that I felt sick to my stomach. Even so, I think I would have let it go and said nothing if the boy who'd just told the story hadn't tried to slide his arm around me provocatively as part of the punch line.

My outrage at his behaviour was really the culmination of two years of hassles and sly smiles and lost boy-friends and not being trusted by the faculty. It was two years of fighting for respect and friendship. It was two years of anxiety and frustration and anger that went into my closed fist as I whirled around to face this young man who towered over me. Without a second thought or a moment's hesitation I carried through with my fist and belted him right in the middle of his stomach. It was so unexpected that he lost his balance, staggered a few steps backward, tripped, and fell into the shallow fishpond. While only the two boys standing next to him had seen me slug him in the stomach, half the student body witnessed his spectacular plunge into the fishpond. Water splashed everywhere and several large goldfish went flying out onto the patio. Everyone roared with laughter at him as he sat in the middle of the pond totally drenched and completely bewildered. After a moment, even I laughed. I walked away with a feeling of silent triumph.

But I knew I couldn't go around punching people when they said something that I didn't like or that hurt my feelings. I was getting worn out fighting for every single accomplishment each day of my life. I knew I had to have some help. What I needed was a boy-friend, but the boys I liked didn't like me.

Then, like an answer to my prayers, I found Walter. Everyone loved Walter. He was captain of the football team and student-body president. He was built like a defensive lineman and nobody argued with him. He may not have been the most handsome man in the senior class but he was certainly the most respected, the most powerful, and the best liked.

When Walter asked me to go steady with him, I accepted happily. I wore his ring on a chain around my neck and took my place among the 'popular' girls. Now, even when I was alone no one bothered me. I had Walter beside me whether he was physically present or not.

After school ended in June I went home. I made arrangements for one of my girlfriends to take my contraband clothes home with her over the summer so my mother wouldn't find out about them.

Walter had graduated and I didn't know how we were going to keep in touch. I was supposed to come back for summer school and I told him I'd call then. I didn't want him to write me at home because my mail was opened and my telephone calls were monitored.

As usual, going home after several months was a challenge. I was away so much that when I came back everything seemed to be in sharper focus. Before, for instance, I hadn't minded the daily tour buses with their loudspeakers blaring away the brief history of each movie star's home. Now I found them a totally offensive invasion of privacy. Even though we had a very high front fence covered with ivy, I hated the way tourists in those buses would stand up and strain to peek over the fence into our lives. If I happened to be in the front yard, I'd go in the house when I heard the bus coming down the street.

Then there was the small group of women who had been Mother's fans for years and years. They would come and spend an entire day sitting on the garage steps, waiting for a chance to see Joan Crawford. I couldn't imagine why they did that every weekend. It was irksome to know they were perched on those steps like birds waiting for a few crumbs of bread all day long. But week after week, there they were, patiently waiting.

I got to know them very well because they were the same women who were commandeered for the special work details Mother ran when the garden furniture needed washing or the basement needed cleaning or the fan mail had stacked up. These women were mostly secretaries by profession, all were single, and I guess being a 'fan' was more interesting than being alone. So they jumped at the chance to work their asses off in the service and presence of their favourite movie star.

And work they certainly did. Manual labour and menial tasks. Nothing was too mean or too heavy or too dirty for them. I couldn't understand it. I worked right beside them and I hated those jobs with a passion. But they didn't seem to mind a bit. They almost never accepted money for their hours of work, though on occasion Mother did offer to pay them. Their reward was serving their idol. They never spoke up to defend themselves when Mother heaped abuse upon the quality of their work. They just looked heartbroken and worked all the harder. They never disagreed with anything Mother said or did, even when she pushed them to the limit. They said yes to whatever she asked of them, even if it meant giving up their own spare time and energy.

They were like a small band of puppets moving and swaying to her every wish and whim. They served her with loyalty and devotion and were completely self-effacing about it. They wanted no money, no praise; they only wanted to serve.

That behaviour was what Mother eventually wanted from everyone around her. I drove her into a blue fury because I wasn't like the fans. I hated doing the dirty work of the house when I came home from school. I hated being treated like a mute puppet. I had to say 'Yes, Mommie dearest' so many times that the very sound of it nearly made me vomit. She made me call her 'Mommie dearest' now whether I wanted to or not. And even when I dutifully said 'Yes, Mommie dearest', I got in trouble anyway for the tone of my voice or the look on my face. She wanted me to act like one of those puppet fans and I couldn't do it. There were times when I thought the things she did were wrong. Even if I didn't say anything for fear of getting beaten or having my mouth washed out with soap until I gagged, she knew that I disagreed with her and it made her crazy. It was then that she'd fly into one of her fits of temper and accuse me of doing things I'd never done. Then, she'd punish me for the story *she'd* made up! If I denied what she accused me of doing, she called me a liar and told everyone in the house that she was at her wits' end with me because I lied all the time. No one believed me. It was like living with a lunatic. It was a living nightmare.

I guess it was impossible for an adult who had not been present to believe that *she* was the one who was lying and I was telling the truth. She was always so convincing. She appeared to be so genuinely upset over the situation that she even received a certain amount of sympathy for all her troubles.

She couldn't force me to say yes any more or to curtsey or to be the perfect and adoring child. I was becoming a person with my own ideas and dreams and thoughts about what was right and wrong. At school we were encouraged to think independently, but that was forbidden at home. At home you lived by her rules without discussion whether you were her child or her husband or her fan or her servant. She told everyone what to wear and what to eat and what to think as well.

By now the servant problem was acute. The fans filled most of the void. Mother was unable to keep anyone else, even temporary help. We already had one fan as our nurse. She was not nearly as strict with us as Mother wanted, but when Mother was at home, she made us keep all the rules intact. When Mother wasn't there, she was more lenient. She became our friend and we grew to love her.

Unfortunately, she was too good to last. The fan who was now Mother's part-time secretary seemed jealous of the fan who was our nurse and living in the house with us. She consistently made trouble for her and us. She was like a spy reporting back to Mother the minor details of anything she could wheedle out of anyone in the house. After about six months Mommie dearest also became aware that we really cared about our new nurse and she was fired. Luckily, she got a job as a secretary again and never mentioned being a nurse at Crawford's asylum.

Years later I saw her in New York. I was about nineteen at the time. After I'd unburdened my troubles to her for several hours, she told me the real reason she'd had to leave our house many years before. She said that she was sorry about leaving us because she felt that she'd been able to make our lives a little easier, which was true.

After she'd been with us several months, she said, she realized that Mother started drinking really heavily at night after we'd all gone to bed. I knew it had been a bad time for Mother because she was trying to get another film to do and kept complaining about always being in debt with bills piling up and the house under a second mortgage. She was making between $150,000 and $200,000 per picture, and even at one picture a year, that was a substantial salary in the 1950s. It was hard to imagine my mother having no money, but that's what she said, in spite of all appearances to the contrary.

In addition I knew that her drinking was getting worse. Alcohol unleashed so much anger in the woman that it was frightening to be around her. She was never easy to deal with when she was under stress, but when the problem was compounded by her drinking, she was impossible.

The former nurse then told me that one night Mother came into her room and wanted her to have a drink. The woman said no. Mother got angry and stormed back into her own room, slamming the door behind her. A few nights later the woman was already asleep and woke up to find Mother standing next to her bed. Again, my mother asked her to join her in a drink. Mother was unsteady on her feet and must have been drinking alone half the night. Then she said that Mother invited her to come into her room and sleep with her. The woman said no to that proposition. After a few choice swear words, Mother left. From then on, the woman locked the door to her room at night. But, when Mother got drunk she'd come and pound on the door, cursing and demanding that she unlock the door immediately and let her in. The woman would say nothing and not move from her bed until finally my mother left. The woman decided she couldn't stay with us any longer.

It didn't shock me because I already knew about my mother's lesbian proclivities, and this only added to what I had already figured out for myself.

What I did think about was the pieces of the puzzle of my own childhood. I thought about the night raids, the rose garden, and orange-tree decapitation. I thought about the famous movie star with no man and no job who drank herself into a solitary fury and vented her rage on those who couldn't protect themselves. I thought about the drunken arguments, the irrational anger, the fabricated stories, and the lies about me. I thought about how excruciatingly ugly and sad it was.

During the early summer of 1953 when those events were still going on, I only lasted a few weeks at home. With a sigh of relief, I went back to the Chadwicks' house after summer school, since there wasn't anywhere else for me to go.

Walter had come to see me on campus several times during the summer. I guess we were still going together. Towards the end of summer, he came to see me for the first time at the Chadwicks' home to say goodbye before he left on vacation and then went away to college. The only other person in the house that afternoon was a thin Japanese woman who worked for the Chadwicks. When she told me that Walter was at the door, I was surprised and delighted. He stayed for about an hour. We sat outside with some iced tea and he told me about all his future plans. He told me he'd keep in touch with me. I knew I'd miss him very much and it was nice to hear that he still cared. He kissed me goodbye, and after I walked him to his car I went back to finish my work.

I thought it was absurd that Mrs Chadwick was angry with me when she found out about Walter's unexpected visit. She said I wasn't supposed to have any visitors without her permission. For once I stood up to her and said I hadn't asked him to come over, I hadn't opened the door to let him in. What was I supposed to do? Tell Walter to go back outside and wait while I called someone to ask if I could see him?

She and Commander went into a conference right after she

The Pictures in this photo section are all selected from my own scrapbook, which was compiled over many years by my mother and sent to me when our Brentwood house was sold. This was the first photograph of Mommie and me. I was two months old according to her note on the back.

Snuggled with my giant Panda.

With Mommie and my new daddy,
Phillip Terry, shortly after their marriage.

In my nursery with new building
blocks.

Listening to fairy tales.

A typical day in my Hollywood childhood, posing for the cameras.

Even with my father to protect me, I was still quite shy with the clown.

With my brother wrapped in our father's jacket.

With Mommie on the Del Monte Lodge lawn.

Posing for fans outside our back door. Now my brother and I have matching trim on our outfits.

Backstage at the circus, totally awestruck.

Going down to the docks to see Mommie off on her trip to Hawaii. Both my brother and I had to wear white gloves whenever we appeared in public.

With Mommie at Union Station boarding the train for New York in 1946.

At a toy store opening in Beverly Hills that was just for show.

With my newly adopted sisters in the nursery.

I had progressed to the Girl Scouts at about the age of ten.

On one of our 'dates' to a Hollywood premiere.

The last of the matching
outfits for my final piano
recital.

One of the rare photo-
graphs of my mother really
laughing was taken while
we were working together
on a charity telethon
in New York City. It is
the last picture I have of
the two of us.

spoke so sharply to me and I didn't hear any more about it that evening.

It was most unfortunate that my mother called the next night for her weekly report on my behaviour. When she learned about Walter she went into a rage. In no time at all, she was screaming that I wasn't to be trusted and she was going to have to bring me home since I was causing Mrs Chadwick so much trouble. After the phone call I saw Mrs Chadwick crying. She had not learned to second-guess my mother. This time she knew that she'd been responsible for getting me into trouble. She knew I was innocent but there was nothing she could do about it now.

About ten o'clock that night, Mother showed up in the station wagon with her current secretary as a companion. Since she'd been drinking, she at least had the sense not to drive by herself. Lately, she'd taken to putting her vodka in a plastic water glass filled with ice and drinking while she was driving. Tonight was no exception.

I was packed and ready to go. Mother wouldn't speak to me except to order me into the back seat of the car. But before we left the Palos Verdes area, she asked the secretary if there was a liquor store in the vicinity. The secretary said she didn't know anything about Palos Verdes. I volunteered from the back seat that there was a liquor store about two blocks away once we got to the main street.

Mother slammed on the brakes, which sent me halfway into the front seat, the secretary nearly into the windshield, and Mother's drink all over the floor. She slapped me across the face and yelled: 'You *always* know where to find the boys and the booze, don't you?' As I opened my mouth to explain, she slapped me several more times and ordered me to shut up. I sank down into the darkness of the back seat and didn't say another word during the drive home. Silently, I went upstairs to my room to go to bed. I never wanted to say another word to her ever.

The next few days were terrible. She wasn't talking to me, so she'd order the secretary or the nurse to tell me what to do. She kept me working ten or twelve hours a day with no privileges of any kind. I worked, ate my meals in silence, and went to bed. She left orders that I was allowed to have no television, no radio, no books, no unnecessary conversations with anyone.

Mother had a friend who was visiting Los Angeles from the East and she'd invited the woman to have dinner with us one night. The night Dorothy arrived, Mother decided to take us to Don the Beachcomber for dinner and told me to be on my good behaviour.

I was extremely nervous about being in my mother's company for any length of time, particularly in the evening. I found that staying out of her way and saying yes as pleasantly as possible was my only salvation. Anything else I did seemed to irritate her, and I tried to be as inconspicuous as possible.

Dorothy was oblivious to the strained atmosphere and kept chattering away for the duration of dinner. I sat as far away from Mother as possible and tried to do nothing to bring attention to myself. I was a nervous wreck the entire time. Dinner went smoothly even though Mother was drinking double vodkas on the rocks.

On our way home I was counting the minutes until I could safely escape to my room when Dorothy asked me how school was going. I had been sitting silently in the back seat but replied that I liked it very much.

Then she asked me about several people's children she knew who were also at Chadwick. One of the students she mentioned had had some trouble and been expelled. I relayed that information as diplomatically as I could. With that, Mother turned half-way around to momentarily face me, while driving full speed ahead, and icily inquired who was I to say anything about anyone else since I'd been expelled too!

I was so shocked that I didn't have an answer for her. What she had just said was a total lie! I had *not* been expelled from school. Mother had created a scene and taken me away from the Chadwicks' home when school wasn't even in session.

I didn't utter another word during the rest of the drive. But once we were inside the house I went to my mother when she was alone and asked her why she'd said that I'd been expelled when it wasn't true. Mother hauled off and hit me across the side of my head so hard it made my ears ring. She told me that she'd decide what the truth was and that considering how much I lied, no one believed me anyway no matter what I said. All I said was, 'That's not true.' She slapped me hard across the face.

I was so mad I didn't even cry, although it really hurt. I just stood there staring right back at her, determined that I wouldn't give her the satisfaction of seeing one tear. She hit me hard several times again and then stepped back saying, 'You love it, don't you . . . you just love to make me hit you!'

Only because Mother didn't want her friend who was sitting in the next room to have any peculiar information about our happy Hollywood home, Mother called me into the bar to finish our conversation. I followed her into the little room. She sat on the counter and demanded to know why I insisted on arguing with her. I answered that I didn't wish to argue, but that I didn't appreciate her telling people that I'd been expelled from school when it wasn't true. I said I thought that she was supposed to be the one who was more understanding since she was the parent and the adult.

From the distance of time, I know that it was the wrong thing to say to my mother at that particular moment in our lives. It triggered something in her the likes of which I never saw before and hope never to see again in anyone. It struck at some volcanic trauma in the centre of her being that erupted with a violence, a hatred and a suddenness that plunged both of us into an instantaneous struggle for survival.

She leaped off the counter and grabbed for my throat like a mad dog . . . like a wild beast . . . with a look in her eyes that will never be erased from my memory. I was caught totally defenceless and staggered backward, carried by her weight and momentum. I lost my footing and fell to the floor, hitting my head on the ice chest as I went down. The choking pain of her fingers around my throat met the thudding ache of the blow to the back of my head. She banged my head on the floor, tightening her grip around my throat. Her face was only a few inches away from mine and she was screaming words at me I couldn't even hear. Her mouth was twisted with rage and her eyes – her eyes were the eyes of a killer animal, glistening with excitement. I gasped for air and felt myself sinking into unconsciousness as I tried desperately to fight back, to free myself.

All I could think of was that my own mother was trying to kill me. If something or someone didn't help me very soon I was going to die. I tried with the last bit of my strength to struggle free of those choking fingers and managed to wedge one of my knees between her body and mine. I pushed upward on her ribs with my hands, which loosened her grip. At least it allowed a trickle of air down my throat and kept me from losing consciousness. Now I fought back harder. I didn't want to die. I completely forgot she was my mother. She was trying to kill me and if I had the strength I would try to kill her first. She was terribly strong and all I could do was concentrate on loosening her grip on my throat.

The next thing I knew, the new secretary burst into the small room.

'My God, Joan ... you're going to kill her,' the secretary yelled. She tried to pull Mother away from me. Though she was also a strong woman it took some time to separate us. Mother continued to hit me across the face. I felt her ring cut my lip and saw some blood on her hand. 'Joan ... Stop! ... Stop! ... You're going to kill her!' the secretary yelled again.

Finally Mother allowed herself to be pulled away from me and started crying. I lay on the floor trying to catch my breath. My head was throbbing and I had a hard time swallowing. I raised myself slowly, testing to see if anything was broken.

Mother ordered me to go upstairs to the 'middle room'. Some-one would be up shortly to lock me in there.

The middle room was a servants' room off the back stairs, used primarily for storage, although it still had a bed and dresser in it. Being locked up in the middle room was another punish-ment Mother had devised for my brother and me.

I put myself into bed. I lay in the darkness for a few minutes before I heard the key turn in the lock in the closed door. I felt a peculiar numbness throughout my entire being. Each time I tried to sort out what had just happened, the memory of that look in Mother's eyes flashed across my mind.

It must have been several hours later when I heard a knock on the door, then a key turn in the lock, and a voice telling me to come downstairs to the bar.

When I entered the room a man I'd never seen before stood up and Mother introduced him to me as a juvenile officer. I had no idea what a juvenile officer was doing here in the middle of the night. The man asked my mother to leave the room so that he could speak to me alone, and she did not seem surprised by his request.

I was still standing in the doorway to the bar, but after she left the man asked me to come and sit beside him. He looked at me carefully for a long time as we sat silently in semi-darkness.

'She beat you pretty badly, didn't she?' he asked softly.

I looked down at the floor and nodded my head yes. I didn't know what she'd told him. I had no way of knowing what I looked like since the middle room where I'd been locked up didn't have a mirror.

'Your mother told me her version of the story. Now I'd like to hear yours.'

I looked at him carefully. He was a man of about forty, plain-looking. His eyes were very direct. He seemed concerned but not sympathetic and he looked tired.

I related the events as simply and honestly as I could. I said she lied about my being expelled, which was what started the whole argument. When I got to the part about my saying she ought to be more understanding since she was the parent and adult I looked him directly in the face and said, 'That's when she tried to kill me.' I added that if it weren't for the secretary, she might have succeeded.

When finally he started to speak it was slow and deliberate. I knew he was choosing his words very carefully. He said that there was nothing he could do to help me. He said that I'd have to try harder to get along with my mother because if she called the authorities again, he'd have no choice but to take me to Juvenile Hall and book me as an incorrigible.

He tried to explain the situation more fully to me, but I could hardly hear anything more he said. What kept racing around in my mind was being taken off to Juvenile Hall as an *incorrigible*!

What kind of world was it that allowed Mother to nearly murder me and then call *me* incorrigible? What kind of world was it that always punished me for her insanity? It was a crazy world.

'I'm not going to take you to Juvenile Hall tonight, even though that's what your mother has requested.'

149

I had no words. I stared at him speechless. I couldn't believe this was really happening to me.

'I'm going to tell her that we've had a talk and that you're going to try harder to get along with her and not cause any more trouble in the household. But I have to tell you honestly that if she calls again, I'll have to take you down to Juvenile Hall.'

I didn't say a word but tears streamed down my face. It was so clear to me that I was alone. I had to live with whatever chaos she chose to create whenever she got drunk.

I knew this man was trying to be gentle with me but it didn't help. I hated him and all the others for being too weak to stand up to her. I hated her for what she did to people, for the way she bullied them with her stardom and her influence. I hated the society that allowed this woman to live outside the rules of common decency and the law. Even when they knew she had tried to kill her own daughter, they didn't want to interfere, they didn't want to get involved.

I decided that from now on I would not ask anyone for anything. I would not show anyone how I felt. If I was to be alone in this, so be it, but I would not give anyone the satisfaction of knowing how much it hurt.

'I wish there was something more I could do to help you, but there isn't. You don't want to go to Juvenile Hall, do you?' He waited until I shook my head no, then he said, 'Then remember what I told you and try to get along here.'

The next morning when I went to my own bathroom to wash I understood why it took the juvenile officer so long to start talking to me.

I had one black eye and a cut on my upper lip which was swollen and covered with blood. My whole face was puffy and I had a perfect handprint bruise across one cheek. My eyes were also swollen from crying during the night. I looked awful. I started crying again and had a clammy, shaky feeling. I thought maybe someone should take me to the doctor but nobody did.

A few days later I was on my way back to the Chadwicks'. Mother told them that I was incorrigible and that she couldn't handle me any longer.

I was a virtual prisoner now in their home. I wasn't allowed any phone calls or mail or visitors. I had to do extra work as a further punishment and wasn't allowed to go anywhere except to church on Sunday.

During those days alone while I worked I tried to sort out the mysteries of my life. I saw it all melting into a pattern of troubled times, never feeling at ease, always being on the alert for the first signs of renewed outbursts from my mother. I had been unhappy for so long I couldn't remember being any other way. I began to be adept at skirting the fringes of her recurrent insanity and at walking the tightrope of my own loneliness. I did not feel I was a bad person. But I had a terror of being locked up. Under the constant threat of Juvenile Hall, I retreated as far into myself as I could without losing touch with reality. I lived my life in daydreams. I made up stories about where I would go and what I would do when I grew up.

Towards the end of that miserable summer, the Chadwicks took me camping with them for two beautiful weeks in the high Sierra mountains, where we fished and communed with nature.

THIRTEEN

That fall, Mother told the school she was unable to pay full tuition for my brother and me. Therefore, I was put on partial work scholarship and both Chris and I were expected to work at the Chadwicks' house, where we lived. I worked in the office at school too.

On Saturdays we worked all day doing the laundry, cleaning the house and the yard. On Sunday morning I finished the ironing and then had the afternoon off. The Chadwicks paid me thirty dollars a month for my work, but we received not a penny from Mother, nor did she pay any of our tuition that year. I couldn't figure out where her money went. It certainly wasn't being spent on the two of us, even though she made us feel as though we were an intolerable drain on her finances. She was making one picture a year and I knew she also owned an apartment building called Grosvenor House in Beverly Hills because I had been there with her several times to check on the fully furnished apartment she kept for herself in the building.

She said it was good for me to have to work and learn to appreciate the value of money. During this period of time I began to get the eerie feeling that Mother was somehow making me relive the penance of her own childhood. I'd heard the story of her having to work her way through school a dozen times. She even told me once that my real mother was a scrubwoman. She had created this 'family tradition' that was inescapable and I was to carry it on.

Mother's mood changed for the better whenever she was working on a picture, and I went to visit her on the MGM lot many times while she was filming *Torch Song*. The school bus dropped me off every other Friday afternoon at the studio gate and I'd stay with her on the set until she drove home. I particularly liked watching the dance numbers, which I knew she'd been rehearsing with director-choreographer Charles Walters since late summer. She did most of her own singing, too, although it was later overdubbed. It was the first time she'd been back at work on the Metro lot in about twelve years and she received a royal welcome from all the people who were still there from the old days. It was a time filled with nostalgia for her but it was nostalgia mixed with anxiety and very hard work. She was singing and dancing her way through another kind of comeback, proving herself all over again at almost fifty years old.

The picture was mediocre but she received ample publicity from both her return to the MGM studio and from the dance numbers.

I had already decided what I wanted to be when I grew up. After realizing at about the age of ten that there was no future for me as a cowboy, an accidental turn of events formed the basis of my new decision to be an actress. It really had very little to do with my mother's being a movie star, because I did not equate wanting to be a stage actress with what she did in the dark, quiet sound stages I'd visited since infancy. She neither encouraged nor discouraged me; all she said was that I had no idea what was waiting for me, which was true. But in the beginning it was all excitement and good times.

Each year the Chadwick School put on a Gilbert and Sullivan musical. A few days before my first elementary school performance in sixth grade, the girl playing the lead came down with the flu, and since I was the only soprano who could fit into her costume, I got the part. By dress rehearsal I knew all the songs but I was scared to death. All I could think of was my total failure as the mother in my Brownie troop's production of *Hansel and Gretel* some years before. Mother had never allowed me to appear in any movies, even though she'd had many requests from producers and a serious offer for me to appear in *Cheaper by the Dozen*, so I had practically no acting experience.

By some miracle the show was a success and afterwards everyone rushed up to me with congratulations and hugs. Right then I decided that being an actress was going to be better than being a cowboy. Just to be on the safe side, I didn't give up horseback riding but I did appear in all the regular Chadwick School productions.

Mother had seen me in *H.M.S. Pinafore* at the end of sixth grade but she didn't come to another school play I was in until tenth grade, when I landed the part of the old woman in *Mikado*. The part was supposed to be comedic. I'd done things on stage before that had got laughs but not all of them were intended. Now that I had the challenge of doing a real comedy part, I felt like a fool rushing around with this exaggerated characterization our music teacher had given me while trying to manage the Japanese kimono and tall wig.

A dramatic entrance had been staged for my character, and from the instant I appeared, singing my lungs out in my ridiculous wig, exaggerated movements and funny walk caused by the kimono, the audience roared with laughter.

What I did not know then was that my mother's original ambition had been to be an actress in musical comedy theatre. She had not intended to be in films, but before she ever got further than the Broadway chorus line, she signed a contract with MGM, came to Hollywood, and never appeared in the theatre again.

After the school performance was over, students, parents, and faculty members went to Mother to tell her how much they'd enjoyed my performance. When I asked her how she liked the play she replied that she'd enjoyed it and I'd done a good job, even if I did overact. She wasn't smiling at me as she said that I was going to have to learn more subtlety if I was going to be a professional and most particularly *not* to use my hands so much. *Good* actresses didn't gesticulate.

I was crushed. I hardly heard the people who told me how terrific I'd been. All I heard was Mother's stinging criticism. Abruptly she announced that she had to leave immediately or she'd be late for an appointment. I kissed her lightly on the cheek she turned to me and she drove away. I was heartbroken.

Fortunately, everyone else loved the show and in a few hours

I was laughing with the rest of the cast, the pain of Mother's reaction almost forgotten.

A few weeks later, Mother gave me a surprise party for my fifteenth birthday. She'd invited my boy-friend and two other school friends to join us for dinner and dancing at Mocambo's nightclub on the Sunset Strip. She'd also invited her agent, Jennings Lang, and his wife.

We had a really good time. There was a beautiful cake with fifteen candles and the entire club sang 'Happy Birthday' to me. Mother also arranged for all of us to have champagne, even though my friends and I were under age.

In one of her complete transformations, Mother had planned the perfect teenage birthday. She was gracious to my friends and she looked beautiful. She had the photographers take pictures and was a most charming hostess. I was thrilled and delighted by her affectionate attention.

The beginning of that summer at home was going better than ever before. Mother was making plans for one of her big parties and asked me to co-hostess with her. She even bought me a pretty new dress to wear. The whole house filled with excitement as the evening of the party drew near.

Since the weather was warm, the party was being held in the garden. Mother arranged for a large tent canopy to cover the entire back lawn, and a portable dance floor was fitted over the badminton court. The day of the party, trucks carrying tables, chairs, buffet tables, several bars, and all the tableware started arriving quite early in the morning.

All day long the delivery people scurried back and forth transforming our large yard into a party paradise. By late afternoon servants started arriving dressed in their black-and-white uniforms. There were several bartenders, maids, and butlers and some cooks' helpers. Some of the food was catered and some was being prepared in our own kitchen.

I was dressed and ready when the first doorbell rang. Mother was not finished yet, as usual, so I was delegated to greet the early arrivals and show them upstairs.

Mother had invited nearly two hundred people, including her entire agency, the casts from her last two films, producers, directors, writers, and a group of wealthy Texans who flew in for the occasion. I helped with drinks as usual and chatted with all the friends I hadn't seen in a long time.

Later that evening Judy Garland arrived with her husband, Sid Luft. Judy was noticeably pregnant and dressed in something resembling a brightly printed tent. Mother didn't like Sid Luft for a variety of reasons, but Judy Garland was a definite attraction at a Hollywood party. Later on in the evening, Judy could usually be persuaded to sing. That event would be talked about for weeks in the newspaper gossip columns and at other local show business gatherings.

About eleven-thirty that night, after I'd said goodnight to the party guests and got ready for bed, I went into my mother's bedroom and sat down in front of the window overlooking the garden. I turned out the lights so no one could see me and watched the party below for about an hour. Sure enough, someone persuaded Judy Garland to sing. With the small dance band accompanying her and a microphone amplifying her voice, I had no trouble hearing Judy clear as a bell from my second-storey hideout. She sang 'Over the Rainbow' and followed with almost the full Garland repertoire.

It was magical sitting there in the dark, watching her perform and listening to all the familiar songs. When she finished singing, the entire party gave her a standing ovation. I applauded too, even though I knew she couldn't hear it.

A few days later I heard Mother tell several of her friends that the party had been an enormous success and worth every bit of the five thousand dollars it had cost her.

When school started again a month or so later, I was still on a scholarship. Mother told the Chadwicks she was having a very hard time financially and still couldn't pay our tuition. She now owed the school two years' tuition for my brother and me. The Chadwicks believed her. They not only allowed her to keep the two of us at school but they also accepted my two sisters into the second grade as boarding students in the fall of 1954.

Although Mother was paying no tuition for us, we were now all four boarding students at Chadwick. The girls went home nearly twice a month but Chris and I usually stayed with the Chadwicks at school. Mother had the big house on Bristol all to herself. Why she sent us all away to boarding school when she couldn't pay for it I don't know. We could just as easily have gone to the local public schools.

Despite the fact that our unpaid tuition now amounted to a sizable debt, Mrs Chadwick assured me that she would let me finish out high school even if I had to continue on a total scholarship. I was very grateful to her. She and Commander Chadwick and the school had become my family and my home. I had struggled for a long time. Now I had a real place and a sense of belonging.

In addition to recognition for scholastic and acting ability, success had come on the school swim team. Our young coach, Nicki, had worked long, extra hours battling my own lack of competitive self-confidence, improving my lap times, and almost forcing me to want to win. One of the very best days of my life was at our first big swim meet when I heard the official results booming over the public-address system: 'First place ... Crawford ... lane three.'

I decided to go for another brass ring: I wanted to be a cheerleader. Every candidate had to audition in front of the entire student body and be voted into one of the six available cheerleader spots. I held my breath as the votes were being counted. I had worked hard but the other girls were good, too, and this was also a popularity contest. When the votes were tallied, I'd won a position as cheerleader! This particular accomplishment was a long awaited vote of acceptance.

My college entrance exam scores were in the top 10 per cent of the national average although I was still a junior. That meant I didn't have to take them again next year and could apply to college early. Mrs Chadwick was very pleased and we began exploratory talks about which colleges would be best.

Life had become everything I wanted it to be. I had good grades, good friends, and social acceptance at a school I loved. I didn't go home very often because Mother said she was too busy for us, but my days were happy and productive.

FOURTEEN

Mother had followed her musical at MGM with a Western for
Republic studio called *Johnny Guitar*. In spite of the efforts of a
good cast, good director, and interesting locations, it wasn't a
very good movie, although again, Mother received ample
publicity for doing a Western. She brought Chris out to Arizona
to visit during the summer while I was at camp. Chris had a
good time with the cowboys and made friends with the director,
Nick Ray, whose son, Tony, also went to Chadwick.

The trip was good for Chris in another way. He was the
only family member included in this visit and it was important
for him to feel a little special. He had his share of problems
trying to grow up in a houseful of women. He'd run away from
home on a number of occasions when he couldn't stand being so
cooped up and had been harshly disciplined. Once he lived down
on the Santa Monica pier for almost a week before the police
found him. I admired his bravery.

Even before the disappearing acts, Mother was entirely too
strict with Chris. She made no allowances for the normal
energies of a growing teenage boy. He stood almost six feet tall
when he was just thirteen, but she still treated him like a baby.
She kept trying to force him back into the mould of her image
of the perfect gentleman with impeccable manners and a quiet
demeanour. He was a boisterous, rowdy, fun-loving teenager.
She was simply unable to cope with his eventual manhood in
any constructive way. What she couldn't control, Mother either
dismissed or destroyed.

158

When we were at school, Commander Chadwick was the closest to a father figure Chris had ever known. Phillip Terry had left our house when Chris was so young he barely knew him. In the divorce agreement, Phillip tried to provide some measure of security for his son. He agreed to give up all rights to see the boy on the condition that a trust fund be established for his college education and to assure some financial security when Chris grew up.

It wasn't until after Mother's death that we discovered no such agreement had ever been filed with the divorce proceedings in Los Angeles. Whatever it was that Phillip negotiated and signed disappeared before it became part of the record. We also found out that Mother went to great lengths to adopt Chris by herself in Las Vegas *after* she and Phillip separated, although my brother and I both grew up believing that Chris had been adopted by both Phillip and Mother.

Subsequently, Mother never provided Chris with the college education or the trust fund or the financial security.

The week before Thanksgiving vacation in 1954 I called Mother one afternoon to find out if I should take the school bus home that coming weekend. I knew immediately that she was in a foul mood and wished I hadn't called. Just as I was about to say goodbye she asked about my Christmas card list.

I honestly had to say that I hadn't even thought about it yet. That was all she needed to launch into a tirade about how thoughtless I was, how disorganized, how sloppy. *She* started planning Christmas six months in advance, she said, and I couldn't even get my Christmas card list prepared without her having to remind me.

It wasn't true about her starting to prepare six months in advance of Christmas. It was a story she made up that sounded good to anyone who didn't know any better. It was like those publicity stories about how she scrubbed floors on her hands and knees. Nonsense! I scrubbed floors, my brother scrubbed floors, the fans scrubbed floors. All she did was give orders. The turmoil over the Christmas card list was ridiculous, particularly when our lives had been peaceful for months. This bizarre behaviour plagued my relationship with Mother. You couldn't protect yourself against it because you couldn't anticipate when it would happen. There was no warning except perhaps a tone of voice. Then it would come like a tidal wave, destroying everything in its path.

I had known from the moment I heard her voice that it was going to be a precarious conversation. I tried to be polite and brief in order to avoid anything unpleasant. But here it was anyway.

She made me feel as though I'd done something wrong even though I knew I hadn't. It slowly dawned on me that she was setting up a confrontation, a fight. I told her that I'd try to have my list made up in the next two days. She said I'd better have it done tomorrow. Okay, I said, tomorrow. I'll have it done tomorrow.

I didn't have to tell Mrs Chadwick about the conversation because she'd already got her own phone call. Things had been going so well that Mother's rage over the stupid list caught even Mrs Chadwick by surprise. But that night I sat down and tried to make up an appropriate Christmas card list.

When I called her the next day, Mother was still furious with me. She was acting demented. She told me that if I didn't have the *right* list with *all* the addresses by the next day, I couldn't come home for Thanksgiving. She overlooked the fact or refused to hear that most of the addresses were at home, not at school. At this point I was beginning to feel that old sense of hopelessness. No matter how hard I tried, no matter how many months went smoothly, there didn't seem to be any way to get along with her.

That night she and Mrs Chadwick and I had a three-way phone conversation that degenerated into a disaster. Even Mrs Chadwick couldn't hold her temper. Mother was at her very worst: drunk and angry and irrational. She had deliberately caused this whole turmoil and now she was using it as an excuse to unleash venomous insults at both Mrs Chadwick and myself. It was the only time I ever heard Mrs Chadwick raise her voice expressing opposition to Mother. She told my mother to stop swearing at me, to stop speaking to me in such a degrading way.

Mother yelled at me that she didn't want me home for Thanksgiving or any other time. 'Fine,' I said. 'That's just fine with me.'

My reply sent her into a new fit of rage. She accused Mrs Chadwick of turning me against her. She couldn't stand it that Mrs Chadwick was actually trying to help me. That's exactly what she had fired many servants for, that's what she would not permit.

Then Mother dropped the final bombshell. *None* of us were coming home for Thanksgiving. Even though they had nothing to do with the argument, she was going to make my brother and sisters stay at school over the vacation.

I was willing to bet that she never had any intention of having us home for the holiday and this whole fight was just another of her excuses to blame me for what she wanted to do all along.

But then she screamed: after vacation, *we were all leaving Chadwick*! She would decide later where we were going to be sent, but she was transferring all of us out of that school.

I hung up the phone. In that moment I hated her so much I wanted to kill her. I think I would have tried to kill her if we'd been in the same room. It didn't even matter to me that I'd have to spend the rest of my life in jail. Just the thought of being able to rid the earth of her evil would have been satisfaction enough. I hated her so much I was shaking all over.

Mrs Chadwick met me halfway down the stairs. Her face was ashen and I could see her hands shaking. Commander was with her.

The three of us sat in silence in the large Spanish living room. It was a cool November evening and the room had a chill to it. I looked carefully at each of their faces. This was not the usual meeting between us. Commander and Mrs Chadwick looked different from how I'd seen either of them before. It was as though the three of us were family and the enemy lurked all around us. The room was in semi-darkness and no one spoke for a long time.

Finally, Commander said in his gruff voice, 'Tina . . . I don't know if there's anything we can do to help you, but we're going to try.' Mrs Chadwick was near tears. 'This is wrong, Tina. It's not your fault.'

I wondered if, indeed, the Chadwicks could do anything to help me. No one else had ever been able to. Evidently they had some plan that would allow me to remain in their custody until I finished high school.

Two days later, it was Thanksgiving. My sisters arrived and the Chadwicks tried to make it as festive a day as they could for all of us. I did my best to enjoy the meal but every bite of food stuck in my throat. As I looked around the table at my sisters, my brother, and the two elderly people who had come to be my parents, I could hardly imagine life without them. I belonged here now, these people loved me.

Someone came to take my sisters away from school before the weekend was over. I didn't see them again, after that Thanksgiving, for almost a year. Next, someone came to take Chris away. I had tears in my eyes the entire time I was helping him pack up his things. I felt that all this was my fault and he was being punished for something he didn't do.

During these few days, Commander and Mrs Chadwick were rarely off the phone. They called half of Los Angeles trying to find a way to keep us in school. I gave them the name of the juvenile officer who visited me the night my mother had tried to kill me and I talked to him at some length. I even tried to be made a ward of the court, released in the Chadwicks' custody, but he said he couldn't help me.

In desperation the Chadwicks called a prominent attorney to see if there were any laws or legal proceedings that might be able to help. If I'd been sixteen there would have been a few options but since I was just fifteen there wasn't anything anyone could do.

The time for me to leave seemed ominously close. Mrs Chadwick was getting frantic as it became clear that no one was going to help us. I seriously thought about trying to run away but I knew I'd be hounded until I was caught, and then it might be even worse.

So, when I went to bed Saturday night, it was a long time before I could fall asleep. I dreaded what would happen the next day. Late that afternoon the secretary had called. She would pick me up Sunday. I was to have everything packed. I was going home.

Sunday morning I woke up with a dull, sick feeling in my stomach. Outside it was cool and crisp; a slight breeze was blow-

162

ing through my half-open window. As I lay in bed the cool air blew across me, but it didn't matter. I felt an oppressiveness, a heaviness, that made me feel as though I could barely breathe. I couldn't believe this was the end. It still didn't make any sense to me that what had started as a minor flurry could have turned into a major catastrophe.

I tried again to follow the slim threads of reality through the events of the past week. Each time I ran headlong into an abyss, that black hole where nothing followed logically, where fabrication and anger and turmoil ruled supreme, that place where there was no help and no peace, no escape from the juggernaut of chaos. From her throne in the eye of the hurricane, brandishing her magic wand of obsession, ruled the queen of chaos herself: Mommie dearest.

I could find no reason, no justice, no solace. Powers far beyond my control seemed to have taken possession of my life, my future. I was a being without volition, without a voice in my own existence.

I thought about the four years I'd struggled to overcome the shame of my childhood folly with the stable boy. I thought about the hundreds of hours of manual labour and mental anguish. I thought about my slow, gradual, determined climb to a place of respect, trust, admiration, and accomplishment over the past five and a half years at this school. One third of my entire life had been spent with these people in this place. These were the people who loved me, who had spent years helping me, encouraging me to excel, working with me to assure a successful future. The Chadwicks had become my parents and their school my home. At long last I knew I belonged here. And now, through a chance mis-spoken word, a few bottles of alcohol, and tears, it was all being whisked away. We were all powerless to stop it. Our thoughts, our feelings, our years of hard work, were being swept away while we stood by helplessly watching with horror and disbelief. Legally, my mother had the right. No one could stop her.

At breakfast I could see that Mrs Chadwick had been crying. Commander was gruffer than usual, but I knew that was just his way of trying not to show any emotion. We ate in silence.

It wasn't an uncomfortable silence. It was the silence of three

163

people in pain. It was the silence that happens when someone dies. It was the silence of sharing a moment of mutual anguish. It was also the silence of defeat.

I finished packing and took the sheets off my bed. I cleaned my room thoroughly. I could hardly manage the last of the ordinary little tasks of leaving. My eyes were filled to the brim with tears. Every once in a while they would fall randomly on the sheets I was carrying to the laundry room or on the dresser top I was dusting. My tears fell onto the clothes I was packing in the suitcase and on my own hands as I finished dressing. I didn't try to stop them now because I was determined not to let anyone see me cry when the time came to leave.

The morning hours flew by faster than any I remember. I couldn't hold back the time any more than I could change the situation.

When lunchtime arrived, the three of us reassembled in the kitchen, but no one could eat and we didn't even really try. There were no more words. Each of our minds was racing in different directions wondering how we would manage the final moments of our togetherness.

As much as I'd tried to prepare myself for the moment, it came as a terrible shock to see that the station wagon had already pulled up in front of the Chadwick house while I was next door saying goodbye to the neighbours. I had one last fleeting urge to run for my life ... to run anywhere, to escape this dreadful moment.

I saw three people standing by the car: the secretary, the man who was evidently the driver since he wore the cap of a chauffeur, and another man whom I'd never seen before and who was standing apart from the rest, looking ill at ease. He was heavyset and his eyes continually darted from one face to the next.

Silently I walked past this unwelcome group and realized my knees were shaking as I descended the long flight of stairs to my room. A moment later, as I was just gathering the last of my things, Commander and Mrs Chadwick appeared in the doorway. I knew they were there but I couldn't face them. I pulled my lips inward and held them between my teeth to keep from crying. I felt immobilized. I couldn't believe this was really happening to me.

At last I turned to face the Chadwicks. I went first to her and put my arms around her. Then I hugged Commander. He was not gruff. He was a kind, middle-aged man who was feeling the pain of a battle lost and the casualty count beginning to come in. He insisted on taking my suitcase. I tried to refuse, but he marched stalwartly back up the two long flights of stairs ahead of Mrs Chadwick and me. I felt as though I was dying. I think a part of all three of us died that November day.

Just before we reached the landing of the second and last floor, Mrs Chadwick told me that the heavyset man was a private detective and that he was carrying a gun. I looked at her in astonishment. She said that my mother was afraid there would be trouble. She was afraid that the Chadwicks would interfere with my leaving and she'd ordered this armed guard to accompany us. Mrs Chadwick whispered to me to be careful and remember they loved me like their own child.

We held each other for one last moment. I couldn't stand it any longer. 'Oh ... Mrs Chadwick ...' I moaned. My throat ached from trying to hold back the sobbing.

Commander put my suitcase in the back of the station wagon. I saw the three hired abductors standing silently around the car. I took another deep breath, pulled myself up straight, and walked out of the Chadwick house for the last time.

The secretary said something to me which I ignored as I opened the back door of the car and took my seat by the window. The driver and the hired gun got in the front seat. I sat silently looking straight ahead as the long station wagon made its turn in the driveway and headed down the hill. I did not turn back to catch a last glimpse or wave goodbye. I looked out my window and remained mute. My childhood nightmare had come true after all. I really was being kidnapped, complete even to the guns. My childhood terror of that recurrent nightmare swept over me in silence.

I knew that wherever these people were taking me, it wasn't home. The car was headed in the opposite direction.

So, I'm not going home, I thought. I guessed that I was going to another school, but I wouldn't have been surprised to pull up in front of Juvenile Hall. Everything was so out of hand that I could no longer trust my own intuition to guide me. Since I was damned if I was going to ask any of these kidnappers where I was being taken, I had no choice but to wait it out.

After an hour of steady driving, the station wagon swung onto the Pasadena freeway. Finally the driver chose an exit and we started through a residential district. I thought fleetingly about opening the door and jumping out, but that would get me either shot or run over and I didn't really want to die.

The driver made a sharp left turn and we began climbing a winding mountain road. There were a few houses scattered on either side of the road at first, and then there was nothing but scrub brush and empty hillside.

At last I saw a sign that said Flintridge Sacred Heart Academy and an arrow pointing to the left fork of the narrow road. We turned and continued until a huge old Spanish fortresslike building came into view. The station wagon pulled into a small parking lot at the bottom of a long, wide flight of cement stairs with wrought-iron railings. There were no people around.

The secretary, the driver, and the hired gun got out of the car, stretching themselves after the long, tiring ride. The driver opened my door and then went around to the back to take out my suitcase. I sat immobile for a minute looking at the forbidding building which sat alone on the top of this mountain.

The driver put down my suitcase just inside the school lobby entrance and told the secretary he'd wait for her in the car. Directly in front of the entrance was an enormous statue of Jesus holding a bleeding heart. I stared at it, horrified. *Where was I?* After a moment I looked at the rest of the lobby. It looked rather like an old hotel with dark-red carpeting, wooden floors, leaded-glass windows, and old-fashioned overstuffed armchairs directly out of the 1920s. I heard a soft voice directly behind me and turned to see a woman dressed in long white robes with a black stiff veil over her head. She was standing beside what could have been a hotel check-in counter. Every part of her body was covered except her face and hands. I knew from the movies that she must be a nun, but I'd never seen such a person in real life.

Sister showed us to my room, introducing me to my new

166

roommate, Marilyn. After Sister left, the secretary told me to take out whatever essentials I'd need because except for necessary personal items and my school uniform in the closet, she was taking the rest of my belongings away with her. I looked at her with all the venomous hatred I had stored inside of me, but I said nothing.

After I did what she ordered me to do I think she actually expected me to pick up my suitcase and take it back to the car for her. At that moment, hell could have frozen over before I'd have lifted one finger. I stared at her, daring her to ask anything more of me. It was only an instant. It was only a small, minor instant before she reached down and picked up the handle of the suitcase. I said nothing to her. She left.

Marilyn sat speechless on the edge of one of the beds. 'What is this place?' I asked my new roommate. In the next few minutes I found out that I was in a Catholic girls' school near Pasadena. The school was proud of its scholastic standards and the fact that none of its girls had ever successfully run away. After the drive up here, I understood. When she asked me why I was here, I related a brief and bitter account of the past few days.

After dinner, Sister asked me to come into her private office. She closed the door and we sat across from each other in two small chairs. I waited for her to speak.

In a soft voice she told me what the rules were to be for me here. My mother had told her that I was very difficult to handle and that I had got into trouble at my former school. Mother had requested that I receive very strict discipline and not be allowed any privileges. Sister said that meant I would not be allowed to leave the school or to use the phone to make outside calls. I was to receive no mail, no visitors, and no incoming calls. Since all outgoing mail had to be checked through the office, it would not be possible for me to send letters to anyone but my mother. In addition, I was not allowed to have any money. There was a school store where I could charge up to five dollars per month for toothpaste, shampoo, or school supplies and that was all. As I listened to Sister, it became clear to me that I was being held prisoner. I was under virtual house arrest in this convent. Since no one from Chadwick knew where I was and I was not going to be allowed any communication with the outside world, I was a prisoner. I was incommunicado and in total exile.

My willpower and determination began to crumble. I couldn't hold it together any longer. I began to tell Sister what had happened to me during the last week. It was so fresh in my memory that I related every last detail, including my drunken mother, the Chadwicks trying to save me, and the final abduction scene, complete with the private detective and his gun. As I poured out my story I was only semiconscious of the woman who sat across from me. She was still a total stranger, but she was the only person I had, the only one who would listen. Half the time I was sobbing and trying to talk at the same time. My story, I'm sure, initially made no sense. But as it unfolded, I saw the expression on her face change. I was sure she wouldn't believe me; why should she? So I gave her the Chadwicks' telephone number and begged her to call them and find out if I was telling the truth.

Sister did call the Chadwicks in a few days. She now had a much better understanding of the situation. She said that no matter what the truth was, it wouldn't change the restrictions Mother had placed on me.

As for me, something had broken and I just cried uncontrollably. I cried through morning prayers, through religion class, through lunch, and on into the afternoon. Sometimes I tried to stop crying but it was too much effort. I'd given up being embarrassed about the other girls looking at me. Who cared? During the day, I took a seat in the back row of the class and cried. I have no idea what the nuns talked about, nor did it seem important. I turned in no papers, did no assignments, spoke to as few people as possible.

After four weeks of continual crying and numerous talks with Sister, who was trying to find some means of consoling me, it was time for Christmas vacation. I knew I wasn't going anywhere even before Sister told me. I knew that I was a prisoner in this dreadful, strange place where I didn't understand the people or the religion or the prayers or the talk about hell and sin and damnation. Having been brought up in Christian Science, I'd never heard any talk about that. I'd never thought about sin. I'd known only the gospel of God's goodness. I told Sister that I'd never been baptized and saw the look of horror on her face. I asked her if that meant I was going to hell and she couldn't look at me. I felt as though I'd been thrust through a time machine back into the Middle Ages.

Christmas vacation came and most of the students went home. A few girls from Central and South America stayed at school, but they went shopping and to the movies and visited friends.

It was cold on top of that mountain. The winter rains came early that year. It was grey drizzle outside and damp dreariness inside.

After four or five days of the vacation, crying alone in my room most of the time, I got a stomach ache and told Sister I was going to bed.

I had no more fight left, no more anger, no more spirit of survival. My entire life, built over the last five years of pain, of determination, and finally of success, had suddenly been wrenched away from me. I had cried my eyes and my heart out for a month and I was exhausted by the sheer onslaught of so much sorrow. My eyes had no more tears, my body had no more strength. I was worn out with the years of doing battle and ending up nowhere. I was drained of the last shred of hope. Everything I held valuable, everyone I loved, every bit of success, was gone. It was all gone. It was all gone . . .

I lay in bed, vaguely hearing the rain outside, and slowly felt myself slipping away. I was too tired to think any more, too tired to move. I was overcome with total exhaustion. The world faded away from me and I sank into a kind of limbo world where nothing hurt. If I lay very still and kept my eyes closed, it didn't hurt any more. Everything was muffled. The world was at a distance from me. Time slipped away unnoticed. Day melted into night melted into day again, and it was all the same.

At some point, day or night, but which day or what night I don't know, I was dimly aware of Sister trying to talk to me. Her face floated above me swathed in white with a black halo shimmering above it. Through the haze I noticed her mouth moving but the sound was so faint that it didn't matter. I didn't understand what the words meant and I didn't make any effort to ascribe meaning to the wavering sounds. I closed my eyes again and the floating face with the black halo disappeared like magic. Once or twice in the total darkness, I got up and went to the bathroom. I noticed a small tray of food by my bed and stared at it curiously. I had no feeling of hunger, so it went untouched.

I didn't care any more. I wanted to die. I lost all desire to think. I just sank away into peaceful floating where there were no harsh voices, there was no pain, there was no terror. It was very nice here . . . very quiet . . . very peaceful. Nothing hurt me any more . . . it was all very far away . . . soft and muffled.

Once when I opened my eyes in the dark I saw a stack of envelopes on a small table next to my bed. Christmas cards. Christmas cards . . . Christmas card lists . . . I sank away again, never touching the envelopes.

Time . . . people . . . voices . . . meant nothing. Nothing could touch me here. I didn't care any more. I melted into the darkness and floated through the empty space. I didn't dream. I didn't think. I heard my own breathing and floated on the rise and fall of the air. Air and space and darkness melting and drifting away. Every once in a while a white floating face with a black halo held me upright and forced me to drink some water. Most of it spilled.

The white faces and black halos gathered around me from time to time. I dimly heard the heavy black wooden rosary beads rattling as the litany of their prayers wafted across the bed. Then the black halos drifted away into the rain.

One day I felt hungry. I had to rest several times before I was able to reach the dining room. A nun came out of the kitchen and looked at me as though she were seeing a ghost. A younger nun quickly assisted me back to bed, assuring me she would return immediately with some food. I was so weak that she had to feed me. I fell asleep.

When I awoke, Sister was sitting on the edge of the bed, saying her rosary. I looked at her and tried to manage a smile. When she realized that I actually recognized her, tears welled up in her eyes. She took my limp hand in hers and said, 'We've been praying for you.'

'Thank you, Sister.'

Most of the cards and letters stacked beside my bed were from friends of mine at Chadwick. I don't know how they found me but most expressed love and sadness at the terrible circumstances surrounding my sudden departure. I sat on the edge of the bed, sobbing with loneliness and despair.

The last envelope I opened was from Mother. The stationery was imprinted with a green wreath and 'Happy Holidays to You' in red script across the top. I stared dully at the familiar scrawled handwriting. She had thanked me for the handmade sachets I'd sent her and my sisters for Christmas. Then she asked me to write thank-you notes for the cards and gifts she'd had sent to me at school. She wanted them as soon as possible. The brief note ended with her saying that she hoped the New Year would bring me great joy and happiness. It was signed: 'Always – "Mommie".'

My hands were shaking by the time I'd finished reading. I looked for 'all the gifts' but saw only three small boxes. I turned the letter over and reread it, even though it made me feel ill. How the hell was I going to get 'great joy and happiness' when I was a prisoner, locked up on top of a mountain, with every single shred of my life taken away from me?

Insensitive, cruel, monstrous bitch! The impotent rage inside me welled up and overflowed into hysterical laughter. Tears streaming down my face, I laughed and danced wildly around the room, bumping into furniture and waving the 'great joy and happiness' letter above my head like a banner. My foot caught on a chair leg and I collapsed across my bed sobbing again.

I can't stand it any longer. I cannot take it any more.

But slowly the bleak routine of the girls' school began to be my way of life too. I went where I was supposed to go, did what I was told to do, and spent the weekends by myself reading. I had become numbed into subservience. The penalty for thinking was pain beyond my endurance. I walked in line and went through the motions of being alive. I cried by myself and ate candy because it was the only pleasure left. I had given up hope now, so one day or one week was the same as another. I was serving time in purgatory and no one could help me. I was serving my sentence for crimes beyond my undoing. Institutional life and punishment had become the ordinary course of my days. At least no one here beat me.

I felt that Sister understood me better than anyone else had. I didn't really know how she achieved that, but she had strength and courage I wasn't used to seeing. After a while she even began to bend some of the restrictions I was supposed to live under.

I wrote to my mother regularly and usually called her once a week. It was partly out of habit and partly because I was afraid that if I didn't have any relationship with her at all, at least to remind her I was still alive, she'd get crazy again and transfer me somewhere worse. I'd heard about the county detention homes. However much I disliked being at Flintridge, I knew there were worse places and I didn't want to be sent to one of them. I also didn't want to disappear.

On 5 February 1955, I received a second letter from mother. This one was typewritten. Its scant eight lines thanked me for my 'sweet' letter of last week and again requested thank-you notes be sent to her promptly. She said she hoped I was feeling better and signed the note: *All my love, "Mother".*

She had forwarded a few Christmas presents and now all she cared about was the formality of thank-you notes. She didn't care about anything else except how she looked in the eyes of the public. Her correspondence with me picked up and about a week later another typewritten letter arrived. This one enclosed some Valentine cards sent by fans of hers. She said she was sure I'd be grateful for them and for everyone who was thinking of me. She said it was sweet and thoughtful of me to call her on Valentine's Eve and that she was deeply grateful. She hoped my school term was happy and that I was well adjusted. This letter was signed: *My love to you always, "Mommie".*

I had been at Flintridge three months but it seemed like a year. I wasn't interested in schoolwork any more. It was easy and I was far ahead of most of my classmates. But I discovered that Catholic education contained unexpected pitfalls.

My first shock came in English class during book reports. When my turn came, I gave my report on a book I'd read at Chadwick. Though I was cheating slightly by not reading a new book, I gave the report my very best, complete with selections of the poetry which I read aloud to the class. When I finished, it was usual to ask for questions. But I was met with silence. I turned to look at the nun who taught the class only to see that her face had turned purple! This plump sister managed to splutter that the book was on *the Index*. A gasp went up from the class. I had no idea what she was talking about but she went on at some length to explain that the 'Index' was a list of books Catholics were forbidden to read.

Now it was my turn to be stunned. A list of forbidden books? I couldn't believe it. I knew by the state of extreme agitation in the room that it was no joke. Sister asked me to see her after class.

I couldn't bring myself to apologize. All I said was that I was not a Catholic and that I'd never heard of the 'Index' before today. Sister told me that from now on I was to confine future reports to books found in the school library.

Since I received no spending money, Mother sent a cheque for the school annual around the beginning of March, accompanied by a handwritten note which simply said she loved me and to forgive her for the brief note but she was rushing to a script reading for *Queen Bee*.

When I saw *Queen Bee* about a year later I hated it. I found the entire film horrifying. That wasn't any acting job on Mother's part. It was *exactly* the way I knew her at home when she'd been drinking and was at her very worst. That woman on the screen really was my mother. It gave me cold chills and I had to leave the theatre. Bosley Crowther's review in the *New York Times* summed it up perfectly when he wrote: '[Miss Crawford] is the height of mellifluous meanness and frank insincerity. When she is killed at the end, as she should be, it is a genuine pleasure and relief.'

On 28 March she sent a typed thank-you note for the small birthday gift I'd made. She also complained about the weather being hot, about not having air-conditioning where she was shooting her current film and about having to wear fur coats in the summertime. But, she said, it all made life interesting. At the end of the letter she asked me if I had received the bras and if they fit. Because, she said, pink or black bras couldn't just be purchased, they would have to be dyed to those colours and she didn't want to go to all that expense unless the two she'd already sent were the right size. She called me 'darling' and signed herself: *'All my love, "Mommie".'*

It was all pathetic. Even though this letter was longer than the usual perfunctory notes acknowledging a card or gift I'd sent her, they all made me feel like I was part of the fan mail. The paragraph about the bras was ridiculous. It sounded as though she'd dictated it in front of an audience. I had no money to buy anything and had asked her to send me some underwear, specifying the sizes. What she'd sent were two custom-made bras that were all wrong because I think they'd been made for her. I never asked for pink bras or black bras either. What would I have done with them? I was living in total isolation in a convent. What on earth would I do with pink and black bras? All I wanted was some ordinary underwear and I couldn't even seem to get that.

Furthermore, all the 'darling' business was for the benefit of her own self-image. She knew that the sisters opened all incoming mail and were free to read the contents. So the 'darling' business was not for my benefit because she never called me anything resembling 'darling' over the phone!

Two days later, the following letter from my brother arrived. It was dated 28 March, the same day as my mother's letter about the bras.

Dear Chris,

I called mother last night and asked if 'the whole family would be there for Easter' she said 'you mean Tina too' I said 'yes' then she said 'do you want happiness and fun or sadness' of course I said I wanted fun and then she said 'that's why, Chris, Tina isn't coming home until she can bring some love and happiness to us.'

So if you would please come out of your shell and give instead of take you will find lots and lots more love and joy than hate.

So if you want to be a great success like mommie is, be sweet and loving and you will find that you will gain lots more friends and have lots more fun. O.K.

Just try it and see.

> *Your friend and loving brother,*
> *Chris*

My brother was now under her spell. It had only been about five months since I'd seen him but through his well-intended letter to me I heard Mother's propaganda machine grinding out the lies about me. She may as well have written the letter herself, because in it my brother had captured her total philosophical insanity. She really was the 'Queen Bee' and her influence was all pervasive. I wasn't mad at Chris. I was inexplicably tied to Mother too, but my God how I hated her.

Easter vacation came and went. I never set foot off the convent grounds. There was a short note from my mother wishing me a 'Happy Easter' and a few cards from her fans whom I barely knew.

Easter was an important religious holiday at Flintridge, so the few of us who were left at school had to go to Mass every day. I was more familiar with the ritual by now but even so, I was terribly lonely and felt like the outsider I was.

It was the middle of April before I heard from Mother again. I'd sent her another of the little gifts I made and she sent me a thank-you note. It was a paltry exchange.

Then, right on the heels of her Easter letter came another, dated 21 April. In it she congratulated me on my fine report card, saying that she was very proud of me. Then she replied to a request I'd made to do something for Mrs Chadwick's birthday which was in about a week. Mother suggested that I do for Mrs Chadwick what I'd done for her – send a telegram, or did I have something more extravagant in mind? Mother said she couldn't tell if I was asking for money or for a gift so why didn't I call her secretary as soon as I received this letter. She signed her sarcastic note: *My love to you as always, "Mommie".*

I was livid. The telegram she referred to was something that happened just once, a year ago. I didn't have the money to buy her a present on her birthday and I'd misguidedly thought that a telegram would be more important than just a card. She interpreted the telegram as a last-minute remembrance, as not caring about her. When I sent it, I had no idea it would displease her so very much.

From that point on until her death, she sent me a telegram on my birthday. There was not another birthday card from her as long as she lived. She became fixed on that birthday telegram, though it happened only once. Over the many years that followed, I sent her cards and I sent her presents, and still I got a telegram from her on my birthday. I sent her *one* telegram when

I was fourteen years old and I got birthday telegrams in return for the next *twenty-two years*!

The strangest thing is that I understand what happened. Mother tended to become riveted on what she considered a personal slight or insult but she would not discuss it with you. Later, she wouldn't remember what the explanation for it was or that it may have been unintentional. She silently brooded over the incident and carried it with her inside. She remembered only the insult, however accidental, and it grew as time passed. Usually, such a misunderstanding fades away with time. But for Mother, the process was the opposite. She clung to the image of the old hurt, to her own secret image as the deprived, somehow cheated and unloved person.

That image was the bottomless pit into which you could pour years of loving, kindness, and attempts at reconciliation without visible results. It failed to erase the one mistake. It put you at a permanent disadvantage. Your unpremeditated error in judgment became part of a larger aberration that existed privately in the far reaches of her own childhood deprivation, her own alienation and loneliness, her own insatiable need for love. There just wasn't enough love in the whole world to fill her need. She didn't allow enough space for other human beings to be themselves and give her anything real. She demanded such constant reassurance of devotion that she left no room for love. It was impossible to satisfy her.

Over the years, most of the people who really did love her, in spite of her demands, were pushed away because she seemed unable to accept others as totally separate from herself. So she forced herself into settling for subservience.

To her, devotion meant saying yes to her. You didn't have a genuine relationship with her. You did what she wanted and said what she wanted to hear or you were banished. You treated her like the Star always. You behaved enough like a fan to make her feel comfortable. Inevitably, you were placed in a position of servitude, however subtle. Under these conditions, she was generous. She showered gifts and thoughtfulness beyond anything remotely required. That was the price and those were the payoffs.

The other part of the twenty-two years of telegrams was just bookkeeping. You went on a telegram list of hers. A secretary either sent the telegrams or reminded Mother to dictate personal notes. The secretary simply copied last year's message, looked in the black leather phone book, and sent all the telegrams for that particular day.

The next message from Mother, dated 3 May 1955, was only three lines long. It told me she had not yet received thank-you notes for the Easter cards she'd forwarded to me from my brother, sisters, and two fans.

Ludicrous as it now sounds, I had to write formal thank-you notes to my family and they had to do the same. Then I had to send their thank-you notes to Mother instead of simply mailing them from school. Besides checking up to make sure I actually wrote them, the manoeuvre was designed to keep me uninformed as to their location. I was not allowed any direct contact with either my sisters or my brother.

The next letter is chilling in retrospect. Not just for what it actually said, but more importantly for what it neglected to say. It was dated 9 May 1955. Mother thanked me for my Mother's Day present and said she was sorry we didn't get to talk on Mother's Day. I had called her at home three times. At nine o'clock in the morning I was told she wasn't up yet and I left the first message. I called back around two in the afternoon and was told by the secretary that mother was in the back yard being photographed for *Look* magazine and couldn't come to the phone. I left a second message. When I called back around seven o'clock that evening, I was told that my mother had gone out. Nevertheless, Mother ended her letter to me saying that I was sweet to call and that she sent me all her love, as always.

On 10 May 1955, Joan Crawford married a man by the name of Alfred N. Steele in Las Vegas, Nevada.

At my school on a mountaintop near Pasadena, I heard about the marriage for the first time over a radio news broadcast. In his school, somewhere else in Los Angeles, my brother also learned of the marriage over the radio. Mother never mentioned her plans to any of us, never introduced us to her future husband even over the phone. She had never mentioned her plans to marry Mr Rachmil two years before in what turned out to be only a carbon-copy dress rehearsal for this wedding and she never said one word to us in advance of this one.

I was stunned. I hadn't heard of the man before that very moment. I had no idea what he looked like or where they'd met. The radio said he was president of Pepsi-Cola.

I was furious with Mother's insulting behaviour that considered me no more important than the general public, getting their information from the news media. Since none of the broadcasts mentioned the newlyweds' location, it was several days before I was able to reach Mother, though I left messages with the secretary at home.

In the meantime, I received her 'Mother's Day' letter, which only added to my humiliation. It was a devastatingly rotten feeling to be treated as inconsequential. She did not care about me, she did not even consider me worth common courtesy.

Mother didn't call me back. I kept calling until I found her at home again. The instant I heard her voice, I could have strangled her. She was arrogant, pompous, condescending, and every inch the consummate bitch.

She inquired why it had taken me so long to congratulate her! I told her the radio hadn't given any location and I'd left messages with the secretary. Then she said something that is emblazoned on my memory for ever: 'Christina, *all* you had to do was call Las Vegas . . . the whole world knows who *I* am. It's very simple, the operator would have been able to locate me. Obviously, you didn't try very hard. Hundreds of *other* people found us!'

'Fine,' I said, shaking violently from head to foot. 'I hope you're both very happy.' I hung up. I pounded my fist against the wall. She was despicable. It was useless.

Call Las Vegas, indeed. I'd rather be dead first. Can you imagine? 'Hello, Las Vegas information? My name is Christina Crawford. I heard on the radio this morning that my mother, Joan Crawford, the movie star, just married a man named Steele. You wouldn't happen to know what hotel they're staying in, would you?'

I did not speak to Mother for several months. I didn't bother calling her again and she didn't phone me at school. Mr Steele took her to Europe on their honeymoon. I received a telegram for my birthday in June and a week or so later a note from

Paris. Mother congratulated me on being made vice president of the student body, saying how proud she was of me. She added a brief tour itinerary covering the south of France and mentioned that she'd be sailing to New York soon.

Unlike Chadwick, Flintridge Sacred Heart Academy had no summer school programme and was closed during the months of June, July, and August except to the nuns who lived there. I had several invitations to spend time in friends' homes and asked Sister to ask my mother's permission. There was no expense involved since the families would provide transportation and Sister knew the parents were responsible people. Sister received a letter of reply which was mailed from Rome. In it, Mother said that she preferred to have me stay at school for the entire summer. The reason she gave was that I could not 'behave' at home so she had no assurance I would do better as a visitor. In addition, she said, it would be good for me to have time alone, not having anyone to 'show off to', a thinking time she felt I needed. Mother followed that by saying that I never said 'love' in my letters to her, only in my letters to other people which I knew she would read. She also complained that I hadn't written her a thank-you note for my birthday gift until eleven days after receiving it. Then she reiterated that she wanted me to stay at school all summer and continue my enrolment there until graduation the following year. She signed the letter '*Joan Crawford*'.

This was just plain meanness on Mother's part. All that was required of her was simple permission. I had done nothing wrong, caused no trouble. I had been at Flintridge for seven months. During that time I had not seen Mother, not set foot off campus. For seven months I continued to be punished severely, denied normal school privileges, and virtually locked up. I had done nothing that could even remotely have been considered wrong. My report card was excellent. I had been elected student-body vice president for my senior year. I had not broken any rules, got in any arguments with Mother, or in any way strayed from the narrow path allotted me. Even under circumstances that depressed and discouraged me, I had achieved everything my present situation could bestow upon me.

Sister knew the truth. I knew the truth. But the truth didn't make any difference to Mother. She was off on a honeymoon in Europe and couldn't be bothered with me. So she trumped up feeble excuses, mostly constructed of her own cruelty, to punish me further.

It was excruciating for me. There didn't seem to be any connection, any relationship, between what I did and what I got. No matter how hard I tried, no matter how long I worked, it didn't seem to be enough to get me out of this everlasting punishment. It didn't make sense any more. She held all the cards: 'Her will be done.'

So I stayed at Flintridge that summer. The days dragged by interminably. The Dominican sisters went on a retreat, which meant that for two weeks, not one sister said one word. They prayed and listened to religious lectures, but they remained silent. It was eerie. I no longer found the entire surroundings so strange, but it was lonely and depressing.

Sister had asked me to work in the office during retreat. I was glad for anything to occupy my mind, so I answered the phones and opened the mail for eight hours a day. The rest of the time I spent taking walks by myself, going for an occasional swim by myself, and reading alone in my room.

If I'd had a notion of loneliness before, it was nothing compared with this summer. I was so lonely I felt hollow. The office telephone sounded like a cannon. The closest thing to companionship I had was food. It was the one and only source of anything even remotely resembling pleasure. I was so unbelievably alone that I wondered if I was going to lose my mind. I thought about prisoners locked away in solitary confinement and marvelled that they retained the will to live at all. I thought about hermits and the mountain men of the old West and wondered if they too battled the enticing seductress of insanity. I now knew how people went mad: they gave up fighting. They went mad because it was a hell of a lot easier. They went mad because it comes to be a far better place than dying from the slow pain of loneliness. You just ease into being crazy; it doesn't happen overnight. You get tired of the constant battle with no victories. You become exhausted hoping for the ceasefire. You lose your grip on the world slowly and drift into the chasm of your own hopelessness. You have no mirror in which to confirm your own being. The *now* of your grief stretches endlessly into the future – no hope, no relief, no rewards, no change – ever.

During that summer I stood shakily on the tightrope of my lonely self. Each time I wavered I saw below me the pit of madness, beckoning me to join the other lost souls who had given up the fight and slipped into a special world. It was a terrifying journey. I was the solitary traveller, somewhere during each day, suspended just above the beckoning chasm, hovering unsteadily, feeling my grip slipping. I was sixteen years old.

I had got some postcards from France and Italy as the honeymoon progressed. Mostly they held glowing praise for the lovely countryside and fabulous meals Joan Crawford and her husband were enjoying. On 8 July she scrawled a strange letter to me detailing a school in Berne, Switzerland and enclosing a pamphlet about it. The girl on the cover of the pamphlet was Bridget Hayward, Margaret Sullavan's daughter whom my mother referred to as being very happy at the school. I had written Mother that I didn't want to go to school in Europe, preferring to go to an American college. She responded by saying: '... remember me – I've been around since your birth and have taken very good care of you – watched your grades, etc.' She said I would stay at Flintridge another year and then a decision would be made. The last sentence read: 'Bless you – have a good summer – think good thoughts and my love always – "Mommie".'

I wanted to go to college, and the places Mother was talking about were the equivalent of finishing schools. I didn't want to go to school in Europe because I was sure I'd just be stuck there without money or friends. Mother considered that putting us away in schools counted as taking care of us.

The 'have a good summer and think good thoughts' part of her letter was facetious and cruel. She knew exactly what my summer was going to be. After all, it was on her specific orders that I continued to be locked up without parole. Who did she think she was kidding? Is that how she deceived herself so that she could go on playing martyred mother for the public?

Why in God's name did she adopt all of us in the first place? Sure we served a purpose when we were adorable babies. She got years of prime publicity out of us. She built a public image on us as her career began to decline. Millions of unsuspecting fans thought: 'What a wonderful woman ... to take *four* little orphans into her home.' Hundreds of pages of movie-magazine garbage were turned out on what a wonderful mother she was. We were paraded out one by one, in our darling little starched outfits and pseudo-British manners. We were photographed from every angle and cooed over by pandering publicity hacks, we were sent presents from fans all over the world – presents we were not allowed to keep. We were the best-mannered, best-behaved, most perfect child-mannequins the queen bee could produce.

After we had served our purpose and got all the publicity that could humanly be turned loose on the adoring public, we made a fatal error: we started growing up. We started becoming people. It was no longer possible to control our every thought, our every gesture, our every move. We were no longer the perfectly manipulated, camera-ready puppets that spouted, 'I love you, Mommie dearest', at the slightest indication of her whimsical displeasure.

Mommie dearest got her feelings hurt. Mommie dearest became distressed. Mommie dearest became enraged when she perceived that all was not well in mannequin-land. The children, the babies were in a state of mutiny! Mommie dearest has to make an example of eldest daughter. Mommie dearest has to punish bad babies ... Mommie dearest beat bad babies ... Mommie dearest try to kill bad babies ... Mommie dearest doesn't want to have anything more to do with bad babies ... Mommie dearest put bad babies away from her ... Mommie dearest find a prison for bad babies and lock them up to punish them for being such bad babies.

FIFTEEN

When the honeymoon was over, I received a note on Sutton Place South stationery. Mother called herself Joan Steele on the envelope's return address. She thanked me for the tie I'd sent Daddy for his birthday, saying that 'your father appreciated it'. She said the humidity in New York was worse than the summer heat and that she would be back in Los Angeles within a week. She was starting another picture immediately since the director and dress designer had already been in conference with her during these few weeks in New York.

I had still never met this man she called 'your father', but I had sent a small birthday present to him.

The picture she was about to make was *Autumn Leaves* with Cliff Robertson, directed by Robert Aldrich. Though she was working in Los Angeles, I didn't see Mother during the months she was in town. In fact, I barely spoke to her on the phone because she said her schedule was so hectic that she didn't have much free time. Truthfully, I was just being ignored.

It was October when the announcement came out of the blue. Mother called to say that she was taking the entire family to Switzerland for Christmas! There was no explanation, no discussion, no mention of the year it had been since the family had seen one another. No mention either of my lengthy punishment. She just said that I would be coming home for Thanksgiving and she was getting me all new clothes for the trip. I'd have to miss some school, but that could be arranged.

I stared at Sister in total disbelief. This had to be some sort of trick, some sort of game I was just too stupid to recognize.

I had not been home or seen Mother even once in the last eighteen months. I had been *persona non grata* for a long time. What had changed? I racked my brain, but I couldn't find any answers. I still had not met Alfred Steele, her husband of five months. I had not seen my brother or sisters in a year. What had changed?

Sister did confide in me that after Mother and Mr Steele were married, all my back school bills started being paid. I took a chance and called Mrs Chadwick. She confirmed it. The back bills at Chadwick were also being paid. Since nothing else had changed, I could only guess that Mr Steele was the reason we were all going to Europe on this trip. But I really didn't care what the reason was. I was actually going to get off the top of this mountain and out of these buildings. I didn't care if they wanted me to turn upside down and walk on my hands backward. I was getting out!

Just before Thanksgiving vacation, a letter from Mother arrived with a Detroit, Michigan postmark. This letter was totally different than any I'd received over the past year. She called me her 'darling angel' and sounded excited by all the attention she was getting on tour with Daddy for Pepsi-Cola. She talked about the schedule and the public appearances with a delight I hadn't heard from her even when she wrote about working on a film or in a television production. She ended the letter by sending me her love and saying that she'd see me on Thanksgiving.

I was so excited by these sudden changes I could hardly think about anything else. We were all going to Europe for Christmas. I was getting new clothes. I could hardly believe it.

Mother sent a car and driver to pick me up from school. I was very nervous during the ride home. As we got closer to the house I started getting scared. What if something happens and I don't get to go? What if Mr Steele doesn't like me? What if I do something foolish? I hadn't been home in such a long time. I hadn't been anywhere in such a long time, I wasn't sure I'd remember how to act with people. What would I do . . . what would I say? Is the past year just swept under the rug and forgotten? Is it a trap? Thoughts tumbled one after the other through my mind faster and faster.

At long last we turned onto North Bristol Avenue. It was just as I'd remembered it. There were one or two new houses but the rest was the same as before.

Chris and my sisters were home from their schools too. We rushed into one another's arms, laughing and hugging. They were just as surprised as I'd been to hear the news of our trip. Chris had grown more and was taller than I. The girls hadn't changed much except they were of course a year older. I was sixteen and a half, Chris was thirteen and the girls were almost eight.

I first saw Alfred Steele swimming in our pool. I remember standing on the steps leading out to the garden and asking Mother what I was supposed to call him.

'What would you call anyone who was your father?' she asked me. I had to think about that for a moment. It had been ten years since she'd been married before. I'd really never had a father. There had been lots of her lovers I'd had to call 'Uncle' but that didn't seem appropriate. The problem was that it seemed preposterous to call a stranger 'Daddy'. I'd never even been introduced to him as Mr Steele. I'd never seen him before in my life. It was very confusing but I wanted to be as polite as possible and do anything I could to please her, so I finally decided on 'Daddy'.

Mother turned to me and said, 'He's too fat, he wears glasses, and he's slightly hard of hearing in one ear, but he's a nice man. Go introduce yourself.'

It was getting dark and I could not see her face too well. But I didn't have to. I'd heard that condescending tone of voice all my life. She didn't love the man swimming in our pool; of that I was positive. Fortunately, I realized that she couldn't see me very clearly either and would never know my look of shock. This was how she described her husband of less than six months? I felt sorry for him already. The disdain in her voice transmitted her message clearly.

I walked down to the pool alone. When I got near the edge I stopped and waved at the man in the pool. He swam up to where I was standing and smiled at me. I kneeled down and stuck out my hand. 'Hello . . . Daddy. I'm Christina.' He took my outstretched hand in his dripping-wet one and I knew immediately that I was going to like him.

Alfred Steele was a very direct man. He'd started out as a geologist, graduating from Northwestern University in Chicago. By what path he went from geology to sales at Coca-Cola, I never quite understood. But from Coca-Cola he went to Pepsi-Cola. When Alfred Steele took the job at Pepsi, it was little more than a regional Southern drink with a loosely knit group of family-owned and -operated bottling plants and not much national distribution. By the time he married Joan Crawford, he'd driven Pepsi into national prominence and distribution, second only to his former employer, Coca-Cola. Pepsi was giving Coke a run for its money in every nook and hamlet of America. Al Steele welded a national network of bottlers together, standardized the syrup formula, introduced Americans to the 'Pepsi generation', brought the distinctive logo into mass consciousness, and was on the brink of going international for the first time. He was a marketing man, he loved jazz, had a deep respect for excellence, and told good jokes. He was a self-made man who inspired the people around him to do their best. He did not seem to have that obviously driven quality so often the earmark of successful men, but he never stopped planning ahead. He did not stand very tall – five foot ten maybe – but Al Steele was a big man and people loved him.

Thanksgiving vacation went wonderfully. We had a family dinner in the formal dining room. All of us were on our very best behaviour, trying very, very hard to make everything go smoothly.

The Saturday before I was to leave for school, Mother had a man come to the house and fit me for a fur coat. I wasn't allowed to open my eyes, so I couldn't see the fur, but I could feel its softness. There were lots of new clothes for all of us too. The store brought them to the house, where they were spread across the beds in our rooms.

It was better than any Christmas I could remember. We were all jumping with glee. The girls and I had been in boarding schools and Chris had been in a military academy. We were sick to death of uniforms, and this was a bonanza.

I went back to Flintridge bubbling over with the story. Sister was reserved and even sceptical, but she prayed for me and wished me success.

The next weeks flew by. I had extra schoolwork to do before I left and homework to take with me on the trip because I would be a month late returning.

At long last the moment had come. Mother, the girls, Chris, and I were boarding the train for New York. Mrs Howe was also with us to take care of my sisters. It was 8 December 1955.

This trip was such a monumental event in my life that I decided to keep a diary of it. I wanted to remember all the details, all the people and all the places we were going to see. My brother and I also collected souvenirs during the trip and made a scrapbook filled with matchbooks, menus, photos, and samples of foreign currency.

It snowed during our first day aboard the train as we watched Arizona and New Mexico speed by our windows. The second day we arrived in Chicago around noon and had lunch with Mother in the famous Pump Room, and Mother ordered more clothes for me, which were to be delivered to New York City.

Every time I turned around I seemed to get presents. I didn't know why, and I gave up questioning it. This whole adventure was like a dream come true.

We arrived in New York early in the morning of the third day. Daddy and the press photographers were there to meet us. I realized I wasn't used to having pictures taken any more and my mouth began to hurt from trying to smile for the cameras. These were the first 'family' pictures we'd had taken with Daddy. In fact, these were the first family pictures we'd had taken in almost four years.

That evening Mommie and Daddy took all of us to dinner at Voisin and afterwards we went to the Stork Club. I slept soundly that night for the first time in a week.

New York was a whirlwind of a time. This was just exactly like the fantasy *other* people always had about what it was like to be a movie star's daughter! It was all right here. I was experiencing it right now – the beautiful, expensive clothes, the long black limousines, the best tables in the best restaurants, the photographers wherever we went, the shopping sprees and the seemingly endless stream of money. I saw Daddy tipping twenty and fifty dollars at a time, I saw Mommie signing for hundreds and hundreds of dollars of clothes and accessories in New York stores. I saw the world at our fingertips, everyone smiling and bowing and doing our bidding. I saw more money and the things money could buy than I'd ever seen before in my life. Mommie had always spent money on herself but not much on us. Now that Daddy was paying the bills, the pace picked up considerably and we were all reaping the benefits.

Maybe it was all the time I'd spent alone in the convent. Maybe it was the years of no clothes and no money at all, no privilege of any kind, that made all this seem like such an extreme contrast. Maybe it was the speed with which these changes had happened that made me begin to feel uneasy. Maybe it was just too much, too fast that unsettled me.

Friday, 16 December 1955, we sailed aboard the Cunard luxury liner *Queen Mary* for Europe. Mommie and Daddy had a party in their stateroom suite for friends and the press. We dutifully waved and smiled for all the photographers and then we were sent back to our own rooms.

Once the ship sailed, we were pretty much on our own. Except for a visit in the afternoon and an occasional dinner, we didn't see much of Mommie and Daddy for the next five days. Jimmy, Daddy's valet, took Chris and me on a tour of the big ship. He was wonderful to us, keeping us amused and entertained.

After five days of rain and stormy seas, we arrived in Cherbourg, France, where we waved and smiled for the photographers again and then boarded the boat train for Paris.

It was a beautiful ride through the French countryside. To my amazement, we were assigned two entire railroad cars all to ourselves. Mommie and Daddy had their own car and we were in the adjoining one. Shortly after we boarded, a steward announced that lunch would begin in about an hour.

That 'lunch' turned out to be a seven-course gourmet feast that lasted the entire journey to Paris! I'd never seen anything like this, either. The tables in our private lounge car were set with silver, crystal, fine linen, and beautiful china. Each course was served on a different set of dishes with separate silverware. With each succeeding course, the steward brought another bottle of wine. We had a perfectly wonderful time drinking our way across the country and into Paris. We learned that in France there is no minimum drinking age and that children were often given wine. I thought that was very civilized.

In Paris we took the waiting limousines to the George V Hotel to bathe and change clothes. Before we got on the next train for Switzerland that night, Daddy took us on a brief tour of the city.

The overnight train was elegant. All the rooms had wood panelling and red carpets. Early the next morning we changed trains again and took one of the narrow-gauge trains for our final ascent into the Swiss Alps.

The entire country looked like a Walt Disney movie. The white snow covered everything and the Swiss chalets looked like picture postcards.

Finally the narrow-gauge train stopped at St Moritz station. There were horse-drawn sleighs waiting to take us to the Palace Hotel. The bells on the horses jingled just like Christmas carols and the big furry lap robes in the sleigh protected us from the cold. The sky was crystal-clear blue and the entire valley sparkled. I was sure I was dreaming. I was sure I was going to wake up soon, back in my room at the convent.

The Palace Hotel was something out of another century, another time. A bygone elegance had been captured in its spacious halls, antique furniture, gracious formal dining rooms and well-trained staff.

During the next few days, we barely saw Mommie and Daddy. Chris and I went skiing all day, the girls played in the snow and went ice skating, and we all checked in once a day with our parents. I was even allowed to go out dancing at night with the young men I met on the ski slopes. I was surprised and delighted.

On Christmas Eve the whole family gathered for presents. Mommie and Daddy had ordered caviar and champagne for everyone to be served in their suite of rooms while we opened the gifts. Daddy was a terrific storyteller and regaled us with his own skiing escapades in the Austrian Alps. Mommie was quieter than usual as she presided over the family event.

Christmas day was a peaceful one. My brother and I went

skiing all day and then met the rest of the family for dinner. By staying out of the way, we also managed to stay out of any possible trouble and the trip progressed smoothly.

The next day, Daddy planned to take us to the Olympic ski-jumping trials, but when Chris and I met him it didn't take us long to figure out that something was beginning to turn sour in paradise. My guard went up immediately and I secretly nudged my brother to stay quiet. Daddy was plainly aggravated as he told us, 'Your mother prefers to stay at the hotel this afternoon.'

Daddy's spirits picked up during the sleigh ride which took us to the jumping trials. It was the first time we'd been with Daddy alone, and he seemed more relaxed after he got over being upset with Mommie. Chris and I stood on either side of him watching the trials, and once he put his arms around us. I remember looking at Daddy a long time, as long a time as I could without just staring at him and making him uncomfortable. I thought about how wonderful it was to have a father at long last. I thought about all the people who simply take it for granted that they have a mother *and* a father. A daddy who helps you and takes you places and maybe even loves you. I thought it was probably too soon to expect Daddy to love me, but I was hoping with all my heart that someday he might. He was very kind to me and sometimes, when he looked me directly in the eyes, I thought he just might understand something about the person inside me, but I never tried to say anything about it.

Though it was very cold in the bleachers set on the side of that mountain in Switzerland, I was basking in the happiness of being with my daddy, even if it was a sort of instantaneous father-daughter relationship and even if we didn't talk too much with each other and even if we didn't know too much about each other. It was a daddy – a nice daddy – and that meant the hope of having a chance for a real father as time went by.

During the sleigh ride back to the hotel, we sang Christmas carols until Daddy's valet, Jimmy, broke up the songfest with one of his off-colour limericks.

We were still laughing when we got back to Mommie and Daddy's room, bubbling over with stories about the afternoon and ready to share all of it with Mommie.

The moment she opened the door, a cold chill ran through

me. I knew before the rest of the group that Mother was in the midst of one of her rages. I suspected that she'd been drinking while we were all away and had got herself into a full-fledged temper. It had been evident from Daddy's mood earlier that they'd had a disagreement and in our absence the situation had not improved.

From years of past experience, I knew my only salvation was to get the hell out of there as quickly and unobtrusively as possible. I managed some fast pleasantries and took my brother out with me.

Before we walked any distance down the hall, the door behind us slammed shut. Just as I had predicted, Mother and Daddy launched into one hell of a fight. We stopped momentarily to listen but then scurried back to our rooms for fear someone might catch us eavesdropping.

Except for 'checking in' around six each evening, that was just about the last I saw of my parents until New Year's Eve.

The last night in St Moritz my mother gave a dinner party for the writer Paul Gallico. Her guest list read like an old European movie cast with a baron and baroness, a prince and princess in attendance. I had asked an Englishman named David to be my escort. To my horror, I realized only an hour before the party began that my mother had become confused and invited a young American named David to be my escort. She'd mixed up the two Davids so, while I was inviting one, she was inviting the other. I had two young men, both named David, as dinner partners that evening. My daddy thought it was terribly funny.

The overnight train took us back to Paris, where we checked into the George V Hotel again. Three days later and a whirlwind tour of Paris barely completed, we took the Blue Train for the South of France, arriving in Cannes the next morning to await our ship home.

After a rather strained luncheon with Mother and Daddy, we drove down to the docks and boarded a small boat that took us out to our liner, the *Andrea Doria*.

The next morning our beautiful and luxurious ship stopped in Naples to pick up more passengers. Since there was enough time to leave the ship, I badgered Daddy to take us to Pompeii.

I was not prepared for what I saw during our brief stay in

Italy. Until now, all I had seen of Europe was luxury hotels, ski resorts, and expensive restaurants. It never dawned on me to think of the devastation of World War II or of hunger and poverty.

Mother was upset when she saw the limousines. They weren't regular limousines at all. They were two strange old rickety jalopies that had recently been painted black.

Pompeii surpassed even my own vivid imagination of what an ancient Roman city would look like. The temples and the open forum were so beautiful that you could almost hear the ancient orators echo across the thousands of years.

Word had spread that Joan Crawford was visiting Pompeii. When we left the protected part of the ruins to return to the cars, there were nearly a hundred people gathered at the gates yelling, 'Joan Crawford ... Joan Crawford ... hey ... movie star ...'

I had an uneasy feeling about it. These people reminded me of the New York mob that descended upon us many years before. Instinctively I reached for my brother's hand and checked on my sisters, who were several paces behind me. These people weren't the usual crowd of fans; there was something different about them.

Our drivers came to the entrance to escort us back to the black jalopies. They insisted on hurrying us and kept Mother between the two of them, trying to protect her. Mother was actually pleased with the crowd's attention and thought it quite natural to give them autographs, since she thought that's what they wanted. But the two burly Italians who were our chauffeurs of the moment propelled her briskly towards the car. The crowd was upon us in an instant. They didn't want autographs. They wanted money, jewellery, anything of value. People were pulling at us now and the drivers were yelling at them in Italian. One man in the crowd tried to pull off my mother's gold earrings and the biggest driver hit him.

We were running for the waiting cars now – all of us. Daddy, Mother, and the rest of us were running for the frail safety of the old black jalopies. Once inside, we slammed the doors, quickly locked them, and rolled up the windows. It was only then that we fully appreciated the skill of our drivers. They managed with amazing speed to get us out of that angry crowd without hurting anyone. Mother was quiet the rest of the drive.

Once aboard the *Andrea Doria* again, the ship's photographer chronicled our every move. We posed for pictures with the ship's captain, in front of the sculptured wall murals, and up on the bridge. I had lost my convent-school shyness during the last six weeks and was now quite the young lady, dressed in all my fine new clothes, having my hair done once a week, and even having my nails manicured.

Mother had my hair cut short in Paris. I wasn't thrilled with the way it looked, particularly after Mother said I reminded her of Norma Shearer. I knew that was no compliment from her. In fact, Mother did not like Norma Shearer and once told me the story of the time she sat on the set at the studio, just beyond camera and microphone range, knitting furiously the entire time they were shooting Norma Shearer's close-ups when the two of them starred in *The Women* at Metro in 1939.

Mother and I only had one unpleasant encounter on the ship returning to New York. She and Daddy hadn't been getting along very well in private ever since that day Daddy took us to the Olympic trials without her. You'd never have known that they were having such terrible fights by their public behaviour, though. As long as there were other people around and especially if there were photographers or the press with us, they were the epitome of happy newlyweds.

But on the train back from Switzerland I had the room next to theirs and I lay awake half the night listening to them call each other awful names. Finally I heard Daddy hit her, after which things quieted down. By the time we boarded the *Andrea Doria*, nothing was going smoothly. Mother was drinking heavily again. She always had her one-hundred-proof vodka with her in little flasks that had specially designed covers to match her clothes. We'd brought a couple of *cases* of that vodka with us to Europe, hidden throughout all our luggage. We were never stopped at customs, however, because I heard Daddy say that he had Jimmy make all the necessary arrangements.

One night Mother had been drinking steadily since long before dinner and when time came to say goodnight, she was in a foul mood. I kissed her on the cheek and turned to leave the stateroom. Daddy came back into the room just then and I went to him to kiss him goodnight too. She whirled me around and slapped me hard several times. It was the first time she'd hit me in front of Daddy. I blushed crimson. But she slapped me again, saying, 'I got my man, now you damn well go out and get your own.' She shoved me towards the door.

I didn't know what to say. I couldn't believe what I had just heard her say to me. I was stunned by the suddenness and vehemence of her outburst. Daddy started to say something to her but she told him to shut up. I left them arguing.

Damn her! Why did she always have to ruin everything? How in the world could she possibly be threatened by me? All I wanted was a father. I certainly had no designs on her new husband. I barely knew him. Sure, I wanted a father very much. Sure, I hoped that eventually he would think of me as his daughter, but that was *all* I wanted. Nevertheless, from that point on, Mother never allowed me to be anywhere with Daddy alone.

When we arrived in New York City, there was a large crowd of Pepsi people and photographers on hand to greet us. Again we smiled and posed for the 'happy family' pictures.

Although Daddy had a big apartment on Sutton Place, the entire family stayed in a hotel. Mother didn't like the apartment. It had about eight rooms, but she said it was too small.

Daddy took Chris and the girls to the airport the following day but I stayed for another week. The last day aboard ship Mother told me that a magazine called *Woman's Home Companion* wanted to do a story on us. It sounded very exciting to me. She said that they'd heard I wanted to be an actress and thought it would be a wonderful story to see mother and daughter together with Mother teaching me 'the ropes'.

So, Mother and I went on various show-business appointments and bought *more* clothes while the photographers snapped pictures of us and the writer followed us around constructing a story. By now, new clothes were nothing special. If I'd gone to a party every night for a month, I couldn't have used them all.

Each evening I got dressed up and went with Mommie and Daddy to dinner, to the theatre, or to a different night club.

After two months of smiling and being all dressed up for photographers, I was beginning to tire of the public spectacle. Finally, the picture layout and story for *Woman's Home Companion* were finished. I said my fond goodbyes to Mother and Daddy and flew back to Los Angeles by myself on a cold day near the end of January 1956.

SIXTEEN

When I returned to school on Sunday, Sister's gentle face was a welcome sight.

During the next few weeks I told everyone about our fabulous tour of Europe. My stories were the absolute centre of attention. I regaled the girls with every detail about the different countries, the grand hotels, the dashing young men, the wonderful food and the beautiful clothes. Of course I didn't have any of the clothes here at school because Mother said I didn't need them. They were being kept at home until I had further use for them.

On 4 February, a letter arrived from my mother who was still in New York at the Hampshire House. She thanked me for my sweet letters, saying that she'd mailed the ones I'd written to people who were particularly kind and helpful to me during my stay. She also gave me permission to spend the weekend with my friend Gay if her parents would provide transportation. Gay had her own car and her parents never drove her to or from school, but I hadn't mentioned that to Mother. She concluded the note by saying that she and Daddy were going to Jamaica, he on business and she for a rest. She told me to be a good girl and sent her love.

In this letter she had enclosed notes to me from Paul Muni and Shirley Booth. I'd written each of them after seeing their current Broadway plays. I was most impressed that they had taken the time to answer me.

In reply to my Valentine cards, Mother wrote me a letter with some bad news. After she opened with a perfunctory thank-you for thinking of her and a brief synopsis of the beautiful Jamaican beaches, she said that my brother had been expelled from school again. She said she didn't know what to do with him, but she'd been talking to California three and four times a day. She wouldn't be back in Los Angeles for almost another month but she sent me her love.

I had gone home with my friend Gay on several weekends between the time I'd returned from Europe and the end of February. Gay's mother had married Myford Irvine a few years before and they lived on the original Irvine ranch in Tustin, California. Gay and I had been friends since we'd both gone to Chadwick and before we'd transferred to Flintridge for very different reasons, at different times.

I talked Gay into driving me to our former school for a visit. It had been a year and a half since I'd seen the Chadwicks and we had a wonderful few days. I wanted to tell them all about our magical trip and to let them know that things were finally beginning to go all right for me again. Mrs Chadwick said I seemed very grown up but she did take me aside before I left and cautioned me about going easy on my make-up. I laughed, Commander Chadwick laughed and I thought nothing more about it. The two days I was with them flew by so fast it seemed no more than a few hours.

At first I couldn't imagine how my mother found out about this visit. I put the pieces together when I learned that Mrs Chadwick had written a letter to my brother mentioning my visit. She had no way of knowing that Chris would be expelled from that school and her letter forwarded to the house on Bristol.

Mother was still in Jamaica soaking up the sun when all hell broke loose in the form of a very long, handwritten letter. It is difficult to paraphrase accurately and retain the scathing tone of her words, but the letter began by saying that she was shocked beyond belief that I went to see the Chadwicks and she forbade me ever to see them again. She said that I had lied to her and to Sister by not asking permission. She said that she wouldn't send me to college if she found out I disobeyed her in the future.

What followed after that was a litany of every foul thing she could gather to say about me. She said I could not be trusted now any more than I ever could, that my enthusiasm and loving attention were merely surface and totally false, that I produced them just to get what I wanted. She said that she and Daddy remarked on my insincerity during the Christmas holiday we had just spent together. She said that I would never be a warm, real human being.

The letter went on to berate me, reminding me of my promise that mother would see a changed person if she would allow me to come home, but, she said, I had not changed. She told me that all the compliments I'd received in New York were just to make me happy, but behind my back people really said that I had sophisticated snobbish manners, a temper and wore too much make-up.

I was shaking with anger, tears streaming down my face by the time I turned the page and read that she'd have something planned for me after graduation but that I was not coming home. She said she would not have me bringing my 'qualities' into our home again, that she would not allow the 'babies' to be subjected to them. My sisters were nine years old now but Mother still called them babies and treated them commensurately. At the end of the letter she repeated her threat of not sending me to college if I disobeyed her.

This handwritten letter had no signature. It just ended at the bottom of the last page.

Well, that was it. I'd made a fatal error in judgment. I thought things had changed. I thought that no one would ever find out if I made a short trip to see my former 'foster parents'. It never dawned on me that it would be Mrs Chadwick herself who would inadvertently give me away.

I had been allowed to do so much over the past few months that I thought my life had changed, that perhaps I was going to be able to live normally now. But I was wrong on all counts.

I apologized to Sister and told her that I knew it was wrong not to tell her, but I also knew that Mother wouldn't give me permission for the visit and I actually thought I was sparing all of them. I thought I could do something I wanted without hurting anyone else. Wrong again. Mother's hatred of the Chadwicks simply because they loved me turned on me full force. She hated them for knowing the secret person she really was and she hated them for trying to help me. Unable to get back at them directly, she lashed out at me. As it turned out, I was hurt most of all.

In reply to my letter attempting explanation and apology, Mother sent another long letter dated 3 April 1956. I had written what I thought was a good and thoughtful letter. She quoted almost every paragraph in her own letter, followed by a cryptic response. At one point I had said: 'I felt guilty not getting your permission, but as I imagined you would not grant it, I made the decision and resolved to take the consequences.' Her reply was that if I knew she wouldn't give me the permission, I should have stayed in my own school. As to my desire to share the experiences of the trip with the Chadwicks, she said I could have written them a letter. She said she knew that all I really wanted to do was go there and show off. She was furious that I wanted to share anything with the Chadwicks and felt cheated, saying where did she come in? After all, she said, she'd done the providing. She asked, what did I give her? Answering the question herself by saying that all she got from me was dishonesty, lies and going where I was not supposed to go. She said that I was unappreciative and extremely ungrateful. She closed by quoting my phrase about 'taking the consequences' and saying that I was once again confined to school, if I made one false move I wouldn't go to college. Then she said that she hoped I enjoyed the consequences and signed the letter *Love, "Mommie".*

I had just handed her all the ammunition she wanted to use against me. She twisted and turned my words until they suited her purpose. She never once called to talk to me about any of this. She just made her pronouncements and issued the orders for punishment. In an odd way, things were back to normal again.

My visit to the Chadwicks took place in February. My punishment lasted until the following September when I was sent off to college. That entire time I was threatened by not going to college at all. All my newfound privileges were removed and I was once again confined to the school campus. This time I admit that I contributed to my own downfall, but I didn't deserve seven months of punishment.

I continued to send the little gifts and cards and to call her on every holiday. I don't know why, really . . . I can't explain it. She was my mother. I didn't know what else to do. Maybe I couldn't admit to myself that it was a completely hopeless relationship, that I was inconsequential to her life. She held tremendous power over my life even when she wasn't present. The fact that she influenced my days so completely even when I rarely saw her made her power seem indomitable. I was dependent on her. I couldn't do anything, I couldn't go anywhere without her permission.

Those little cards and gifts were attempted peace offerings, I guess. They were my attempts to soften the harshness of the conditions under which I had lived so many years now. I used to think that if my mother would only love me, my whole life would be different. I tried every way I knew to show her that if she would just love me again, I'd be a good daughter. But she didn't even know me any more. I'd only seen her for two months out of the last two years! She only knew these pieces of me and what she made up in her own mind about who she thought I was. I never did understand where she got those ideas about me and I was not around her enough to defend myself.

But there was no escaping it – I was tied to her. My entire future depended on her and I tried to do whatever I could not to make things any worse than they already were.

The first good news in months came when I received a letter on 3 May saying Carnegie Tech, the college of my choice, had accepted me. I was overjoyed. In her letter my mother added that she knew my acceptance would make me very happy. Then she added that Cliquot, Camille, and little Chiffon were all well and happy. She said that they were so adorable and that Chiffon hugged her around the neck whenever she picked her up, just like a real baby. It was signed: 'God Bless. Write to me soon. "Mommie".'

The names referred to in this letter all belonged to *dogs*. They were the miniature poodles Mother had collected. That was just what she wanted – dogs and babies. They did exactly what you wanted them to, they couldn't talk back, they couldn't think for themselves, they really were dependent. That was what she wanted in a relationship and that was what made her so furious with me. She was not easily dissuaded, however, and continued to refer to my sisters as 'the babies' until they were ten years old.

School was nearly over now. There was only a month left until graduation and we were beginning to prepare for our final exams. All the other girls were very excited about graduation and their future plans. Most of them were glad high school was over and were looking forward to being included in adulthood. A number of girls were planning to get married, some were going to get jobs and only five of us were going on to college.

I sent Mother and Daddy a card on their first anniversary. They'd been travelling all over the country on business trips, opening Pepsi bottling plants and making public appearances.

I prayed that nothing would happen to me before I got out of this school and into college. Mother's letters to me were so sweet and so filled with 'darlings' that I sometimes wondered about my own sanity and sound judgment, for during this entire time I continued to be punished. I was still not allowed to leave the school. I was still not allowed to go home.

My friend Gay was having a huge graduation party. Her parents, the Irvines, had invited every girl in the senior class and their parents. Everyone had accepted, even the parents of the girls from Central and South America who were travelling thousands of miles to see their daughters graduate.

I had written to ask permission to go to the party. On 31 May, I received a very nasty reply. It began by saying that I was not permitted to go to any of the graduation parties held off the school grounds. The next paragraph said that my graduation and birthday present was to have been an airline ticket to go to London with Mother and tour Scotland and Ireland while she was making *The Story of Esther Costello*. However, since I disobeyed her and visited the Chadwicks, she was afraid this gift was out of the question. She said I had written her that I was willing to suffer the consequences. Now, she asked, did I really think it was worth it? She reminded me again that I would not be able to go to college if I left the school grounds for any reason. She signed this missile of cruelty: *'My love always, "Mommie".'*

I ran to my room and threw myself across my bed, kicking and screaming and crying. That evil goddamned BITCH! She's just a mean, rotten bitch to the marrow of her bones. This letter is only intended to stick the knife in a little deeper, to prove how much and how effectively she can hurt me. This letter was intended to make me crazy and it succeeded. How I wished I'd never been so honest and straightforward as to say I'd take the consequences. She knows she never considered sending me airline tickets. She already told me I had to stay in school all summer again. She's the queen bitch and she'd *never* forget a punishment in just four month. Four months isn't nearly long enough to torture bad, ungrateful, artificial Christina. Four months? Just a drop in the bucket. Not nearly long enough to make the point that 'Mommie dearest' is the powerful one, 'Mommie dearest' holds the only key, 'Mommie dearest's' will *must* be done. Four months doesn't begin to make amends for the crime of disobedience. There had to be other ways to make me pay. This letter was one of them.

My friend Gay brought me the letter my mother had sent her parents on Joan Crawford stationery. It politely said that she had to decline their invitation because her husband would be out of town and she had business commitments that she couldn't postpone. Then she repeated the incident of four months ago when Gay had driven me to see the Chadwicks. She said that I had disobeyed her and she felt I must be punished. That was why she was forbidding me to attend any of my class graduation parties. She said she hoped Mrs Irvine understood that she must deprive me of the things I liked best in order to teach me a lesson. She signed the letter: *'Gratefully, Joan'*.

Preparations for graduation on 12 June were accelerating. I'd sent Mother an invitation for her and Daddy to attend the graduation ceremonies. Since I had no money, I also asked her for a strapless bra to wear under the graduation dress. Her reply was dated 2 June, just ten days before my graduation. There was an acknowledgement of receiving the invitation but no mention of whether or not she and Daddy would attend. Then she lapsed into a long discussion about how the store could put lingerie straps on the dress which would do fine. She also said that I didn't need a new dress for the Sunday Baccalaureate service.

I didn't ask the store to do anything. I asked Sister to write to my mother and explain my request. I still didn't know from this letter whether or not anyone was coming to my graduation. All the other girls were busily making plans with their parents for the parties, trips, and other festivities. High school graduation is a moment everyone remembers for the rest of her life.

I remember my high school graduation as one of the most unhappy days of my life. It wasn't the worst day, but it was one of the most unhappy.

On 11 June, the day before graduation and also my seventeenth birthday, I received a Special Delivery letter. Mother called me 'Tina darling' and said that she was so very sorry but she was working and wouldn't be able to attend my graduation exercise. She had to work all day on Tuesday at the studio to get her clothes ready and then take my Daddy to the airport in the evening. The secretary would bring my birthday and graduation gifts to me along with a strapless bra. She signed herself: '*All my love, "Mommie"*.'

I crumpled the blue Joan Crawford stationery into a ball and clenched it in my fist. God . . . I hated her.

So this was to be the excuse. She had to try on some clothes and he had to catch a night flight. My mother and my stepfather were less than one hour's drive away from the school and neither one of them was coming to my high school graduation.

The secretary arrived early the next day bringing me three small, gift-wrapped boxes and a strapless bra. She stayed through graduation.

I went back to my room about 4 o'clock. I took off my pretty white graduation dress, hung it up carefully and sat down on the edge of my bed. I cried for a while. Everybody knew that I was the only girl in the whole graduation class without my family in attendance. Everybody knew I was being punished on this day too. I could see the look of pity in their eyes. It made my skin crawl with humiliation and anger.

That night while the rest of my class was enjoying the big Irvine party, I ate dinner alone in one corner of the empty dining room, watched an hour of television, and went to bed.

Two days later a letter arrived from my hardworking mother. She said the secretary had told her about the beautiful graduation and how 'exquisite' I looked. She congratulated me on the Scholarship ribbon and the Legion of Honor medal from the

American Legion. Then she said: 'You are a good, sweet girl, and you are behaving beautifully now. I want you to know that I love you very much and am proud of you.' She closed by reminding me to write thank-you letters for my graduation cards and gifts and told me to send the letters to her for mailing.

I seriously wondered if my mother had actually written that letter. It sounded more like the way the secretary talked. I wouldn't have been a bit surprised to hear my mother say: 'You were there, you write the letter and I'll sign it.' But it did gall me that I had to send the finished letters home. I was seventeen years old, for Heaven's sake, and she still treated me like a nit-wit.

But the crowning blow of that miserable graduation day was when I opened the presents from Mother. There were two small matching boxes that had been separately gift wrapped. One box had a birthday card on it and the other box had a graduation card. Each box contained *one* gold earring!

I couldn't find words for my indignation until several days later. It took her until 20 June to write her reply.

She explained that the reason she had the earrings boxed separately was that one earring was a graduation present and the other a birthday gift. In reply to my letter in which I said: 'I'm sorry you weren't at my graduation because it was an experience we should have shared as it happens only once, and can never be recaptured', she wrote that we'd missed many moments together. That there had been years of moments I'd failed to share with her. She said that my sarcastic criticism of her for not being at my graduation made her feel sorry for me! If I really understood about her work, she said, I wouldn't have bothered to criticize her. She said she was standing for clothing fittings that day so that she could pay for my education. After that she said that I couldn't have a room with a bath at college because it was too expensive, then she made a most peculiar request. She asked me to make a list, from memory, of the museum pieces she'd got from the Carmel Museum and given to Chadwick School nearly five years earlier. She told me not to contact the Chadwicks about this matter, just to list the pieces from memory. She put a postscript on this letter asking how I knew about a girl who was my brother's friend, saying that if I didn't tell her the truth within a week, she'd cancel my enrolment at college.

Mother had taken us to the lunatic fringe again. The girl, Kathy, was a friend of my brother. He had told me where she lived. I'd never been there but Mother wouldn't believe me and I didn't feel like arguing with her. It was all too stupid. I wrote her that I'd never been there or anywhere else she didn't already know about and left it at that. She was just going to have to deal with the rest of her paranoia by herself.

But I knew that the response I received to my letter was prompted by a twinge of guilt. She couldn't stand any kind of honesty outside the narrow confines of her work. She couldn't tolerate personal honesty. She interpreted that as criticism of herself. This time in our lives, she'd been wrong and she knew it. Her answer, her reaction, was always to hide behind her work, to play the martyr, to try and make me feel guilty for receiving an education, to make me feel guilty for being alive.

Mother and I had, indeed, missed years of shared experience, but who's doing was it? I certainly never asked to be sent away from home when I was ten years old. She sent all of us away because *she* wanted to. She made the decisions about our lives. We had no choice, we just lived with hers.

I thought back over the last few years of my life. What was it that had brought about two years of punishment? Well, one whole year was for not preparing a list of Christmas cards fast enough. Then, seven more months of punishment were caused by a two-day visit to a middle-aged couple. For these heinous disobediences I received a sentence of one year and seven months of solitary confinement.

I was still supposed to feel unending love and deepest gratitude for the benevolence of my long-suffering, hardworking mother – my mother who believed in a philosophy of 'take away what she loves most and she'll learn giving'. A philosophy of 'maximum punishment for all disobediences and some day she'll learn to behave'.

I had spent about three months out of the last three years off the campus of a boarding school. I had no money, few clothes I had access to, none of the normal privileges given to the other students. And I had no home. I had been orphaned twice: once by my own biological parents and the second time by my adopted parent. Since the age of ten I had grown up in institutions and foster homes, even if they were called by other names. What's more, I had received better treatment, more consideration and basic understanding and fairness at the hands of strangers than I ever had from my own mother. For all this, I was to be eternally grateful.

I had suffered from migraine headaches for the last year and a half. The headaches had got so bad that Sister suggested I see a doctor. I was initially taken to an eye doctor, who checked my vision thoroughly and could find nothing wrong. When I was told I was being taken back for a final eye examination, I found myself instead in the offices of a psychiatrist. I was furious with the deception but I took the battery of tests the woman gave me, stacked up all the cards in 'yes' and 'no' piles, and gave her my interpretation of the pictures she held up.

When all these were concluded, the doctor asked me to come into her private office. She seemed to be an understanding person, genuinely interested in helping me. I told her about the terrible headaches and when they had started over a year ago. She asked me a few questions about some of my answers on the tests and then she asked me if I had any idea what might be bothering me. She asked if I knew what might be causing my headaches.

I looked her squarely in the face and said to her directly: 'Yes. I hate my mother.'

That was the end of the interview. That was also the end of my visits to the doctor. That was not the end of my headaches.

During the remainder of that summer after graduation, I did what I could to help Sister. I worked in the office, answering the phones, typing transcripts, processing the applications of prospective students. I tried to lighten the work load. Sister had been very good to me. She had done everything in her power to make life more bearable for me. She had extended herself beyond any technical responsibility for my well-being.

I realized during the quietness of that summer that I had learned a lesson from the special life of the convent. As much as I had originally hated it and the circumstances that had brought me here, perhaps those lessons could not have been attained any other way. I had come face to face with myself. I had come in contact with my own loneliness, my own abyss of uncertainty, my own hatred and impatience. I had never known the kind of pain I'd felt during these long months of solitude. There was no escape for me. I had to find a way to face myself, learn to live with myself and begin to be patient with myself. Patience. I had come face to face with my own Nemesis. Patience. The curse of the young. Patience. The secret weapon of survival.

I thanked Sister for her understanding, her many kindnesses towards me. I was a difficult person. I tended to brood and to turn inward upon myself. She had met me with gentleness, with wisdom and with love. I admired her deeply.

Shortly before I was to leave for college I read an article in the Los Angeles *Times* about an auction. It was with great sadness that I realized that it was the contents of *our* house going up for sale. I wrote mother a letter inquiring about that auction and received a handwritten reply on 27 August from Great Fosters, Surrey, England. She said it was strange that I never cared about the house, or the running of it, until I saw the ad for auctioning. She hoped the house would be sold soon because she said there was no more love in it. She hated the conditions she was working under in England but she loved the cold, rainy weather. She said the food was horrible 'fish with flies or steak – so thin you cannot find it – everything is cooked in mineral oil so it's a laxative every meal'. She was staying in the suite of Henry the Eighth and 'Ann Bolyn' as she called the unfortunate lady, where the beds sank to the floor and the spiders were as big as 'tarantulas'. She said the 'babes' (my sisters) were leaving for school soon and that she was not able to send me any spending money for college because she'd already spent her cheques.

It was quite clear that she hated being in England. She was obviously miserable and being forced to live under sub-human conditions just to support us. How she sacrificed for us. How grateful that should make us. It didn't surprise me particularly that the two months allowance and food cheques from her business office had been spent. I didn't expect much any more. And I didn't really care about her nightmare. What I cared about was that nothing go wrong in the few short weeks remaining before I was off to college and a new life. It was interesting that she signed this letter 'Mother'. Usually she had signed 'Mommie' with quotation marks as though it were a pseudonym. Perhaps it was.

A car and driver came to pick me up from Flintridge one week before college started. I said goodbye to Sister and promised to write her. I was not sorry to be leaving this mountain-top, however, and breathed a sigh of relief as the limousine descended the hill for the last time.

I also called my grandmother to say goodbye. I knew that I'd be closely watched at home and didn't want to give the secretary any unnecessary information which might get back to Mother. I told Grandmother I'd write her from college to let her know how I was doing and where I was. She always thanked me for my phone calls and for thinking of her.

When I arrived home, I found a big trunk almost packed for me. Elva, Mother's wardrobe woman, had already finished most of the work. I liked Elva. She'd been with Mother for years, travelling with her on occasion to make sure all the clothes for personal appearances were properly packed, ironed, and ready for Mother to just step into.

My brother and sisters were also home from their respective schools. I knew it was the last time I'd be seeing them for a while and we spent a good deal of time talking about the future. I spent hours talking with Chris. I gave him my new address and asked him to try and stay in touch with me, no matter where he was sent. I told him I didn't think they'd censor the mail at college and not to be afraid to write me.

I did call some of my old friends and told them I was going East. Since I wasn't allowed to leave my own house, a few of them came to say goodbye to me. Nicki, my coach from Chadwick, was getting married and I'd managed to save a few dollars for a small wedding present. She and her fiancé, Jim, made the trip out to the house and I gave them their gift. Nicki was her usual energetic self. She brought me the news on all my Chadwick friends during the couple of hours we were able to visit.

Finally it was time to leave for Union Station and the train for Pittsburgh, Pennsylvania. I walked from room to room through the entire house, trying to imprint the memory of it in my brain.

I told Mrs Howe that I didn't think I'd ever see this house again. She looked at me a little oddly, but didn't try to dissuade me from a final tour of my childhood home.

My mother was still in England, but everywhere I felt her presence, almost like the smell of her perfume in the stairway, as though keeping Oscar company while he stood alone in the special niche. The happy memories and the years of pain swept across my heart.

I walked out into the yard, where I could hear the echo of those long ago birthday parties, the clowns and the organ-grinder music. Somewhere out of the past I could catch a long forgotten glimpse of the big parties, the bright canopy, and Judy Garland singing far into the summer night. I walked around the pool where Chris and I had played king of the mountain and learned to talk to each other underwater. I stood beneath the big olive tree where once we'd hung a large stuffed toy in effigy, scaring Mother half to death when she looked out her window and thought we'd executed one of the twins! I looked at the flower beds and the little vegetable garden we'd got one of the gardeners to help us start years ago. I went into the theatre where I had seen Mother walk into the ocean in *Humoresque* and had become hysterical because I thought she'd really died. I looked down at the same chair where Phillip used to spank me, and then I gazed at the little empty stage upon which I'd made my disastrous debut as the mother in *Hansel and Gretel*. I tried to look at every corner and every piece of furniture. I stood under the trees and knelt beside the new rose garden. I knew in my bones that I would never see any of it again. I knew these moments were the last ones of this part of my life.

I stood on the steps leading down into the garden, the same steps I'd stood on so many evenings wishing on the evening star ... 'Star light, star bright ...' wishing for a horse of my very own ... wishing Mommie loved me ... wishing for the strength to stay alive until I could grow up ... wishing for ...

PART
THREE

SEVENTEEN

College surpassed whatever expectations I might have had about it. There was no way I could have imagined what it would be like to live in the East, any more than my fantasies of the first taste of freedom could measure up to reality. I simply had no idea about life outside the confines of boarding school and Mother's erratic discipline. What awaited me was the beginning of a new phase of my life, a phase substantially different from anything I'd experienced so far.

Most extraordinary was the sudden freedom. I ventured slowly into this new world of personal responsibility. The rules were minimal and no one seemed to function as the overseer I was used to having as an integral part of my life. There was an opportunity to be an individual, to grow as a person. I soon realized that I had no idea who I really was. Most of my energy in growing up to this point had been spent coping with school-work and my mother's personality. Very little time had been spent deciding what I wanted out of life. Now each day brought these decisions and their consequences.

I still had to resolve differences between the public fantasy of 'Joan Crawford's daughter' and the reality of my own life. I was, of course, a movie star's daughter, but I did not have the personal life-style to correspond with the image conjured up in the minds of strangers.

Mother was filming *The Story of Esther Costello* in England. She never visited the college campus. She frequently forgot to send my allowance. I did not have suitable winter clothes. I spent Thanksgiving vacation in the college dormitory despite invitations to stay with friends. Then I found out that I was going to have to spend Christmas vacation at college because the picture had fallen behind schedule and Mother was going to remain in London through December.

Almost four months of college had passed. There were new friends, new ideas, and an open exchange of thoughts that changed my perspective on the world. I felt a growing acceptance as a young aspiring actress. It was the commonality of our dreams that bound my friends and me together, not the differences in our backgrounds that mattered so much any more.

I wrote Mother at least once a week. I was so genuinely happy making friends, going out on dates, and working hard at my classes that I tried to share all the details with her. My good fortune was still hard to believe.

She wrote back progress reports on her picture, on the difficulties she was having with threatened strikes, and then added silly things like, 'Please don't wear your evening dresses to classes. Save them for dinner parties. Dress simply and watch the make-up.' I never understood what was in her mind when she wrote things like that. It occurred to me that she didn't always know who I was.

The Pittsburgh papers had been calling me regularly since my arrival. I agreed to do one interview if they promised to leave me alone after that. The interview, I thought, went well. They took a couple of photos and left. They asked the usual questions about 'How does it feel to be a movie star's daughter' and 'Are you following in your mother's footsteps?' I replied that I was going into the theatre. I did the best I could but I made some mistakes. I wasn't sophisticated enough yet to realize that once you become a public person, some of the control over what is printed about you is taken out of your hands. It is possible, I found out, to say something perfectly innocent and have it taken out of context so that the resulting printed article makes your original statement seem quite different from what you intended.

Mother was not pleased about the interview, but I couldn't seem to explain the situation to her. It was the first of many discussions we had about the press. I thought she would know the problem better than anyone. She'd been dealing with the press most of her life, but in relation to me, her daughter, she forgot how hard that lesson was to learn. I took her advice, though, and didn't allow any more interviews.

By the time spring vacation rolled around in March, Mother and Daddy were both back in New York. Although Mother said that there was no room for me to stay with them in their Sutton Place apartment, she sent me a ticket and allowed me to stay with a girlfriend's family in Brooklyn.

I was a little nervous riding in the cab to meet my parents for lunch at '21'. I hadn't seen them since we returned from the European trip more than a year ago. It was odd meeting in so public a place. There were the usual greetings, Mother gave me some spending money, and they briefly inquired about college. It was just as though I'd seen them in the past few weeks. I experienced a sense of disorientation at the casualness with which everything was done.

After my first visit with them, neither Mother nor Daddy asked me anything about myself. When I saw them it was usually in a restaurant or at the theatre and they talked business with their friends. It was all very chic and pleasant and impersonal. Coming from my college atmosphere, I was unable to be blasé about the expenses they took so for granted. Each lunch came to over a hundred dollars and I thought wistfully about struggling along on my twenty-five-dollar-a-month allowance. But I know it was useless to think in those terms. I had learned a long time ago that there were two distinctly different standards when it came to my mother and money. It was the ordinary everyday concept of money that totally eluded Mother, but the one with which I had to live. On the other hand, whatever Mother wanted, Mother got.

So, back at school I typed term papers in the dorm at night to make some extra cash. I thought about getting out on my own during those quiet hours. I was bored with being in schools for so many years. College was much better than boarding school had been, but I was still feeling helpless. I realized that as long as my mother held the purse strings, she controlled my life. She influenced my thinking even in her absence. I had become so used to being controlled by her that it was difficult to imagine any other way of being. On one hand I rebelled against the confinement, seeking to free myself, and on the other hand I assumed there would always be this invisible connection between us, guiding my life even against my own will. For me Mother was like the legendary Lorelei. I felt the pull and lure of her song even when it was silent. It was the memory of her wishes, the need for her love, the sound of the lullaby buried deep in our past. I tried very hard to guide the ship of my life by myself, but I could feel it shudder and wander off course. Then some echo, some fragment of that song of the Lorelei, would reach me and I felt the ship tugging in that direction. But I knew there were only the rocks and a wreck awaiting me. At the last moment I managed to turn, avoiding ultimate disaster, but it was clumsy and accomplished little except the thwarting of annihilation. I had listened to the Lorelei song so many years I could barely distinguish it from reality. I had become so attuned to the melody fragments that they seemed a part of myself. I heard the faraway strains even when no one was singing. I could not seem to break free. It was like being hypnotized. I only needed one faint note to remind me of the entire song and my programmed response followed.

Mother and Daddy had been travelling extensively to Pepsi bottling plants, sales meetings, and conventions all over the country. Mother could be counted on to draw huge crowds since she was the only major Hollywood star to make the transition from films to public prominence in the business world at that time. In the late 1950s no movie star did commercials for television, none were permanently associated with just one product. Pepsi-Cola was getting more publicity, more national press coverage and public awareness from Mother's appearances than they could ever have bought with advertising dollars. Daddy planned the strategy with his marketing executives, then Mother played the part. She had bottles of Pepsi next to her at press conferences, cases of Pepsi backstage when she went on talk shows, and she learned to mention the company name whenever she was interviewed for any purpose whatsoever, including her own films or television appearances. As Daddy pushed the soft-drink company ever closer to the number one market spot in the nation through expansion and promotion, Mother drew the crowds and got the media coverage. They made a remarkable team during those three years. Behind all of it was the product, the soft drink that would mark an entire era. The 'Pepsi generation' was coming of age.

Mother and Daddy were on the Pepsi trail most of the time during early 1957. They covered every part of the United States. No company occasion was too insignificant for a whistle-stop visit to places like Ottawa, Kansas, or Tulsa, Oklahoma, or Joplin, Missouri. It was during these hectic days that Mother was forced to start flying. Until then she had insisted on taking the train, but the schedule Daddy had mapped out required greater speed. Besides, Daddy was now chairman of the board of the company and he had to spend more time running the business from offices in New York.

Though Mother complained about being so busy, I knew she loved every minute of it. For ten years previously she'd struggled alone with a faltering career, four children, a parade of passing lovers and mounting debts. By the time she married Alfred Steele, she was fifty-one years old, she'd sold her apartment building, taken out a second mortgage on her house, borrowed against her insurance policies, and she didn't have a job. After the marriage, someone else paid the bills, bought her jewellery, paid the rent, and took her anywhere she wanted to go. It was an ideal arrangement. She even got to play 'movie star' again to throngs of adoring fans. She considered being Mrs Steele as work for the company, as a job, a performance. She knew the people were coming to see her and she gave them a show befitting the queen of celluloid. She always made a little speech and signed endless autographs. She changed clothes two and three times a day so that the photographs taken at various events would show her in different outfits. She ensured media coverage wherever the glamorous couple went. Mother also made sure the Pepsi name was either in the photograph or in its caption. She was a perfectionist.

Since Mother and Daddy were going to be away for most of the summer, first in Los Angeles and then touring Europe and Africa in preparation for the opening of international bottling plants, it was decided that I would spend just a few days with them in New York and then go to Westport, Connecticut, to work as an apprentice in the summer stock theatre there.

I was in New York on my eighteenth birthday. As a surprise, Daddy gave me his 1957 Thunderbird convertible. We went down to the street in front of their Sutton Place apartment and there it was, parked at the kerb, all shiny and unbelievable. It was really gorgeous. I hugged and kissed both of them and cried.

Westport Country Playhouse was a jewel among summer stock theatres, run by the Theatre Guild in New York. Because it was only fifty miles from the city, everyone wanted to play Westport. We had the best shows and stars of the season.

There were about ten apprentices that summer. At first I was an anomaly to the rest of the group. But after a few weeks, everyone had too much work to spend any extra energy on someone else. We were welded into a team by the work itself and I liked the theatre very much. Each week a new show brought a new cast of people, problems, and challenges.

Carnegie Tech required that all freshman drama students be individually invited to return for their sophomore year. It had to do not directly with grades but with whether they thought you had a real future as a professional. I was sent the letter of invitation but I found out that a number of others had not been asked to return. One girl took the rejection so badly that she committed suicide by throwing herself in front of an express subway train.

I was horrified by the news. She was only nineteen years old. The rejection must have been like telling her she was a failure as a person. She must not have had any way of coping with her sense of shame. I thought about my own life and decided not to waste any of it.

Between the suicide and the news that my favourite acting teacher had left the college, I decided I didn't want to return to Carnegie. I very much wanted to be on my own and go to work.

When Mother and Daddy returned to New York, I called and had a long talk with my mother. Neither she nor Daddy was pleased with my request to leave college and go to professional school in the city, but I pointed out that I'd still be going to school, it would cost less, and I'd have a better chance of getting a job sooner. Mother said she couldn't force me to go back to college even though she wished I would. We agreed that if I wasn't accepted by the Neighborhood Playhouse for that fall, I'd return to Carnegie for another year.

Shortly after that, Mother and Daddy left for Africa and were out of the country for the rest of that summer.

Unfortunately, I spent the last month of the summer sick. I was in the hospital for a few days and then had to rest for a week. As the days passed, I became terribly depressed. Part of it was being sick and the other part was fear about what my future actually was going to be. I was just as scared about moving into the 'Big Apple' as any other eighteen-year-old kid ever was. I had no practical knowledge about how the real world worked. What others seemed to take for granted was a mystery to me. I didn't know anything about getting things done. When a girl from the theatre and I decided to share an apartment in New York that fall, just ordering the telephone or arranging for utilities was a major adventure for me. I was afraid to ask questions for fear of looking like a fool, so I listened to other people. It was a very inefficient way to go about life.

Mother and Daddy returned to New York towards the end of September from a side trip to Washington, D.C. I'd spoken with my mother several times and she'd arranged to send over some furniture from the extra pieces she and Daddy had in storage. When I returned home from school one afternoon, the man from the storage company was arranging two small couches and a glass-top table with four chairs. The furniture was simple and modern. The colours were green and yellow.

My roommate was standing in the middle of the room with a horrified look on her face. There was another man in the room, tacking up a trellis of plastic ivy to one entire wall of our apartment. My roommate came over to me and said that I had to do something immediately. I had to *stop* the plastic ivy man right away. I nearly laughed out loud, but she was so serious I didn't dare. I went to the man and asked him to take down all the ivy he'd attached so far. He replied in a disdainful tone of voice that Miss Crawford had ordered it. I told him I didn't care what 'Miss Crawford' had ordered, he was to stop with the ivy immediately. My roommate sat down. I went to the phone and called my mother.

I thanked her for the nice furniture and then told her I didn't think we'd be needing the ivy on the walls. I said our apartment was just too small. To my surprise, Mother was angry with me. She said it cost money to have the man spend that time. I tried to explain to her that we hadn't discussed ivy before and it just didn't look right. I said I was sorry about any extra expense, but she'd never mentioned the idea to me in advance. She said I didn't have any taste, any sense of design.

I didn't want to argue with her. I just tried to be calm about the entire situation. My roommate was in shock. My mother was being nasty. The ivy man flounced out in a huff, trailing his plastic leaves behind him and slamming the door dramatically.

I started to laugh. Everything was in chaos. I tried to apologize to my roommate for the plastic ivy, even though I had nothing to do with it. She was very New England. She liked antiques and pottery from Bennington. She did not like modern furniture, but she could live with it. What she could not tolerate was green plastic ivy climbing all over the walls. She was also not fond of my mother trying to impose her will over both of us.

If it hadn't been for her I probably would have let the man finish and lived with the plastic ivy rather than risk a confrontation with my mother. It was amazing to me that Mother could make me feel as though I'd done something wrong whenever I expressed the slightest divergence from her wishes. A simple difference of opinion was a major incident to her. So, in the past I would have lived with the ivy, hated it every time I looked at it, and wished I could stand up for myself better than I did. I would have felt a little guilty for not being more grateful.

Somehow in these situations I lost all the way around. She didn't offer alternatives. She acted as though I had everything I needed to live my life successfully and I simply insisted on screwing everything up. It was getting me crazy. I had days of depression so severe that I couldn't face going to school. Instead, I'd stare out at the Fifty-ninth Street Bridge in the rain and write poetry that didn't make much sense. I didn't seem to be able to find my way out of the maze, to deal with it in a way that made things get better. Everything I did just seemed to make it worse.

Then, in a complete turnabout, Mother told me that she'd accepted an appearance on the *Jack Paar Show* for me. She told me what dress I was to wear and had the show send over all the questions I'd be asked. She made Jack Paar promise her personally that he wouldn't ask any unexpected questions and then she coached me on what I was to say in each response. The show was live in the East and a delayed broadcast on the West Coast. Mother and Daddy would be in Los Angeles but they'd be watching.

It was not my choice nor was it my wish to do this show. I was going on as the daughter of a famous person in a segment where they guessed the mystery person. But I was so eager to begin a career and please my mother at the same time that I swallowed my pride and agreed to appear. I'd memorized all the answers perfectly and even though I was very nervous, everything went smoothly during the programme.

After the show was over and I was on my way home again, I realized for the first time that I'd made a fundamental error, one that was to haunt me over and over again during my professional career. I was on that programme only as an extension of my mother. I had no real credentials at all. I was a movie star's daughter, I was just a novelty, a curiosity. The questions were all about my mother, about Joan Crawford, not about me. I was standing in for her. I was important only by association and not because of myself. I had no personal identity.

Down through the years I came to know that pattern so well I could anticipate the questions in advance. But that night was the first time as an adult that I knew I'd been used. That was the first time I felt the public lie I was telling. It was one of those awful trade-offs when you think you'll be able to deal with your own betrayed value system later. The problem is that you never get to 'later'. The lies are always now. The feeling about yourself, your own self-respect, is always now – not later.

Mother sent me a telegram saying how wonderful I was. Her friends said what a credit I was to my proud mother.

I was a credit to my mother. I spoke only when spoken to. I said all the right things. But there was nothing of me in that show except my physical presence. There really was no Christina at all, there was just 'Joan Crawford's daughter'. I felt like a fraud. If I'd had an ounce of common sense, I'd have scrapped my childhood dreams of becoming an actress and done some-

221

thing else with my life then and there. The handwriting was clear that night, but I didn't have enough wisdom to see the pain and frustration that awaited me. Doggedly and single-mindedly I stuck to my plans. I was determined to overcome all obstacles. My dreams of a career were all that had stood by me during the past years of confinement and near-hopelessness. I'd never given any other way of life one bit of serious thought. I saw no alternatives so I was faced with no decisions.

EIGHTEEN

Our house in California was finally being sold to Donald O'Connor. Mother sent some of her furniture to storage in New York, auctioned off some, and gave a good deal to charity thrift shops. She and Daddy were letting the Sutton Place apartment go and lived at the Plaza Hotel while they awaited the reconstruction of their new penthouse condominium at Seventieth Street and Fifth Avenue.

The workers had already torn down the top two floors to the steel beams. This was no ordinary remodel. Where there had been sixteen rooms there would now be eight. The plans called for two master bedrooms, two master baths, a living room, library, dining room, kitchen, and maid's room. Despite the fact that between them Mr and Mrs Steele had five children – her four and his one son – there was no guest room. Construction went on for over six months, causing other tenants to complain bitterly and finally try to sue the Steeles for completely disrupting the lives of everyone else in the building. Before it was all over, the delays and unexpected problems, the new furniture shipped from California and hauled up through the window openings by giant cranes, the cost escalated from an expected $500,000 to nearly a million.

At first glance it was spectacular. The space and view were unexcelled in Manhattan. But there was something barren about it. There were none of the beautiful antiques from our California house, none of the old paintings. Everything was new and modern and plastic. Even the flowers and plants were plastic. Mother preferred them because they could be kept sparkling clean and were regularly washed in soapy water. There were plastic covers on all the upholstered furniture that crinkled and stuck to you when you sat on them. All the windows were sealed. There was no fresh air. The temperature was regulated at about sixty degrees both winter and summer so that it was always freezing cold in the apartment.

When guests came for the first time, Mother gave them the grand tour. She showed them the apartment, then she showed them all her closets. She proudly opened the rows of mirrored doors to show off floor-to-ceiling racks of clothes, each garment carefully covered with plastic. That was followed by an inspection of the hat closet, the shoe closet, and the handbag closet. I wondered if she'd got the idea of this closet tour from our visit to Shirley Temple's house when I was a little girl.

Upstairs, Mother's pink-and-white bedroom was the larger of the two master suites, and downstairs the white, green, and yellow rooms reflected practically nothing of Daddy except a chess set and some carved-ivory elephants in a bookcase.

The wood floors were polished to a dangerously slippery shine and, where rugs existed, they were pure white. No one was allowed to wear shoes beyond the entrance hall because Mother didn't want those white rugs soiled. Many an unsuspecting guest was unpleasantly surprised by Mother's edicts before word got out about having to go bare-foot in her apartment.

I felt exhausted when I left there. It wasn't the constant work of cleaning and recleaning, it wasn't the minute attention given equally to small details and major jobs, it wasn't just the freezing-cold temperature inside the house. It was something else, something I couldn't quite define. Everything was such a big deal. Nothing was ever simple. The household was in a permanent state of agitation and I was continually worried about whether I'd make a mistake or say something wrong. It was just exhausting to be there any length of time. I loved my mother and I wanted to help, I wanted to please her, but each time I left it was with a sense of relief.

My mother was totally oblivious to everyday realities. Her life-style was created out of fantasy, a manufactured public image, now financed from the chequebook of big business.

After one of their many trips that fall, I met my mother and father for lunch at '21'. The meal was pleasant enough, and after the meal Mother and I stopped at the ladies' room. She discovered that she didn't have any cash with her and asked me to leave a dollar for the attendant. Before she departed I whispered to her that I only had one dollar with me. She smiled, patted me on the shoulder, and said that Daddy would reimburse me.

The ladies' room attendant smiled when I gave her my dollar and said: 'Thank you, Miss Crawford. You know, your mother is a wonderful person. She's my favourite movie star.'

By the time I caught up with Mother and Daddy they were already in their limousine and Daddy was just shutting the door as Mother waved goodbye, saying how nice it was to see me again.

It happened so fast I never got a chance to say one word. My heart sank as I watched the big black limousine pull away into traffic. The wind was blowing and it was cold. It looked as though it would begin snowing any minute now. I pulled my coat around me. The restaurant doorman asked politely if he could get me a cab. I turned to face him and managed to say nonchalantly, 'Oh, no, thanks. I think I'll walk.'

During the rest of that winter and into the spring of 1958 I called, I visited their apartment, I wrote them when they were away. I remembered all the holidays and birthdays and anniversaries. I tried to be what Mother wanted me to be, but I knew in my heart that my own life was changing and it was harder and harder to reconcile the two.

What today would be recognized as a classic teenage process of self-definition and evolvement was interpreted by Mother as my defiance of her wishes. It was impossible for me to be her ideal child. No one could live the way she did except herself. I could never have my own identity under her rules. I would always be an extension of her own personality. She projected onto me both the best and the worst of herself. When we were together she trained me to be just like her. When we were apart she attributed to me all the qualities she most disliked about herself, whether founded in my reality or not, and then behaved as though her own fantasies about me were real. It forced me to defend myself against accusations that were fabrications.

Once she called in a rage demanding to know why I was going out on the town every night when I was supposed to be in school. It took me almost an hour on the phone with her to discover she'd just read one of those silly gossip columns which had an item in it saying I'd been seen at a restaurant with Peter Duchin. I was unable to convince her that I didn't know the young man, had never set foot in the restaurant mentioned, and had nothing to do with putting that item in the newspaper. These conversations with her were madness and folly for me. She yelled and I cried and we never quite resolved the point in question.

Because of the way our family had been constructed, there was no relative I could go to for counsel or help, no family friend with whom I could talk. I simply had to do the best I could at a time when Mother was immersed in Pepsi business, travelling with Daddy and renovating her own acting career. Because of the extensive publicity she'd got through her soft-drink promotion campaign, she was now getting offers to do television shows and started working in Hollywood more frequently. It had been a good arrangement. As the company stock advanced, so did her career.

The way Mother lived was so far removed from anything even remotely available to me that sometimes just that insight alone left me feeling helpless. How could I explain what was important in my life when her main concern was the plastic covers on her clothes or making sure no one walked on the white rugs without taking their shoes off? Where could I begin relating what I was seeing for the first time in that massive jungle city when she had a screaming fit if I wore jeans to move furniture? She'd done an incredible job of erasing every single trace of her own growing up, she'd launched such a total campaign into public elegance that there were no visible elements of a mother who might listen to my discoveries or relate to my questions. She was not good at relating to personal things, anyway. She was uncomfortable talking about feelings or subjects that might prove embarrassing. She preferred to keep conversations centred on external trivia or business. If there was something crucial I needed to talk to her about I had to announce it by saying, 'Mommie, I need to talk to you alone.'

When I thought it was time to know something about contraceptives I did just that. She looked at her hands and then at the floor. She mumbled something about not staying in bed too long and then called our family doctor to make an appointment for me to talk to him. That was it. The conversation was never mentioned again. Mother had simply not developed a way of dealing with a relationship that required give-and-take or the effort of working through any misunderstandings. It was as though learning to cope with emotional development had been left out of her personality when she had completely remodelled herself thirty years before. Unexpected moments of real closeness between us always brought tears to her eyes.

Just before Mother and Daddy left for a long weekend in Bermuda during early August, Mother sent me a note and part of my allowance saying: '. . . with all my expenses and practically no salary coming in, and Daddy not on his salary yet, I just can't make it any more.'

I discovered that a peculiar thing had happened to them. The apartment had overrun its original estimated cost to such an extent that not even the money my mother received from the sale of the Brentwood house combined with their savings could begin to pay for it.

Alfred Steele made money on salary and benefits from his company, but he had no inherited wealth. He was also paying child support to his first wife, who had custody of their boy, Sonny. So there came a time when Daddy had to borrow against his future salary from Pepsi just to meet the immediate payments coming due. That meant he borrowed against money he hadn't yet earned. That also meant that he didn't get his salary at the present time. It must have been a well-kept secret, because it probably wouldn't have been good publicity for the chairman of the board of a family company to be so in debt because of his personal life-style that he had to borrow against money he hadn't earned. He was only about fifty-three years old at the time, but what if something should happen to him? After all, there wasn't any collateral for the loan other than his own physical presence and his personal reputation. But what he had done for the company during these last few years was extraordinary and since only a few people had to approve, the private loan of company money went through.

On the surface, Mother and Daddy continued to live as they always had. Yet in August 1958, nearly eight months after moving into their sumptuous new apartment, Daddy was still 'not on his salary yet'.

This was the year, on 14 August 1958, that my grandmother died. Maybe it was Grandmother's death that reminded me of a story Mother told me about her own childhood. They were living on the outskirts of town, in Kansas probably, and Grandmother kept some chickens in the dirt yard out back. Mother was fascinated by the baby chicks. She'd go out there and play with the little yellow chickens, picking them up and hugging them. She loved the pretty little things so much and squeezed them so tightly to her that they went limp in her arms. When a chick didn't move any more, she'd put the limp one down and pick up a new lively one to hug. She told me she'd squeezed nearly a dozen baby chicks to death before her mother caught her and punished her severely, making young Lucille promise *never* to go near those chickens again.

When she first told me that sad, strange story many years ago, it hadn't made much sense to me. But in the days after my grandmother's death as I struggled through a miserable, hot New York summer, I thought about it over and over again. It became like a flash of insight into mother herself. How many times I had felt like one of those baby chickens in her hands as I yearned for the fondness and love only my mother could give me.

Now at this time of my life, the story held quite a different meaning for me. I felt as though I were in real danger of being squeezed right out of my own life. I felt as though I could not survive as a separate person if I remained under her control and influence. I knew the significance of the chicken story for me now was that I had to struggle free or I, too, would go limp in her arms and be discarded. It was not my physical being I was so concerned about any more; it was the preservation of my psyche and my soul.

The last time I saw my father was during a heated discussion about the future course of my life that took place in their apartment during September 1958. My parents wanted me to stay in school and I wanted to get a job. It was a typical parent-child communication problem being shared by millions of private families across the country. But, we were not a private family, nor did we have a particularly resourceful relationship. Mother wanted things her way, Daddy tried to mediate, she told him to shut up and before it was all over I was on my own. It was time for that anyway. I was nineteen years old now. If I was old enough to make life decisions, then I was old enough to find a way to support myself.

One night a few weeks later there was a knock on my door. I was afraid to open the door, so I asked who was there. A muffled voice replied, 'Jimmy ... open up.' There before me stood Jimmy, Daddy's valet and bodyguard. He seemed in a hurry and was talking very fast, looking over his shoulder down the hallway as though he was afraid of being followed. He made me nervous, but I asked him inside. He stepped through the doorway but wouldn't come any further. 'Your dad sent you this,' he whispered, thrusting something into my hand. Then he said, 'Don't let anyone know ... it's just between your dad and you. Don't say nothing about it!' I nodded okay.

In my hand was a hundred-dollar bill. Tears welled up in my eyes and I was about to ask Jimmy to thank Daddy when he said, 'Your dad says to tell you he sends his love and hopes you're getting along all right.' As Jimmy was nearly out the door, I grabbed his arm and said, 'Tell Daddy I'm just fine and thanks.'

After I'd closed and locked the door, I sat down on the edge of the kitchen chair staring at the money from my father. As much as I needed and appreciated the money, I appreciated the thought even more. I wished I could have called him and talked to him, but I was afraid to for fear it would cause trouble. Then I started thinking about my father, chairman of the board of a major corporation, a responsible adult, having to sneak around my mother to do something decent for me. She had finally got to him. People gave up so much of their own free will just to be around her. I couldn't understand it and I couldn't do it. I had never been able to do it. She was my own mother but there was no way I could live my life solely according to her dictates. For me, that wasn't living at all, that was no better than being a slave. She had a way of holding out the promise of great rewards in return for voluntary slavery. She held out the promise of undying love in return for total devotion, but in my experience with her it never quite happened. Now she had Daddy playing slave too. She'd got him to buy her everything she wanted. She'd got him into debt. She'd got him to live according to her schedules and prerogatives. And now he was sneaking around behind her back for fear of her anger. Poor man, I thought. Poor Daddy. I wonder if he still thinks he got such a bargain. I wonder if he knows he's already sold his soul to the devil herself. I wonder if he knows she's already got him and he'll never get out alive. There's nothing I can do but watch it all unfold like a movie plot.

My initial attempts at earning a living were chaotic, to say the least. I worked as night cashier in a friend's restaurant, I worked part time for an employment agency, I typed scripts for writers who composed in longhand. I got 'island fever' in New York and saved enough money to live in England for three months.

Alfred Steele died of a heart attack in April 1959, just one month before the celebration of my parents' fourth anniversary. He was fifty-four years old.

I was still in England and heard the news over the radio. I called my mother but was unable to return in time for the funeral. I cried for a long time over the loss of a very fine man who for a brief time had been my beloved daddy.

When I returned to the United States I discovered that Mother had been made an honorary board member of Pepsi in memory of her late husband. She had also been put on the official Pepsi payroll and continued the work she'd begun with Daddy. The *Journal-American* carried a touching article about how she was carrying on with her husband's mission now that he was gone and she was a widow.

I heard that his will had been offered for probate and that his first wife was contesting on behalf of their son. Beyond that I was uninvolved and uninformed.

What followed was a year fairly typical of an aspiring young actress. I did summer stock and winter stock. I did a small part in an independent film. I went from job to job, trying to make ends meet and learn my craft. There were no guarantees, no 'going home again' as some of my friends were able to do, no assurances during these days. I lived a good deal of my life scared. Scared of being alone in the city, scared of not being able to pay my bills, scared of walking the streets at night by myself, and scared most of all of failing. I was still young but I dared not look ahead too far into the future. It was enough to get through each day.

During those inevitable quiet moments, those moments when even the big city seemed to pause imperceptibly, I sat alone trying to deal with the knot of fear that felt like a clenched fist surrounding my life. I made friends but I didn't really trust anyone, there were a few brief affairs but I didn't fall in love, and there was professional progress which seemed tenuous at best. It was as though I'd had to begin at the very bottom and experience growing up into a person by some condensed process even I didn't completely understand. Since I had no value system, I had to try out each concept that seemed acceptable and learn by eliminating what didn't work. It was inefficient but it was the only way I knew. Slowly, out of the muck and constant flux of the city, out of my encounters with the people in it, I began to feel myself emerging as a person. I was very lucky. Nothing really terrible ever happened to me. There is a saying that God protects fools and children. I was nineteen years old, but when I began this part of my journey, there was enough of both the child and the fool to protect me too.

Looking back, it seems a great irony that these days actually brought me much closer to an appreciation of what my mother had been through. I began to have a fuller understanding of the process of her early years when she, too, was a struggling actress. Those were the years she never mentioned. Those were the years she'd tried so hard to erase from both her own and the public's memory. Those were the years that I now knew were filled with pain, frustration, and perhaps even humiliation. I wrote her letters about my feelings, about the experience of setting foot on a sound stage myself for the first time to perform rather than just visit her. I'd felt her presence everywhere. The years of my childhood spent sitting in the quiet darkness watching and listening and being swept away in the magic came flooding back as I heard the familiar cues and followed the routine patterns involved in making a picture. The theatre was different. I felt it was more mine. I felt more comfortable in front of an audience; it was somehow more alive for me.

Mother had gone out to the coast to do a cameo role in Jerry Wald's production of *The Best of Everything*. It was the first film she'd done since completing *The Story of Esther Costello* in 1956. Jerry and Mother had been close friends since *Mildred Pierce*. He helped her make a comeback then and he was the first to step forward now and offer her another film. It was a small part, but he must have realized what a difficult time it was for her right after Daddy's death and it was a considerate gesture.

Before leaving for Miami to do my first film, I'd had several long talks with a freelance writer who was interested in doing a national magazine story on me. I was one of the first 'Hollywood kids' to go into the business as an actress, and there was evidently story value in that as well as my own personal experience. The article was published in October 1960. It was well researched and the writer had tried to be fair. The title was not of my choosing but designed by the publisher to sell magazines. In fact I had no knowledge of the title until I saw it in print. I had a dreadful sinking feeling. The story was called 'The Revolt of Joan Crawford's Daughter'. It caused quite a stir.

In addition, there were quotes about me attributed to Mother in that article which were simply untrue. True to her behaviour in the past, she continued to present her own fabrications as fact, disregarding both reality and truth. She even repeated the accusation that I'd been expelled from Chadwick, which was a lie. But there was nothing I could do about that once it was on the news-stands.

I sent a copy of the magazine with a short note to Louella Parsons, the Hollywood columnist, saying that I hoped she'd be able to understand the spirit in which the article was written and not just its title. She wrote back a sweet note saying that since she'd known me practically all my life, she was indeed aware of the intentions of the article and wished me all success with my career.

Less than a month later, I received a wire from Jerry Wald offering me a part in his next picture starring Elvis Presley. Then came an offer of a long-term contract with 20th Century–Fox studio and I was summoned to the West coast for a screen test. It was just like all the movie-magazine stories, only it was really happening to me. I tried to remain calm through the whole uproar, but it was impossible.

When I saw the test, I didn't like it very much. There were a multitude of things I would have done differently the next time. But it was good enough to get me the part in Jerry Wald's next picture with Elvis and the studio signed my contracts. My mother also saw the test and wrote me.

It was an exceedingly brief note, dated 5 November 1960, which said that she thought I was lovely in the test. She added: *'I am sure you will have great success, and nobody wishes it for you more than your – "Mommie".'*

There was something about all this that was like ghosts on parade for me. It was a peculiar homecoming. I felt uneasy. In the interviews that were systematically arranged by the studio I tried to emphasize only the positive. I talked only about the happy years with my mother. It seemed every time I turned around someone else would begin a conversation with 'I bet you don't remember me, but . . .' I began to think that half the world must have passed through the gates of our Brentwood house when I was a child. I listened to their stories with that fixed, polite smile on my face so many times it's a wonder I didn't forget myself and curtsey as well.

My part in the picture was small. My billing in the picture was much larger. The publicity was a classic Hollywood hype. It started to make me feel very crazy. I was beginning to realize that I was no match for the experts.

Before I finished shooting my small part, Jerry Wald called me into his office. I didn't think much about it, since I'd been to see Jerry numerous times over the past two months.

He was clearly uncomfortable. 'Your mother has just informed me that she is unable to do *Return to Peyton Place*.' He almost had tears in his eyes. He went on to say that she told him she was very sorry, but other commitments prevented her from doing his film. He looked at me and said, 'We've been discussing this for months. It was all set! All that was left was to sign the contracts. What do you think happened?'

I honestly didn't know what to say. Jerry was extremely agitated now, pacing up and down behind his desk. He said that he got the impression she wouldn't do his next film because he'd hired me to do the Presley picture. He had the distinct feeling that she was angry with him for helping me. He looked directly at me again.

'I'm sorry, Uncle Jerry. I didn't know anything like this would happen to anybody.' I felt terrible, both for myself and for him. I felt ridiculously naïve. If he was right, then she was punishing him where it really hurt. It was innuendo and intimidation of the most insidious sort. Hollywood always had been a town run on fear and gossip.

A week later I finished shooting and the next day my long-term contract was cancelled. I was told it was due to overall financial difficulties resulting from *Cleopatra*. I never worked at Fox studio again. But there had been so much publicity already churned out that the studio-sponsored interviews continued to appear in print until the picture was released many months later.

For nearly a year I continued to get a few acting jobs in Hollywood but without much success. Finally, I just gave up. To all intents and purposes, I disappeared. My life was in a shambles. Whatever progress I'd made during the New York years seemed to fall apart now. My personal stability turned out to be mere quicksand and for a while all I could do was try to put myself back together.

I lived quietly in a little house in Laurel Canyon. Eventually I took an undemanding job at a savings and loan in Hollywood, spending my free time fishing, working in my garden, and reading books on Eastern philosophy. The man I lived with was my first real love. Through him I began to learn trust in another human being. He was my initial glimpse into another way of life. This was the first time I sensed some order to the universe, some meaning to my lifelong pain. If my relationship with Mother had something to do with the concept of karma then perhaps it wasn't total absurdity. There was a reason I was put

234

on earth, a life lesson I had to learn. I would continue to have to learn it over and over until it was resolved. Until there was some peace in my life, I could go no further. It was a time of inner speculation. It was a time when I was forced once again to come face to face with myself. I must admit I didn't always like what I saw in my own mirror, but it was also a time when I gave up blaming others for what had happened in my life. I stopped blaming my mother or trying to make excuses for either one of us. I began to treat myself with greater gentleness. My life had to be put together again based on something other than insanity, cruelty, insecurity, and the hype. I think those few quiet years probably saved me from destroying myself.

NINETEEN

Whatever Happened to Baby Jane? was released in 1962. It was the most successful picture Mother had made in many years and the last important film of her career. When I read the stories about her feud with Bette Davis I could just imagine the trauma of those two women working together. How Bob Aldrich even finished that picture is a feat in itself. Bette Davis was the consummate match for my mother's storehouse of intimidation tricks. She was as shrewd a professional and every bit as indomitable as her co-star. Years later, Mother would only have to hear the name mentioned to start a tirade.

It was 1964 before I ventured into show business again. When I returned, it was to the theatre, where I felt most secure. The world had changed over those three years. Kennedy had been assassinated, the civil rights movement was well under way, and now the peace initiatives had begun. Personal expression and political freedom were familiar topics now. The young and the disadvantaged were fighting to be heard. I felt more comfortable in this emerging climate of social change. Professionally, I was no longer an oddity. There were now a number of successful 'second-generation' Hollywood actors and actresses.

My last stop on a road tour that summer of 1965 was a theatre in an amusement park in the coal mining region of Pennsylvania. Before the week's run was over, I received word that I'd got an audition in New York for the Chicago company of *Barefoot in the Park*. I went straight to New York the night our play closed and two days later my agent, Sue Mengers, accompanied me to the audition. I was so nervous I was visibly shaking. I'd never auditioned in a Broadway theatre before. I did the best I could in a sort of unconscious state. When it was over, there was dead silence in the dark house. I was on stage and didn't know whether to leave or stand there or just sit down and wait. I was immobilized.

Then the voice of the producer came out of the darkness: 'That was probably the worst audition I've ever sat through. You haven't seen the play, have you?'

I thought surely I was going to throw up all over their pretty set. I managed to shake my head no, but I couldn't say anything. The voice from the darkness said, 'See the play tonight and be back here at ten thirty tomorrow morning.'

I laughed so hard at the play it was nearly impossible to remember everything. But I stayed up most of that night memorizing the lines and working out blocking as best I could.

The next morning my audition was light-years better than the disaster of the day before. After three scenes, they said, 'Thank-you-we'll-let-you-know', and I left New York without a clue as to my chances.

Nearly a month later I got the call in Los Angeles that I'd been hired. I was beside myself with happiness. This was the best job I'd landed and I was proud of myself. The work went very well. The reviews were terrific. That season I received the Chicago Critics' Award for Best Young Actress.

It was April of 1966 after a hurried courtship that Harvey, my director from *Barefoot in the Park*, and I decided to get married.

Harvey asked me to come to New York and meet his family. Several days after my arrival, I called my mother. I told her that I was planning to be married. 'I'd like you to meet my fiancé. I'd also like you to be at the wedding. It just wouldn't seem right without you.'

It was a combination of many things, but I was so choked up I could barely finish the sentence. I waited for her reaction for what seemed like an eternity.

What happened next was a miracle in my life. My mother was genuinely delighted. She was delighted with the whole idea. She instantly invited the two of us to come for drinks that evening and to join her at a dinner party with Marty Allen and his wife. It was complete acceptance.

From that point on, Mother and I were in daily contact. She decided to plan the wedding, the reception, the whole thing. We wanted only a civil ceremony so she arranged for a New York Supreme Court judge to perform the ceremony. She booked one whole floor of the '21' Club for the luncheon reception. She helped design my dress and told me to register at Tiffany's and Georg Jensen so her friends would know exactly what to get us. She had the announcements engraved and her secretary made out the guest lists and mailed the invitations. I was overwhelmed. Harvey became understandably glassy-eyed about this time, but he handled himself admirably. In fact, he and Mother became good friends and liked each other's company.

Mother was superb. She managed every last detail of the event. We were married on 20 May 1966, and I was on cloud nine. People had flown in from Chicago and Los Angeles. There were friends of Mother's, Pepsi people, relatives of Harvey's. Guests included Mike Nichols, Neil Simon, the Werblins, Kriendlers, Burnses, and my cousin Joan. Neither my brother nor my sisters were there, but I talked to each of them on the phone and knew they were with us in spirit.

After our honeymoon on Cape Cod, my husband and I returned to our New York apartment to find a veritable mountain of gifts and my furniture from Los Angeles. Only a few weeks later, Harvey left to direct the London production of *Odd Couple*.

I was not in the least bit lonely. I visited Mother nearly every other day, basking in our mutual homecoming and enjoying every minute of it. I had a new apartment to settle, a new life to manage, letters to write, and my mother's love.

I spent many evenings at Mother's apartment. For the first time I felt really comfortable with her. She seemed to feel the same and went out of her way to plan fun things for us to do together. I was almost automatically included in her social events, met the majority of her New York friends and business associates, and spent quiet evenings with her just watching television and talking.

There were still some days when she was in a bad mood and

she drank quite a bit, but her fits of anger were never directed at me. A German woman worked for her whom she called 'Mamacita' or just 'Mama'. Interestingly, I learned that the middle-aged woman's real name was Anna, the same as my grandmother. It was upon Mamacita that my mother vented her fits of bad temper and impatience even though she loved the woman dearly. I wondered if it could be pure coincidence that Mother named her maid 'Mama' and then took out all her spite on her. My mother acted out all the rage with her own mother all over again. At times it was just like watching a child having a temper tantrum when she didn't get things exactly her own way. I felt very uncomfortable during these episodes but didn't interfere. Mamacita was devoted to my mother, but finally she had to leave due to ill health and advancing age. She was close to eighty years old when she retired. I'm sure she never imagined she'd actually outlive her former employer.

Christmas was a joy. My husband was home and we spent half the time with my mother and then went to Connecticut to visit his family. Harvey and I had spent very little time together since we'd been married, and it was over this holiday that we both realized we had some difficulties to work through.

My brother had got married and divorced and had moved back to New York. He was drafted into the army at the height of the Vietnam War just two months after his draft status changed due to the divorce. I was scared to death. We spent many nights talking about our worst fears. He called me from San Francisco the day before he was shipped overseas. I followed the daily reports in the newspapers and on television and prayed for his safe return.

During all these months, my mother and I remained very close. The subject of my brother was usually off limits but once in a while when the two of us were alone in the room, Mother asked if I knew where he was. She wouldn't look at me but busied herself with some small task as she waited for the answer. At those times I told her quietly where he was located in Vietnam, where the enemy attacks had just taken place, and that he was fighting in the field but had not been wounded.

She knew that we had remained close over all the years and I was the one person in the world she could ask for information about her son. Except when she asked these private questions, we never spoke of him.

We were having so many moments together that were filled with real understanding and genuine friendship that it was a wonderful time for both of us. Something seemed to have changed her ability to relate to me. She trusted me now and would even look to me for my opinion. She knew that I would tell her the truth as I perceived it. Most people only told her what they thought she wanted to hear. I didn't do that. I tried to always show her respect, I tried to help in any way I could, but I was not a servant. She was perceptive about that. If you were clear as a person she tried not to overstep the defined boundaries. If you were unclear she would push you to the limit and then smile when you fell on your face. Once she had you on her territory, it was her game, her rules, which she changed just in time to expose you as an idiot.

She began talking to me more and more when we were alone. She told me some of the personal difficulties she was having. It was the first time we'd had talks like this since I was a little girl and too young to fully understand. She'd rarely go into great detail, but she'd outline what she worried about. She talked about Daddy. After his death she had romanticized him and their relationship. When he was alive they had their share of battles and she'd had her share of black eyes. Now that he was dead it was safe for her to transform him into the ideal husband and their relationship into the perfect marriage. On my wedding day, she gave me the pearl necklace he'd given her. Later she gave me the gold watch she didn't wear any more. She wanted me to have something they'd shared together. During their four years of marriage I had witnessed few moments of genuine affection between them. But for many years after his death, Mother expressed great love and a deep sentimental attachment towards him.

Daddy had been dead seven years now, but the will was still being contested. She told me that after he'd borrowed against his salary in order to finish the apartment, they'd had serious financial problems. Neither his borrowed future salary nor the sale of her Brentwood house was enough to pay the accumulated bills and debts. Daddy then borrowed from Mother. She'd done some television shows and had borrowed against her insurance policies. She gave him the combined amount, taking the company stock he owned but could not sell as collateral. When Daddy died suddenly and unexpectedly, his financial affairs were in disarray. He had not lived long enough to repay the original company loan. Mother was put on the company payroll almost immediately. Because she was already holding most of his assets as collateral against the substantial amounts of money she'd loaned him, there was nothing much left over to be willed to anyone else.

I thought back to all the presents Daddy had given her. The sets of diamonds and mink coats and lavish vacations. They were just like two kids, for God's sake. She was a movie star and he was chairman of the board of a multimillion-dollar company. Daddy always said you had to spend money to make money, but somehow it had all got out of hand. They spent according to their fantasy of each other. Mother gave me the impression that if it hadn't been for the box-office success of *Whatever Happened to Baby Jane?* and her lucrative percentage deal on that picture, she'd be having financial difficulties right now even with her regular salary from Pepsi.

In April 1968, I started work on a daytime soap opera at CBS. Mother loved the soaps and we had fun discussing my new job on *Secret Storm*. I played a neurotic young wife with a passion for mischief who developed a drinking problem when she suspected her husband of seeing other women. Mother watched every show I was on, even when she was out of town. I gave her a list of air dates, which she carried with her and even sent to her friends. Her own fans started writing her about how much they liked the show. She was visibly pleased with their reaction. My soap-opera character 'Joan' always had some trauma going on in her life. The crew told me that they looked forward to the days I worked because sparks were guaranteed to fly. Fred Silverman was head of daytime programming at CBS and the soap operas were beginning to get a new recognition.

Although my free time had dwindled to almost zero, I managed to have Mother over to our apartment for dinner several times. It was quite a challenge. My kitchen was no larger than a closet. I loved cooking, but it was a minor miracle that I could create a dinner party out of that closet without losing my mind or breaking every dish we owned.

The first night my mother arrived for dinner was an event of magnitude. She was just as unused to being invited to a 'family' dinner as I was to giving one. She had invited our longtime friend Cesar Romero to accompany her and at exactly the appointed hour they arrived in her limousine. When I opened the door to greet them, I saw Mother and Uncle Butch carrying Pepsi coolers up the stairs as if they were coming to a picnic.

Mother had brought nearly an entire meal with her. She'd even brought her own one-hundred-proof vodka. Maybe it was her way of feeling comfortable and maybe she was taking out some 'insurance', but whatever it was we had a good laugh. It was a happy moment in my life. I was able to give her something she genuinely appreciated. Mother relaxed after a few moments and enjoyed herself. That was the best part of all.

My husband was away most of the summer. For the first time I was really lonely. We had not been getting along well lately and even my going into therapy didn't seem to be helping our relationship substantially. I spent most of my free time with my mother.

Our roles of mother and daughter had changed over these past few years. There were times when I felt as though I was taking care of her, as though I had become the parent. I worried about her. The apartment was too large for just one person and a maid. I knew Mother was drinking heavily again and taking prescription drugs from more than one doctor. She had sleeping pills, other medicine for her nerves, and something different for what had become a chronic upset stomach. She was sixty-three now and usually alone with just an elderly maid for a companion. I worried about her getting up during the night and falling, as she had already done several times, hurting herself rather seriously. Usually she only received bruises from these falls and covered them up with her clothing. But lately she'd begun to take bad falls, hurting her back once and her foot several times. She blamed either antibiotics or other medication for the falls, but she drank every day and took sleeping pills every night and I was worried she'd accidentally kill herself. I spoke with one of her doctors about the problem but it didn't do any good. No one wanted to bring the subject out into the open with her.

When she started talking about selling the apartment I was much relieved. Another, smaller apartment without the staircase would be an improvement.

Mother managed to conceal the effects of her drinking by maintaining a rigid schedule. I'd see her take a few drinks in the morning, but she ate lunch and took a nap every afternoon. She'd drink during the evening but she'd usually have a small dinner and go to bed early. She was still going out at night occasionally but she insisted on being home by nine-thirty or ten. When she was working for the company, she kept everything tightly controlled with detailed schedules which followed the routine she knew she could manage. I don't know how many people were aware of the seriousness of her drinking problem during these years. No one ever spoke of it openly.

By the middle of summer, I decided it would be best for both my husband and myself if we got a divorce. It was better, I thought, to admit we'd made a mistake and separate rather than continue causing each other misery. We had no children to consider, no shared property.

I moved out of our apartment just before Labor Day weekend. Mother arranged for my things to be put in storage until I could find another apartment. I'd been looking for weeks, but was unsuccessful at finding anything decent. I stayed with a girlfriend for a week and then moved into an apartment hotel on Central Park West. At best, getting a divorce and beginning your own life anew is a painful and solitary process. There is the inevitable hurt, anger, and sense of failure that you simply have to face and work through. I was grateful that my job kept me so busy. Being alone was unwelcome and depressing during these initial weeks of reorientating my life.

Early in September, I went to Philadelphia to do the *Mike Douglas Show* with Mother. We had just returned to the hotel after taping the programme when the New York secretary called. I answered the phone. It was sad news.

I walked into the next room and asked my mother to sit down on the bed. Franchot Tone had just died. I tried to tell her as gently as possible. She buried her face in her hands and

243

cried. I held her in my arms for a few minutes; then she asked to be alone. We returned to New York the next day and Mother went to his funeral. It was a difficult time. Many of her friends and contemporaries were beginning to die. She said this seemed to be her time to go to funerals.

The beginning of October, I flew to Mexico to get my divorce. Mother had helped make the arrangements and everything went as smoothly as possible. But my whole life seemed to be in upheaval.

I thought it was just the strain I was under with the divorce and the long hours of work on the soap opera that were making me feel ill. I was tired and losing weight. There was a lack of exuberance and a grimness to my everyday existence that I couldn't seem to shake.

One cold October morning I woke up at the usual time, around six o'clock. Before an hour had passed, I knew I was terribly ill. I broke into a cold sweat as the pain in my abdomen became worse. I wasn't going to be able to go to work. I was scared. I was very scared. The last thing I was able to do was call my mother.

From then on I remember nothing except sirens and doors opening, people in white moving me from place to place. The doctor at the hospital was only a blurry image, though I could hear him say I had to have an operation immediately.

I was sure I was dying. I was terrified. I was all alone and dying. I prayed to God to help me. I never said goodbye to my mother. The anaesthetic was administered and I slipped away.

In the recovery room, I dimly saw the face of a doctor I recognized. I managed to whisper, 'Tony, am I going to die?' He assured me I was going to live. The operation had been successful. The fallopian tumour was benign. I slipped away into unconsciousness.

The next morning I awoke to see the doctor with my mother and Gloria, my director from the show. They were standing around my bed, but my vision still had a surrealistic quality to it. Everyone looked worried. Mother stood somewhat in the background. Quietly, Gloria started speaking to me. It took a while for the information to penetrate the fog of pain and the heavy medication. She was trying to tell me that ... my mother ...

had offered . . . to play my part on the soap. CBS had accepted her generous offer.

I just couldn't think with all the medication and the awful pain. The doctor told everyone they would have to leave right away. I could not stand the slightest strain right now. He asked me if I was all right. I couldn't answer him. I tried to tell Gloria to take care of my mother, but I don't know if anyone could understand me.

After that I was not allowed either visitors or phone calls for several days. I was much too weak from the major operation and too heavily sedated because of the excruciating pain to do anything but rest. I was grateful to be alive but too exhausted to think of anything but sleep.

On the fourth day, Mother called me in the evening just after I'd tried to eat dinner for the first time. I had to eat now even if I didn't want to. It was just like being a little girl again.

Mother's voice over the phone sounded happy and excited. She said work was going very well, everyone was so helpful, and she thought there were just a few things she wanted to ask me about the part. She chatted on, asking questions I tried my best to answer. My hands started shaking. The nurse looked at me closely before she took away my tray and left the room. I tried to talk normally to Mother, who sounded as though she was having a great time. I told her that I had to say goodbye because I was feeling weak, but thanked her for sharing all the news with me and I wished her luck on the show.

I didn't know whether I felt so bad because they were beginning to cut back on the pain medication or because of the phone call. I had an awful sinking feeling all through me. I was shaking.

The doctor appeared in the doorway of my room, followed by my nurse. He asked if I'd like a cup of coffee. I had tears in my eyes so I just nodded my head. He asked the nurse for two coffees and then came to sit on my bed.

'I think you'd better tell me about it,' he said gently. I realized for the first time that he knew. It all started pouring out of me. Mother taking my job, Mother an alcoholic, I didn't know if she could hold up on the show, how helpless I felt, how humiliating it was. She kept calling me to tell me how wonderfully she was doing, how wonderful all the people were to her. She sounded like she was having such a good time. All the newspapers wanted interviews. It was going to be in *Time* magazine. She was a star again, the focus of all the attention. It was my job she'd taken. What could she be thinking of when she did that? She said it was to save my part so they wouldn't replace me, but it was the absolute end of my character's credibility. I was playing a twenty-eight-year-old woman. My mother was well past sixty!

In truth, nothing in recent years had given Mother as much publicity as taking over my part in the soap opera. It was in all the papers, in many national magazines, and remembered long after my part and even the show itself were over. It was a perfect publicity hype. It was an event that overshadowed the rest of the work and even the programme itself. Years later when people asked about my professional background and I'd mention doing the soap, they'd reply, 'Oh, yes, I remember that. Your mother took your part.'

Before it was time for me to be released from the hospital, the first of the shows Mother did was aired. My nurse and I turned on the television a few minutes before the programme began. I realized that I had butterflies in my stomach, just as though it were a show of my own. Mother had already said that everything went wonderfully well during the two days of taping and I prayed she was right. I had not spoken with the director and I had no other information.

At the very beginning of that day's episode of *Secret Storm* the announcer stated that my part was being played by my mother, Joan Crawford. Then the music came up and the show began just as it always did.

The moment her scene began, I had that strange sinking feeling all over again. I watched every move she made. She was nervous, I could see that easily. As the scene progressed, my heart sank into the pit of my stomach. She wasn't just nervous. Mother had been drinking when this scene was taped. She was not sober when she did this work.

After the show, I called her. I was not at all pleased with what I had just seen but the way she sounded on the phone was almost a plea for everything to be all right. I didn't have the heart to say much more than 'Thank you'. She seemed delighted but there was a vulnerability to her voice. She said, 'I hope you're proud of me.' Again, I didn't have the nerve to say anything except, 'Of course . . . I'm very grateful.'

When I hung up the phone I felt ill again. I felt sick about what I'd just seen on television and sick about the lies I'd just told.

The national publicity hit that week and I tried to be gracious, saying that it was a very kind gesture on Mother's part.

But, as the days progressed and the remainder of the shows in which she had taped scenes were aired, I sat in my hospital bed watching the television set with a growing sense of humiliation. My mother was appearing on the programmes drunk. I couldn't believe it. It was a nightmare.

I am not proud that I never told Mother how I felt about her performance. I did not have the courage to be honest with her. What I should have said to her was what I said to myself. 'How could you humiliate both of us by getting drunk before the show? Jesus Christ, Mother. Don't you have any self-respect left?'

What I didn't realize until many years later was that a basic part of our relationship had shifted. For years I had been the one on the outside looking in. Mother had held all the cards. She had been the star, the success. As I grew older and began to achieve my own progress, our roles began to change imperceptibly. Now I was the one who had what she wanted to keep for herself. I had youth, I had work as an actress and she had neither. I was the one who looked after her; slowly, over the last few years, I had almost become the mother. She was beginning to relive her life through me. It was onto me that she had projected herself. To me she had attributed those qualities of her own that she both despised and admired. Somehow I was the palette upon which she had painted her innermost being. Through me she lived and now relived her own childhood, her own relationship with Grandmother, and finally even the acting work, the profession we both shared. It is extraordinary how entangled in each other we had become. Now it was my mother looking to me for the same love and approval I had always sought from her. Now it was Mother who needed the youth and the vitality of my life. In that context it is not so impossible to understand how she could even consider playing a woman thirty years younger than herself. The boundaries of where she left off and I began had become so enmeshed in the projections and imaginings of our lifelong relationship that there were times when we were one and the same person.

I did not have the perspective then that only time can bestow. I still found myself caught by the song of the Lorelei, still saw myself as her child, still thought that she was the adult. The pain and frustration of continually trying to extricate myself from our melded image and establish myself as a separate human being was too much with me to be able to see her chaos clearly. I heard the pleading in her voice and was not able to give fully the acceptance she so desperately wanted from me. She could not even see the turmoil I was going through, helplessly imprisoned by my hospital bed. She had succeeded in becoming me for a while and I felt I was sinking into oblivion. It was insanity for both of us.

A month later I had moved into a new apartment and was back at work. Everyone was wonderful to me upon my return. They treated me with both kindness and loving care.

I finally mustered the nerve to ask someone I trusted what happened in my absence. Evidently, Mother had arrived at the studio with her entourage, the Pepsi coolers filled with food, and her vodka. She also had her California secretary with her, who was reportedly rude to many of the cast and crew. Mother had arrived in full regalia, every inch the star. I was told that she was drinking most of the time she was at the studio and that her scenes had to be taped many times before they had enough material to edit into scenes suitable for the air show.

Weeks later, a few people told me privately that they were very sorry about the entire situation. I could see, once again, that old look of pity in their eyes.

After I was well enough to resume some sort of normal activity, my mother gave me tickets to see shows she'd been invited to attend. She asked me to stand in for her and accept numerous awards on her behalf. The events centred around business and charitable activities she was involved in and she requested that I go in her place.

She told me it would all help my career and most of the time I was more than glad to do the favour. I became so involved with my mother again that I'd break dates and rearrange my own plans to accommodate her. She finally asked me to travel with her on company business. I went on the chartered jets to Virginia and Pennsylvania, attending dinners and plant openings. There was eventually an inquiry as to whether I might be useful to the company in a capacity similar to Mother's but geared for the younger generation since I was not quite thirty. But every time the subject of formalizing the work I did was broached, Mother acted as though she hadn't heard it.

Because of the two life-styles I lived, I had to have two complete wardrobes. One set of clothes I bought for myself and my own life. The other set Mother contributed to because they were for the occasions when I substituted for her at a public event or accompanied her on company business. The requirements were quite different; so were the clothes.

During this time, Mother's drinking increased. It was now so serious a problem that she'd often have a new set of bruises between the time I left her one afternoon and saw her the next day. She still took a variety of prescription medications and I worried for her safety. She was taking bad falls on the polished, rugless floors. It was her elbow one week, her ankle the next, and her back hurting regularly.

One day a doctor she liked and trusted visited her to check on her swollen ankle. When he was ready to leave, I was also on my way out and walked with him to the elevator. I asked if we could talk and he offered to drive me home.

When I felt it was safe and no one would overhear me, I told him how concerned I was about Mother's health and particularly her drinking. I begged him not to tell anyone I'd talked to him, because I knew my mother would be furious if she thought I was going behind her back, even in her own best interest. I told the doctor that something had to be done, someone had to help her, even if it meant substituting harmless pills for some of the different medications she took. I told him that these falls and bruises usually happened in the evening after I'd left or in the middle of the night after she'd been drinking and then took the sleeping pills. I was really afraid that she'd accidentally kill herself.

He looked rather sad. I knew I couldn't say any more than I already had. I realized that there was nothing he could do about it either. Mother just wouldn't listen to anyone. The times I tried to suggest directly that she not have any more to drink, she became very angry and didn't talk to me for days afterwards. Even when she was briefly in the hospital for a face-lift and the doctors there forbade her to drink, she still had the ever-present coolers in her room filled with bottles of one-hundred-proof vodka. The doctor told me that she wasn't healing properly and the swelling wasn't going down as it should because Mother insisted on continuing her drinking in the hospital. I tried to talk her into removing the coolers and the vodka bottles, but again she became angry and told me to mind my own business. Then, afterwards, she'd make a big deal out of having me taste the 'glass of water' she was drinking. When I tried to decline, she insisted even if there were other people in the room. That would last a few days and then the bruises would reappear and the stories about the falls would start.

Her problem was no longer an entirely private family matter. She'd appeared on several television talk shows obviously drunk and slurring her words. She later blamed it on her favourite scapegoat: antibiotics. She also appeared at public functions drunk, even when she knew she had been invited to sit up front on the dais and was expected to make a short speech.

Several of her close friends in the business who were responsible for these charitable or professional events were beginning to realize the seriousness of her problem. They even told her that if she didn't get her drinking under control, at least in public, they'd be unable to invite her to any of their events again. They no longer wished to be embarrassed by her behaviour or put themselves in the position of being responsible for her. The two men I know personally who gave her this ultimatum had been friends of Mother's for thirty years or more. They loved her, admired her as a great lady, and were deeply saddened at being forced into the position of confronting her in this way. But their own reputations were now at stake and they had no alternative.

Mother took the criticism badly. Instead of trying to face the situation or deal with her problem, she became furious with her friends. She said spiteful things about these people, who really loved her and were only trying to help her. She considered it an unfair attack on her and used it as another excuse to drink. She had an opportunity to change and she chose not to.

Sometimes, now, she went an entire month without leaving her apartment except to attend an occasional dinner party from which she returned early. Most of the world she dealt with came to her new apartment for meetings. She rarely, if ever, had anyone over for dinner except me or the people who worked for her. She became more and more difficult to deal with personally. In just a few years her New York secretary would retire early, Mamacita would leave her, and even her devoted cleaning man and valet would have to quit her service because of the way she treated him.

Though she lived a progressively more solitary life, she never allowed herself to be alone in the apartment. That year the maid went to visit her own daughter at Christmas, and I stayed with Mother every night. I left in the morning after breakfast as soon as the secretary arrived. A woman came by in the afternoon to clean and cook and she stayed until I arrived in the early evening. Food was ordered by phone and delivered to the back door.

I tried to get Mother interested in going out for a while, even for a drive around the park for some fresh air. I didn't know how she could stand being in that apartment all the time looking at the same few faces every day. I even tried to talk her into taking a vacation somewhere quiet and private, but she refused. She said she travelled enough for the company.

There were a growing number of people surrounding her in these days that I didn't care for at all. They were the 'star-fuckers', people who went mad over celebrities, who would go to any lengths to have their own names associated with anyone famous. These people were not just fans; they had professions and services to sell. Some of them wanted only the opportunity to name-drop with their friends. Others had something they were hustling. At first they appeared to be great and fond admirers of the ageing star, fawning over Mother and telling her how wonderful she was. I tried in vain to tell her that all they wanted was a quick sale, but she looked at me as though I'd stabbed her in the heart. She'd explain to me how attentive and loving these people were towards her, how good they'd been to her. Didn't they call her every day just to see how she was feeling? Didn't they invite her to dinner? Of course, she was 'too busy' to accept their kind gestures, but it was the thought that counted. I knew that the minute I turned my back some new, dreadful painting would arrive, or some contribution to a cause would be made, or she'd lend her name to another activity she'd never attend, or she'd pay an exorbitant price for some personal service. Perhaps it was ludicrous that I tried to protect her from the con artists that preyed on the ego of her faded image like necrophiliacs, but I could not stand by in silence. Eventually it made me so mad and I felt so impotent that I stopped talking to her about the situation.

She was a woman who prided herself on having indomitable willpower, who was known as a strong-minded person because she gave all the orders, but she could be taken in so easily. The truth never rested easily with Mother and honesty was not her favourite subject. But sweet-talk her, say yes every time she opened her mouth, be at her beck and call, fall all over her with praise and even token admiration and she'd give you the whole world. How could she possibly not see through these people?

It was as though she wanted so badly to recapture the days when she had real power, the days when the praise and admiring throngs were real, that she settled for phony substitutes. She seemed perfectly willing to pay the price. It made me very sad.

In March 1969, I gave Mother a party for her birthday. It was the first time I'd ever given her a party and I don't know where the idea sprang from originally except I thought it would make her happy. Officially she was sixty-one. Unofficially she was closer to sixty-five. By either count, that's a long time to wait for your first family birthday party.

Together Mother and I planned the evening. She insisted on paying for most of it, over my protests. I tried to argue that one shouldn't pay for one's own party, but she was not to be dissuaded.

At exactly the appointed hour, the guests streamed out of the elevators and down the hall to my apartment. The Kriendlers, her friends from '21', Jerry and Minette Pickman, Bob Kelly from Pepsi and his wife, my director and her husband, Mother's doctor and his wife, and Herb Barnett, who was now chairman of the board at Pepsi, all arrived simultaneously. As a surprise for Mother, I'd also invited my sister Cathy and her husband, who drove down from upstate New York.

The party went perfectly from beginning to end. Mother was genuinely touched with all the gifts and the warm feelings expressed by her close friends. I couldn't have been happier than I was watching her open all her presents just like a kid on Christmas morning. It had all worked out just as I hoped it would.

The beginning of August, our new producer at CBS called me into his office and told me that I would only be in a couple more episodes of *Secret Storm*. He said that he was sorry, but the character had lost its usefulness some time ago. I knew there was general housecleaning on all the network daytime shows and the news didn't surprise me. They would pay off the rest of my contract and write me out of the programme in just three more segments.

I called Mother to tell her the news, and to my surprise she was very upset. She told me that she'd spoken with this man several months before and he assured her that they had no intention of letting me go. All I could reply to her was, 'Well, Mother, I'm afraid he lied to you.'

Finally, in June 1970, I mustered up all my courage and decided to give Los Angeles another try. I discussed the plan at some length with Mother and she offered to let me stay for a while in the West Hollywood apartment she had maintained since selling our house years before. In addition she offered to call some of her friends and see what they could do to help me. I sat there looking at her with tears in my eyes. I went to her and put my arms around her, thanking her as we hugged. She said she'd miss me, but she knew I was going to do very well.

Ever since my operation and my first serious brush with death, my entire attitude towards life had changed. It was very precious to me now. I was so glad just to be alive and have another chance that I had a more determined attitude towards work and a more positive attitude towards my whole life. Through my good relationship with Mother I felt a burden had been lifted. I knew she loved and cared about me. We had been together for nearly five years, and I believed that we had finally come to a mutual understanding.

I knew she didn't agree with all of my ideas, nor did I always see eye to eye with her, but we'd had good times together, she was proud of me, and we were showing each other that we really cared. I was her friend, her daughter, and when necessary her companion. She trusted me to tell her the truth as I perceived it and to stand by her when she needed me. We'd shared our thoughts and feelings on many levels and were both quite pleased that, after all these years, we'd really found each other again. I had a much greater appreciation of her professional achievements, having now spent ten years in the business myself. I think that gave us a basis for respect that was an important bond as well. I knew better than anyone that I still had a long road ahead of me, but I was young enough and energetic enough to make it. With her moral support and my determination, I was sure of my good fortune.

I made such a pest of myself on the phone every free hour of the day in Los Angeles and went on so many appointments that very shortly I got work. Mother also arranged a meeting with Lew Wasserman, the head of Universal Studios. During the brief meeting, I told him that I was here because I wanted to work and I wanted particularly to work at Universal. The meeting lasted about fifteen minutes and I sensed that I was talking very quickly. At the end, he leaned forward slightly behind his enormous, immaculately clean desk and asked, 'Christina, are you happy with your life?' I was quite taken aback. The question was so direct, so unexpectedly personal. I replied, 'Yes, very.' He nodded his head and wished me good luck. We shook hands and I left. I had known this man nearly all my life but never before had any conversation with him about my own career.

Not long after this meeting I auditioned for and landed my first part on a Universal television programme. I had been in Los Angeles about six weeks.

Several days later, the Los Angeles secretary called me at seven thirty in the morning. She said that Mother was coming out to do a show, so I had two days in which to move out of the apartment. I was barely awake, but I knew something was strange about this conversation. I didn't trust this woman. Why didn't Mother call me herself? I'd been talking to her every day until now. Why did she have the secretary tell me to move? I asked the woman a couple of questions then decided to call my mother directly. I didn't get through. The operator at the Pepsi switchboard said all her lines were busy, so I left a message. Mother didn't call back.

Instinct told me that this whole situation was smelling like something out of the distant past. Events I didn't have any knowledge about were going on behind my back. There had not been one single indication of trouble from Mother herself. She had done nothing but continue to help me and share the progress I was making.

The secretary, whose voice grated on my ears, called back to say the maid was coming that morning to change the sheets and clean the apartment, so that if I could move out before she finished, she wouldn't have to return before Mother arrived two days later.

Now I knew there was a rat in the woodpile and I suspected the grating voice was to blame. But I couldn't reach my mother and I had no choice but to comply with what her wishes were transmitted as being. I moved in with a girlfriend who had a large apartment in the Hollywood Hills.

After I moved out of the apartment, Mother changed her plans. She didn't come back to Los Angeles for several more months. It was a difficult situation I didn't deal with particularly well. I found it impossible to work these things out with Mother when she chose to be incommunicado.

When I finally reached her several days later to give her my new telephone number and address, Mother behaved as though nothing unusual had happened. The secretary told me that the locks and phone number at the apartment were changed after my departure, yet Mother acted as though everything was normal. It was so strange that if I'd had a brain in my head, I'd have asked Mother just what in the hell was going on. But I was too involved in my own life to expend extra energy on confrontations.

In October, just three months after my arrival, I was offered my first guest-star part on television. The agents called to tell me that the show began shooting on Monday. I dashed to the studio for fittings and could hardly wait to get home and call Mother with the good news.

By the time I returned from the studio it was nearly seven o'clock in the evening. I suppose I should have remembered the lessons of the old days and waited until the next morning to call. But it was only about ten o'clock in New York and I didn't think she'd be asleep yet.

Mother answered the phone and I bubbled over with the news. I told her that I'd got the guest-star part on *Marcus Welby*, that I was playing a nun, and that I was in almost every scene throughout the episode. I was nearly in tears with happiness as I thanked her for her help and said that all the hard work was beginning to pay off.

Then I waited for her response. But I waited in silence. Such a long time passed that I thought we'd been disconnected. 'Hello . . . Mother?'

An icy voice that sent thirty-year chills through me replied only, 'How did you get the job?' I didn't catch on right away. 'You remember, Mother, I did the small part on Vince Edwards' show, they said was like a test. Then I met more people, got another job and some publicity. I guess the meeting with Uncle Lew didn't hurt either.' I realized I sounded defensive, I sounded like a child, I sounded pathetic.

Her voice never changed. It was like stone. We didn't talk much longer. She hung up on me in the middle of a sentence. I stared at the silent phone in my hand. Tears welled up in my eyes. What had gone wrong now? How could such good news turn into this awful feeling in my stomach? What in the world was going on? I call to share the best news I've had and she hangs up on me? What the hell is happening to us?

It was one week after I'd finished shooting the *Marcus Welby* show that I was invited to lunch with a friend of Mother's who had been like family to me. When we met at the restaurant, he seemed unusually distant. After we ordered, he asked if I'd spoken with my mother lately. I told him I hadn't talked to her since I started the show. He looked at me carefully. I asked him if there was something wrong. He looked down at his silverware for a long moment as though he was in the midst of a decision he hadn't expected to make.

I was uncomfortable, but I didn't have the vaguest idea what was going on. Then he said that my mother had called him several nights ago. He measured his words. He said that Mother was in a terrible rage. He said she went on about what a dreadful person I was, how ungrateful I was for all the help she'd given me. Mother told him that the only reason I'd called her was to 'gloat' over the star part I'd got when I knew full well that *Marcus Welby* was *the one show she'd always wanted to do*!

I looked at my mother's friend thunderstruck. I couldn't believe what I was hearing. I asked him to repeat the sentence. Again, he said that Mother told him I'd only called her to gloat over getting a part on the very show she'd always wanted. I was speechless. There was no reason to defend myself because I hadn't done anything wrong. But that's not how he seemed to feel. His experience with Mother and the phone call were somehow designed to make it look as though *I'd* done something awful.

'You simply can't believe that,' I said. 'It doesn't make any sense.' He didn't say anything. 'I mean, for God's sake, I called to share good news . . . nothing else. I didn't do anything to her.'

He looked me squarely in the face. 'Christina, she was on a rampage the other night. I don't know how many other people she called, but I don't think we were the first. It was almost nine o'clock our time when the call came through.'

My mind raced to grasp what he was saying to me. That call he received was made at midnight New York time. God help me. Night raid. This was a night raid like the days of my childhood. Mother was never up that late unless she was crazy drunk and couldn't sleep even with the pills. I'd got those calls from her myself when I lived in New York. She'd have got some paranoid idea about me or someone else and be screaming over the phone from the beginning of the call. I learned not to argue, just to listen. The next day it would never be mentioned. Maybe she didn't even remember calling in the middle of the night.

What was going on in the dark recesses of my mother's midnight mind? What demons and devils overtook her that she made up these things? Why was I the focus of her insanity?

Unless I was right there with her, unless I was a physically present reality for her, she slipped away into these wild rampages about our relationship and attributed to me all the devils of her own soul. This was another terrible figment of her imagination.

I knew there was no use telling this man that the entire episode was my mother's drunken insanity. I knew there was no use trying to tell him that I'd only wanted to bring her happiness and proud feelings. I knew it was useless by the look on his face. I'd seen that look too many times before in my life not to know what it meant.

Several months later Mother came out to Los Angeles to present a Golden Globe Award. It was a hectic evening from beginning to end. That was now customary whenever there was a public appearance combined with a speech. She turned everybody upside down, giving her own publicity people instant ulcers.

A few days after the Golden Globe Award dinner, she called to ask if I'd join her and a friend I'd never met for lunch at the Bistro. I just had time to get dressed and drive to Beverly Hills if I was to meet them on time, but I didn't have anything else planned and it was another chance to be with her before she returned to New York.

I arrived at the Bistro a few minutes late and asked for the gentleman whose name Mother had carefully given me. He was seated at a table, and since Mother had not yet arrived, I introduced myself. He was a charming older man and we chatted pleasantly over drinks. After about half an hour passed he started looking at his expensive watch. Both of us were wondering what had happened to my usually punctual mother, but neither of us wanted to initiate the subject of her tardiness. Finally, we had been waiting nearly an hour. He asked if he should call the apartment. He said he'd just spoken with her this morning to confirm the appointment, which had been made days in advance, so he was quite sure there couldn't have been a misunderstanding about either the time or the place.

I was beginning to have an intuitive feeling that something about this was a setup. I casually inquired what time he'd spoken with her this morning. It turned out to be just minutes before her call to me. I was beginning to realize this was going to be an embarrassing situation. I don't think my mother ever had any intention of meeting the man for lunch. She'd manoeuvred me into substituting for her again and taking the brunt of her rudeness. I suggested that we order lunch. I said I was sure there was nothing to worry about.

Near the end of our meal, he was called to the phone. As he left I thought, Poor man, she just stood him up, plain and simple.

When he returned to the table he looked both hurt and puzzled. The story he repeated to me was so ludicrous and so childish that even he saw through it. After he sat down he turned to me. 'Did you know your mother wasn't going to be here for lunch?' I looked at him with what little compassion I could feel for a total stranger and replied, 'No, I'm sorry, I didn't. When I spoke with her, she asked me to join the two of you.'

He tried to say something polite about my being a charming substitute for my mother and I thanked him for a lovely lunch. It was a meaningless exchange. We parted company on a cheerful note and drove off in opposite directions.

During the time it took to drive home, I thought about all the other times I'd been sent in at the last minute to make things look good for Mother, to smooth over one of these insults. It was always under the guise of how much it would help my career.

I tried to call Mother but I was told she wasn't feeling well and was resting. I didn't speak to her again before she left Los Angeles.

At the end of February 1971, I decided to move to California permanently. I returned to New York for a few months to pack my belongings and arrange for the movers. I went to visit Mother a number of times. I just couldn't figure her out. To my face she was the same as always. When we were together she wished me all good luck and success. It was a strange time because she never mentioned the midnight phone calls or other peculiar incidents. She didn't say anything to indicate there was anything amiss between us. I tried to ask her on several different occasions when we were alone if there was something wrong. I asked her if everything was going all right with her own life, but she brushed off my questions lightly and went on to other subjects. I gave her the air dates for my latest two television shows and she promised to watch. I sensed somehow that underneath all the pleasantry she felt I was deserting her, but she wouldn't talk about it.

During the next months on the coast I worked, I made new friends, and I took up tennis. There seemed to be free time I couldn't fill with appointments or jobs, so like the rest of the town I played tennis.

It was December before I got another show at Universal. It was a strange part on a new ABC programme called *Sixth Sense*. It was also to be the last of my career, although I didn't know it at the time.

Bright and early on Christmas morning I called Mother. She'd sent me a black suit that didn't fit because I'd lost weight and I was going to return it, but I thanked her anyway. She sounded hurt that I was returning her gift but I tried to tell her that I appreciated it and *please* not to be upset.

These conversations with her went downhill. I called to wish her a Merry Christmas and before the call was over, I felt terrible. She made me feel as though I'd done something wrong again. She never came right out in the open and said anything you could deal with directly. It was a tone of voice that sounded disapproving, it was an implication that all was not well, it was some veiled reference to her ill health.

Finally I had enough of it and said: 'Listen, Mother, I'm sorry you're not feeling well, but I called to wish you a Merry Christmas. I don't want to argue, I don't want either one of us to feel bad, but I'd appreciate it very much if you didn't speak to me that way.' She said, 'Merry Christmas, Christina', and hung up!

I slammed the phone down in a fury. Goddammit, lady. That's the *last* time I'm going to allow myself to be sucked into feeling like I've done something wrong when all I did was have the consideration to call and wish you Merry Christmas, or share good news, or ask how you're feeling.

In these years I would have given my mother anything she wanted. I tried every way I knew to show her how much I loved her and how I hoped she'd be proud of me. Now I was feeling like one of those little yellow chickens in the story from her childhood. I felt like she was squeezing the life out of me too. I felt myself being squashed in her grip.

She didn't just want my loving devotion, she wanted my entire life. She didn't just want to be proud of me, she wanted to be me. She wanted to have my career, my jobs. I could give her love, I could give her companionship and compassion, but I could not give her my life. I must not allow myself to be squeezed to death like one of those baby chickens.

She was like a magnet for me. I had dropped everything to be with her. I rearranged my life to accommodate hers. And now she wanted more. But it was not mine to give. I knew there was no way for me to give back her own youth nor return her previous stardom. It was simply not in my power. But I felt her grip closing in on me. I felt the suppressed anger with me for reasons outside my control. I heard the old familiar Lorelei song, promising love, promising acceptance, promising happiness . . . luring me closer and closer to the rocks of my own destruction.

I thought back over all the years. I saw the ghostly faces of all the others she'd squeezed out of her life. I revisited all the times I traded living my own life for pleasing her. The Lorelei splashed her seductive song across the years of my memory and I saw it all.

All the years of worrying, the hundreds of times I'd tried to explain and was never heard, the efforts to do something nice for her, something that would make her happy. I lived my whole life reacting to this woman. Even my brief rebellions were just reactions to her. I lived all these years scared of offending her, of losing her love.

There was no way I could continue this devotion to the Lorelei song. I could not find the magic formula. I knew that we were all just people out there trying to make our dreams come true. But sometimes the ghosts and nightmares of our childhood make those dreams seem impossible.

Now I must set out on a new journey. I must find my own dreams. I will have to face the ghosts and the nightmares or my soul will perish just like the little chickens in that dusty Kansas back yard.

From the time I was twelve I'd wanted to be an actress. My

goal was so clear and my destination so straight that I never questioned that part of my future until now. I was thirty-two years old.

It was clear to me that I had to find something different to do with my life. As an actress I would never find my own identity. I loved the work and had grown to hate the rest. It just wasn't right for me any more.

My dilemma reminded me of the old joke about the man who shovelled elephant dung at the circus. All day long he grumbled and bitched and moaned about shovelling the elephant dung. Finally someone asked him why he didn't find another job. With a shocked look on his face, the circus employee looked up and said, 'What? And leave show business?'

There were many months of soul-searching frustration ahead for me. I spent most of the time alone because it was just too painful to be with anyone else. I knew I had to do something about my life before it was too late, before I was so set in the old habit patterns that I couldn't change. But what could I do? In which direction should I look?

It was a stroke of great good fortune when I met David, the man who was to be my husband. His strength and his confidence in my ability, his belief in me as a human being, enabled me to begin thinking about my life in an entirely new light. I gathered courage from our relationship.

People I thought were my friends fell by the wayside in this searching process. Since I determined that acting was no longer to be the course of my life, these people decided I could be of no further advantage to them and they left. At first it hurt my feelings deeply, but I came to realize that it was only the natural culling process that happens when changes occur.

Then I looked into my life to try and see where its previous success had been. I kept coming back to the joy of learning I'd known at Chadwick and the fine education I'd received there. The next step of my life appeared to evolve quite logically.

I went back to college – first to a small private university, and then to UCLA. I remember vividly the trauma of my first month in that gargantuan establishment. One day I found myself sitting on a stone bench with tears streaming down my face. It was the moment when I could have given up the whole idea.

The pain of trying to do something so different, so new, so difficult, was nearly beyond my coping ability. I was thirty-three years old. I was in class with kids who were eighteen. I was older than some of the professors. There were days when I felt like a dinosaur trying to rise out of the tar pits. I cried all the way home.

David wouldn't let me feel sorry for myself. He refused me any participation in self-pity. He said, 'Either quit and stop torturing yourself or go back there tomorrow and fight like hell.' I chose to fight.

A year and a half later I graduated magna cum laude with a bachelor of arts degree. From there I went to USC and the Annenberg School of Communication. During the next year of graduate school I worked as an instructor at a junior college teaching sales management and communication. In 1975, just three years after I'd begun this process of my re-education, I received a master's degree in communication management and went to work in the public-relations department of a corporation handling films and videotape.

I wrote Mother about each step of my progress. I told her that I had totally restructured my life and was no longer in 'show business'. I wrote her when I received my two degrees and then when I got the new jobs. She replied with her congratulations and warm praise. I continued to send presents on the holidays and on her birthday. She seemed happy for me and pleased about my new venture. I had begun to break free. My survival, at least for this phase of my life, was assured once more.

David and I were married on Valentine's Day, 1976. It was truly the happiest day of my life. We were partners and friends in the truest sense. My dear friend, Nicki, originally my coach at Chadwick, had the wedding and reception in her home overlooking the ocean.

Later that year I heard that my mother had stopped drinking. I wondered what she would be like now. I realized that my mother had been drinking since I was a small child. I'd never really known her any other way. If what I heard was true, I was happy for her. Her drinking was a major cause of many of our personal problems during the years of my growing up and into adulthood. That drinking blurred events of the past out of context and sequence. I knew by things she said that she had much of it confused. Alcoholism preyed on her mind, distorting reality, causing her to blame others for her mistakes and personal weaknesses. In the early years it was the fuel that fed raging fires of her anger chiselled out of frustration and fear, turning our home into a night-raid holocaust without warning. Later on it preyed on her own ego, eating away at her self-respect and good looks. It clouded her judgment about her work, causing her to make films that were embarrassments to a brilliant career. It also clouded her judgment about people, leaving open the door and the chequebook for frauds and the ghouls who fawn over ageing stars.

I had made my peace with her now. I had made peace with myself and my own life. I could only hope that she had made similar peace with me. Her letters indicated she had. I had gone on to build a life that had nothing to do with who she was or the years of our pain. She seemed to understand. We had loved each other with an uncommon passion that turns too easily in times of strife and sorrow. Our relationship with all its turbulence had been more full than most, more challenging than most. It held enough ecstasy and devastation to last several lifetimes.

The last letter I received from Mother was dated 10 April 1977. In it she asked forgiveness for being so tardy with her thank-you note for our two 'adorable' birthday cards. She said that the mail had been extremely heavy this year and she no longer had a New York secretary, so that it was very difficult for her to keep up, as she should. She closed sending love to both David and myself, thanking us for making her day special with our remembrance. It was signed: '*All love, Mother.*'

The weekend of Mother's Day my husband and I sent flowers to both his mother and mine. I remember it was Friday morning when we ordered the spring bouquets to be delivered, one to Detroit and the other one to New York.

When we finished, we were standing in our kitchen. I was overcome with an incredible feeling of sorrow and loneliness for no apparent reason. Then a thought flashed through my head so strongly that I had to sit down. David asked me if I felt ill, I looked so pale. I looked at him through eyes filled with tears. I could hardly say the words, but I had to tell him. 'David, I think my mother is going to die very soon.' There was no way for me to explain what I knew with my whole being in that moment.

My mother and I had been bound together for so many years. We had been through so much it did not seem peculiar to me that I should know she was now dying.

That same Friday, in New York City, Mother gave away her beloved dog. She gave the dog away because she knew she could no longer care for her.

The Mother's Day flowers arrived one day ahead of time, on Saturday. They were brought to her as she lay in her bed, very ill. She was told that they were from 'Tina' and she said, 'Oh, yes. It must be Mother's Day.' She requested they be placed on the television set where she could see them, even lying down.

They were the last flowers she ever saw. I remember she'd always said, 'Send me flowers while I'm alive. They won't do me a damn bit of good after I'm dead.'

My mother died on the morning of 10 May 1977.

IN MEMORIAM

'God has set us free, Mother . . . go in peace.' That's what I was thinking as the man from Campbell's and I descended the stairs and returned to the small blue room where the rest of the family was gathered.

Everyone except the lawyer was still there when I returned. Since there were no further decisions to be made that day, we left Campbell's. It was Wednesday afternoon. David and I had had no sleep since Monday night. I was exhausted. We decided to return to our hotel until it was time to meet later that same afternoon.

At four o'clock, we all gathered again at the Drake Hotel. Two men from Pepsi wanted to discuss some public memorial service with the family. The funeral on Friday was to be small and private. The secretary was calling people close to Mother and making the other necessary arrangements. There were to be no flowers, but of course wreaths were already arriving at the funeral home. There was no way to stop them.

We decided together that there should be some kind of memorial service for Mother. Hundreds of people wanted to pay their respects in some way, and at the moment no such avenue of expression existed. Since we were unable to handle anything of such magnitude as a family, we were grateful to the company for its extremely considerate gesture. We felt we'd done the right thing.

The funeral had been scheduled for Friday. It was not possible

267

to arrange for a memorial service any sooner than the following Tuesday, simply because there were too many people being contacted. Many of the Pepsi bottlers had become personal friends of Mother's. She had taken an interest in them, their wives and families, for many years. They had corresponded regularly and seen one another on occasions other than company business.

I did not sleep well Thursday night. It was after midnight when I finally fell into a light sleep, awakened intermittently by the unfamiliar city noises outside our hotel window. When Friday morning dawned, I felt ill. I knew I wasn't really sick, but it would take every bit of willpower I had to get up and begin getting ready to leave for the funeral. If David hadn't been with me, I don't think I would have had the courage. More than at any other time in my life, all I really wanted to do was stay in bed with the sheets pulled over my head until it was all over and we could go home again. I hadn't been able to eat more than a few mouthfuls of food since Tuesday afternoon. Everything just seemed to stick in my throat. I drank some coffee and ate a few bites of an English muffin David had got for us. I took a hot shower, washed my hair, and was fully dressed half an hour before the limousine was due to arrive.

It was warm for this early in May and I was glad there were no signs of rain. The grey drizzle would make everything more depressing.

Mother's retired New York secretary was riding with us in the limousine and she arrived at the hotel exactly on time. It had been several years since I'd seen her but I'd always liked her very much. She was always direct. It made you feel you could trust her.

After our greetings were over and I'd introduced her to my husband, David, she mentioned the date of the funeral for the first time. I stared at her for a long moment. None of us had thought in terms of dates, we'd been dealing only with days when the decisions were being made. No one stopped to consider that this particular Friday was indeed Friday, 13 May. Unlucky Friday the 13th! My God, that is very strange. I never thought about it and probably nobody else did either. Mother died on her wedding anniversary and is being buried on Friday the 13th. A strange set of coincidences.

We arrived at the funeral home early and were shown into a private room just off the main chapel. There were flowers everywhere. Beautiful roses and other spring floral arrangements that took some of the faint musty odour away from these rooms. I didn't feel quite so shaky now that I'd got a little fresh air. I held on to David's hand. He was always right there next to me.

My sisters and Chris arrived a few minutes later. We went in to look at the chapel by ourselves before people started arriving. The urn was placed on a pedestal in the front of the chapel, surrounded by flowers. To the left of the urn was a small lectern where the Christian Science practitioner would read her service.

Now the people were beginning to arrive, and we returned to the private waiting room. Some of the guests came in to see the family before the service, but most were being asked to wait until afterwards.

I was deeply touched at the kindness and outpouring of sympathy for the family. I looked at the faces of longtime friends I'd known since childhood, the faces of former secretaries and others who had served as hairdressers, manicurists, publicity people, and business associates. This was intended as a gathering of only the people closest to Mother. Most of the people were from New York, but some had flown in from as far as Houston and Los Angeles.

It was getting more difficult every minute. My brother came over and stood with me for a while. He knew only a few of the faces, so I introduced him to everyone that came by to see me. Our cousin, Joan, arrived and stood with the rest of the family. Chris knew her and felt more comfortable now that he had someone to talk to. I sat down on a chair for a minute. David brought me a paper cup with water. He also handed me some Kleenex. The next person who came to speak with me was one of the women who had been a companion to my mother for many years. She had begun her friendship and years of service as a fan. She had been one of the two people left with Mother right up until her death. This woman's face was slightly swollen with crying over the last few days and she was still very distraught. She clutched my hands and held on to them tightly. I tried to say something to her, but there were no words that came easily for either of us. Then she leaned over and said, 'Tina . . . Mother

269

loved you. You were her firstborn ... she always said you were there when she needed you most ... you brought her great joy. Remember that ... Tina. No matter what happens ... your mother *loved* you.' She could say no more and had to leave before she was overcome with grief.

The words of this woman struck at the depth of pain and love in a way that not even the news of my mother's death had done. I started shaking. Tears streamed down my face. I always knew that Mother loved me ... that she really loved me. That was exactly why the trouble we had with each other was so very difficult to understand. I knew she loved me. And every time she levelled her guns at me and tried to annihilate me, when the smoke cleared away and the noise died down, there I was, standing before her. I may have been wounded, I may have been in tatters, but by God, I was still standing! She may not have agreed with me, she may not even have liked me sometimes, but she respected me and she loved me as I loved her. We had been joined in battle for over thirty years. But what this woman had said was true. Mother loved me. This was the first time I really cried in the last four days.

The funeral service was brief. There is no formal burial service in Christian Science. The woman who had been my mother's last practitioner read from the Bible and then passages from Mary Baker Eddy. Those passages were so familiar. They reminded me instantly of all those Sundays of my childhood when Mother and I would read the lessons aloud and then call Sorkie in New York.

I looked at the woman reading in her clear voice that sounded so peaceful. From her face I looked at the urn sitting on its pedestal, so plain and nondescript. I noticed that lying across the base of the urn was a single, long-stemmed red rose that had not been there earlier. It was clearly some very personal gesture of love.

I thought about seeing Mother's embalmed body two days before, lying still with her hands folded, so terribly thin, so old and frail. She was gone now. She would leave an empty space for so many who had been faithful and served her until the very end. It is painful to say goodbye. It is always hard to realize that a life has ended. But for Mother I felt a sense of relief. She was at peace now. And I felt no guilt. There had been nothing left for me to do. I'd done the best I could. I felt David's hand in mine and the strength between us.

The organ music began again and the service was over. The family formed a double receiving line in the small private room. People began streaming through the door, taking our hands and saying what words of condolence they could manage. It was very strange how names I hadn't thought of for several years came back the instant I saw the face again. It was strange how these ghosts of the past, all dressed in black, floated by as just a row of faces that I introduced to my husband. So many people. Each one reminded me of a specific time, a special place, an event in my life. My childhood, the years in New York with Mother, our family trip to Europe with Daddy, all the people that had been intertwined through our lives.

Though the funeral had been very carefully planned, controlled, and arranged, the hype was not absent from it. There was a man hawking old pictures, old photographs of Mother and Daddy. He came through the receiving line going to each member of the family asking if we wanted to *buy* his old photographs! When he went through our side of the receiving line and finally made his pitch to me, David quickly and politely showed him the door. I turned to my husband and smiled weakly. Even in death the hype was still with us.

About forty-five minutes later, we left in the black limousines for the drive to Ferncliff, where the urn was to be placed in a family crypt next to Daddy. None of us had ever seen where Daddy was buried, so in some strange way this was almost like a double funeral.

It was a beautiful day. Once we left the decaying streets of East Harlem, everything was green and the sky was clear blue. It was warm, but the cars were air-conditioned. We managed to talk a little with the two secretaries who accompanied us in the lead car. I had a terrible headache which aspirin wasn't going to help, at least not today. I looked out the windows at the lovely countryside and tried not to think about much of anything.

Ferncliff looks just like a beautiful park. There are large trees and green lawns and flowering shrubs everywhere. If you didn't know better, you might think it was a perfect place for a picnic.

Inside the mausoleum it was very cold. The marble floor echoed our footsteps against the marble walls. It was an ancient, hollow sound that accompanied our walk past the other crypts to the final destination. We'd brought one flower arrangement and the urn with us. Again, the Christian Science practitioner read from the Bible. I stared at the marble crypt cover with the names and dates inscribed on it. The urn was placed inside the crypt and looked very small and alone inside the large space. Then this part of the funeral was over too. We all walked slowly back to the entrance and out into the sunlight again. The family was going back to the Drake Hotel. The lawyer was going to read the will.

We ordered some sandwiches and drinks upon our arrival at the hotel. The lawyer arrived a few minutes later and said he'd like to see my brother first and privately. They went to another room. The food arrived from room service, but most of us took our drinks first. It was a strained and a strange time. It was just family members. My sister Cathy and her husband, my sister Cindy, cousin Joan, Chris, my husband, and myself. We'd never been together in one room. My sisters barely knew their cousin. No one but my brother had met David before.

It wasn't long before Chris reappeared. He looked very much the same as when he'd left. He took his drink off the large room-service table. He said that the lawyer wanted to see David and me next, so we departed for the other room. As we walked down the hall, David held my hand as he had consistently done since we'd left Los Angeles four long days ago. We were both very tired.

The lawyer asked us to sit down. He was holding a copy of the will in his hand. I sat nearest him. He flipped several pages over and then handed me the copy, with only the last page showing. There at the top of the final page of the will was one short paragraph which read:

'It is my intention to make no provision herein for my son Christopher or my daughter Christina for reasons which are well known to them.'

I stared at the words in utter disbelief. I looked up from the page to the lawyer's face. He said only, 'I'm very sorry, Tina.' I

272

looked across the room at David, then I looked back down at the piece of paper.

What in the hell happened to her these last years? '... *for reasons which are well known to them*'? What had this woman done? Tried to reach back out of the grave to slap me in the face one more time? What was she doing – having the final word even after she was dead?

I remember saying to her, 'God has set us free, Mother. Go in peace.' With a growing sense of horror I realized that she had not made her peace with me before she died. All the years we'd been together had somehow slipped from her memory. My first impression was that these words she'd ordered put into her last will and testament were from over twenty years ago. These were the words of the woman who had me locked up in the convent school because of a Christmas card list and then said I'd been expelled from my former school.

These were not the words of the woman who gave me my wedding reception at the '21' Club. These were not the words of the woman who asked me about her son fighting in Vietnam. These were not the words of the woman who knew about the rebuilding of my entire life over the past five years and expressed her love and congratulations. They couldn't be. These were the words of a demon reaching out of the mists of years gone by and buried with her in the grave. She had made no peace with the world. She had gone out of this life carrying all the years of hatred and cruelty and violent rage with her, clutching at the torment of it as though it were just yesterday.

She had tried to reach out of her grave and slap me one last time, just to prove who had really been in control all these years.

I was speechless and stunned. Not because of the money. It would have been a nice gesture, but it wasn't the money. It was the insult. It was the implication that I had committed an unspeakable wrong. It was the humiliating innuendo that was left to be interpreted publicly.

How could one woman carry so much hatred with her so many years? I should think that the venom would eat you alive. But, then, maybe it did. Maybe it just did. The official cause of her death was coronary arrest, but the private conjecture was that she died of cancer. So maybe all that insanity and venom finally did eat her alive. Maybe it did finally kill her.

I flipped the pages of the will back to the beginning and read the entire document silently. All personal property to Cathy. A miserly trust fund to Cindy and Cathy which was spread out over the next twenty years. About $70,000 was divided among secretaries and other people who had served her over the years, basically to the people who had said yes and done her bidding faithfully. Not one cent was left to her two closest living blood relatives, her niece and aunt. The rest was split up among various charities. The date of the document was interesting. The will had been written in October 1976, only seven months before her death. I requested a copy.

The lawyer accompanied us back to the suite where the others were waiting. He spoke with my sisters separately. Then it was all finished. There was nothing more except to attend the formal and more public memorial service next Tuesday.

My sisters and I spoke only briefly. They were returning to their respective home towns in the morning. I didn't think my brother really wanted to stay in the room for the rest of that day, so I suggested that he accompany David and me to a friend's home a few blocks away. He went with us gladly.

Tuesday afternoon the company sent a limousine to pick us up. Again we were accompanied by the two secretaries. There had been some problems getting appropriate people to speak at this memorial. Cesar Romero had topped the list but he was unavailable. Mitchell Cox was unavailable. A number of other people were also unavailable. I had nothing to do with the arrangements other than to submit a short list of people I wished to invite. My brother's daughter had become ill so he didn't make the trip back from Long Island. There was no reason for him to attend. He'd paid his last respects privately and conducted himself like a gentleman. He did not deserve any more pain.

The Unitarian Church was full when the service began. The people who spoke referred to the long successful career, the dedication and the greatness of the star. Anita Loos spoke first. I had always admired her and we had been friends since I was young. She spoke beautifully. Geraldine Brooks went next and spoke of the work they'd done together. Strangely enough, within a few months she too was dead. Pearl Bailey spoke and then sang with a power and electricity that gave me chills. She sang her own mother's favourite hymn, 'He'll Understand'. Cliff Robertson gave what was closest to a formal eulogy that was well written. The minister then read the 'Desiderata', which had been a favourite of Mother's, and the service ended. Again the family had a receiving line and again the ghosts paraded by, offering ther condolences. Most of the people at this service were business associates and bottlers. Pepsi had handled everything beautifully, tastefully, and with fastidious care. The service was dignified, began exactly on time, and was orderly throughout.

A number of people wanted interviews with me or to take pictures of me but I politely refused. Whatever was going to be immediately reported about all this would have to be done without any quotes from me. And that's exactly what happened. What was written by various columnists during the next few weeks was drawn entirely from their own previous knowledge, hearsay, and documents of public record, not from me.

That evening, the paragraph from the will which disinherited my brother and me was reported on the television news. In fact, to my astonishment, the newscaster read the entire paragraph verbatim. From there it was picked up and reported in newspapers. The stories were mostly the same. They mentioned the trust fund for my sisters and the unspecified sums to charity, and then quoted the paragraph ending with '. . . for reasons which are well known to them'.

The entire matter was a disgrace. If Mother simply wanted to disinherit two of the children she'd gone to so much trouble to adopt, if that's all she wanted to do, there are very simple, standard ways to do so. There was no need to use the language she chose. There was no need to do what she did, if all she wanted was to make sure we didn't get anything from her estate. But that's not what she did.

As the days passed after the reading of the will, I tried to put the pieces of the puzzle together. What exactly was it that had happened over the years that intervened since I last saw Mother?

Everyone I personally spoke with was shocked at what had happened. None of them knew any reasons for it, none of them had any explanation. They expressed not only their condolences but their sympathy.

It seems that about two years before her death, a number of different incidents coincided to change her life substantially.

Mother had completed her last picture in 1970. It was a terrible film called *Trog* and is best simply forgotten. Her drinking had got progressively worse over the years until she was nearly unable to go out in public any longer. Her last few public appearances were drunken disasters. It was so serious now that the people in the apartment who worked for her put chairs around her bed so she wouldn't hurt herself in the night and stationed other chairs at various places for her to hold on to. Apparently, during one of the rare times when she was left alone in the apartment during the day, she fell and hit her head on the corner of a table. She was unconscious for several hours before she was discovered with a severe wound to her temple and one eye. Though it was evidently a fairly serious injury and could have resulted in complications from both the length of the blackout and the wound itself, Mother refused any medical attention. She blamed the fall on antibiotics she was supposedly taking, but conjecture is that she was drunk and had slipped on the bare floor. The people who worked for her cleaned up her wound and took care of her as best they could without medical assistance. She categorically refused to see a doctor and the other people in the house felt compelled to follow her orders.

Pepsi had finally retired her. She was well past sixty-five but the retirement hurt her feelings. Part of it had to do with the fact that she knew it was the end of her professional career. There were no more acting offers. She insisted on being the Star and she just hadn't made the transition that other actresses were able to make. She didn't become the grand dowager or the character woman. She wanted to retain the old stardom and she was too old. The world had passed her by because she refused to accept change. Her fierce tenacity had outlived reality and usefulness. So without that 'stardom', the only thing she had left was her job with the company. She finally outlived that too, but she couldn't reconcile herself to the fact that those were the natural progressions of life.

She was finally retired and a fully private citizen for the first time since she'd been about sixteen years old. What she had left was the mail and her prolific correspondence. Without a New

York secretary on company salary, as she'd been used to all these years, even answering the mail was not an easy task.

To the best of anyone's knowledge, the last time Mother saw a doctor was also about two years before her death. Her health began to decline shortly afterwards, but she refused to allow anyone around her to call for medical care. She was terrified of hospitals and of losing control.

After the serious fall and subsequent head injury, Mother is reported to have stopped drinking. The seriousness of the injury and being unable to remember how it happened apparently scared her. How she managed to stop drinking without assistance no one could say. After over twenty-five years of alcoholism it was quite a feat.

During the years I lived in New York and saw Mother nearly every day she had been routinely conscious of household security. After I moved to California she received a crank call from an unknown person threatening her life. The lawyers and her few friends who knew about the call tried to tell her that it was an accidentally dialled number and that the man who called probably didn't even know the identity of the person answering the phone. But my mother was not convinced of the chance nature of the call or the threat. It was reported to the police and FBI but no one was ever found. After the incident, she had extra locks put on the doors. She was suspicious of anything unusual. Everyone had to be announced and checked thoroughly before being allowed on the elevators. Now she never left the apartment except to go to the dentist once or twice. She was terrified that someone was going to kill her. In fact, she tried not to leave her apartment at all for any reason. She refused all dinner invitations even from close friends. She remained in touch with the world only through the telephone, her mail, and her television set.

She continued to have her companion buy things for the apartment such as china and other housewares, though she never entertained. She continued to spend money as though life were going on as usual, but it wasn't. She made the woman companion buy new cotton shifts, but the price tags were never removed because she never wore them.

She made out her last will in October. Until then she had seen the people she specifically invited to the apartment, including Cathy and her husband. In December Mother stopped seeing anyone other than the three or four people who worked for her and the Christian Science readers who came regularly.

The lawyer told us that the practitioner became so concerned about Mother's ability to take care of herself that she arranged for readers who were also practical nurses. Mother wouldn't let them help her in any way or even touch her. By this time her physical condition was deteriorating rapidly. She'd been losing weight steadily. Mother was always very proud of her body, but the weight continued to disappear until she was thin and frail. She was no longer strong enough to bathe by herself but still refused to receive help. She refused to allow anyone to notify the family, to call for a doctor, or to get medical attention. People around her mistook her continuing ability to give these orders as a sign of mental competence and followed her wishes.

Two months before her death Mother also stopped smoking. By now she was confined to her bed and had to be attended by the two women who were left with her. Neither of them was a nurse, but they did the best they could to care for her and make her comfortable.

The morning of 10 May 1977, only one woman was with Mother. She arrived in the morning to relieve the other woman, who had stayed the night. She realized that Mother had been through a very bad night but was surprised at the clarity with which she spoke. There were only the two of them in the room when the end finally came. The woman, realizing there was nothing more she could do, began praying. At first the prayers were silent but as she realized how close the end really was, her prayers became audible. She was praying aloud and Mother heard the words. My mother raised her head. The last coherent words from her mouth were, 'Damn it . . . don't you *dare* ask God to help me!' A few minutes later, Mother was dead.

The memorial service in Los Angeles for the motion-picture and television industries was scheduled for 24 June 1977. It was organized by George Cukor and a committee representing a cross-section of the industry.

There had been a great deal of publicity about this memorial.

All facets of the industry had co-operated to create a tribute to one of their members. The studios contributed the film footage, a number of companies made donations to cover the expenses, and numerous people donated their individual professional skills to make the event a success.

Since I was not involved in any of the preparations, I do not know by what process the committee chose people to speak at the tribute. The programme listed their names and called the event 'An Industry-Wide Celebration in Film and Fond Memories'.

My husband, stepson, and I arrived at the proper time. David spoke with one of the guards at the door of the Academy of Motion Picture Arts and Sciences and they admitted us through a side entrance.

Once inside the new Academy building, a man took us to the elevators. Through the glass partition separating us from the main lobby of the Academy, I could see the crowd. There was a champagne reception in progress before the tribute itself began. There were television cameras and photographers' flashbulbs going off. I stood watching the crowd with fascination. Everyone was behaving as though it were a premiere, a party, or an opening night of some sort. People were being interviewed and posing for pictures. Some of the stars were signing autographs. It was an 'event' and I guess these people just didn't know any other appropriate behaviour.

The entire tribute was being videotaped both for the Academy archives and for future broadcast. So it was definitely the place to be seen that night. And there they all were in the lobby, enjoying the champagne reception and the flashbulbs, the fans milling around outside the building waiting for a glimpse of their favourite personality, and the television cameras inside the lobby. There were also special television interviews going on upstairs on another floor where it was quieter. Up there, former directors and lovers, friends and producers were being interviewed on one subject: Joan Crawford.

The man ushered us upstairs and into a private office that had been turned into a temporary waiting room for the people who were going to speak during the tribute programme.

Once we reached the doorway to the office, the man left us

without making any introductions. John Wayne was just coming out of the room on his way to one of the pretaped interviews. I introduced myself and my family. He hurriedly said hello to us, but I'm not sure he actually heard what I'd said.

Then I led my husband and fourteen-year-old stepson into the office, where a sizeable group was gathered. George Cukor was seated directly in front of me. Kevin Thomas was standing near him, and seated next to Kevin was Robert Young, with whom I'd worked on *Marcus Welby*. Carmel Myers was there and Jack Jones was seated on the couch next to Myrna Loy, with whom I'd done *Barefoot in the Park*.

I said hello but no one moved or greeted me. There was a silence which left me standing in the middle of the room with nowhere to go. George Cukor peered up at me over his glasses, imperiously inquiring, 'Who-o-o are you?' He sounded just like the Chershire Cat in *Alice in Wonderland*. I almost laughed. There was a silence as everyone waited for this intruder to identify herself.

I let the silence last another moment, so there could be no mistake about my introduction. Very clearly and distinctly I replied to George, looking him straight in the eyes as I spoke, 'I . . . am . . . Christina Crawford.'

George Cukor stood up as fast as his elderly years permitted. The rest of the room turned into pandemonium. Several people started talking at once. Myrna Loy got up and left the room. She left her drink, her speech, and her mink coat right where they'd been sitting the moment before.

What a strange night it was, and this was just the beginning. George took my hand and I introduced him to David and my stepson. He complimented me on turning into a handsome woman, for which I thanked him, and I sat down next to Jack Jones in the spot vacated by Myrna. We were offered some champagne while various people began trying to pick up the threads of their previous conversations.

Jack Jones uncomfortably related a peculiar story to me. It was some tale about his being Joan Crawford's godson. It had evolved into a standing joke between them and that's why he was here tonight. He'd been asked to speak at this tribute on the basis of that joke.

When the hour finally came for all of us to go downstairs to the theatre, my husband and I were told to sit in any seat of the first two rows. The second row was already full, so we three sat alone in the first row.

The programme began with an introduction of the speakers by Kathleen Nolan, who also spoke first. Fay Kanin, who had written one of Mother's movies, followed; Robert Young told about her sending presents on his wedding day and receiving her letters; George Cukor read the *New York Times* article he'd written about my mother; Leonard Spigelgass recounted some funny experiences from the old days; Myrna Loy was there as Joan's oldest friend; Steven Spielberg spoke of making his directorial debut with Mother about seven years before at Universal.

I remember the event well. Mother was absolutely furious with the studio for assigning her a twenty-two-year-old kid who had never done anything before.

John Wayne was wonderfully candid and got the best laugh of the show. Jack Jones told his 'godson' story and sang. In between there were film clips from the old movies including a wonderful segment on the early silent films.

At the very end John Wayne stood up and read off the list of participants, asking each group to stand as its particular affiliation was mentioned. As the people in the theatre began standing I thought back over what we'd just seen.

There were several mentions of the letters this woman wrote, several stories about the professional experiences shared years ago, a few silly anecdotes out of nervousness. There was nothing about the woman as a person. There was not one mention about her family. No one ever alluded to the fact that I was seated just three feet away in the first row. In fact, no one mentioned that she even had a family and no one offered condolences to me. Neither the private funeral, the New York memorial service, nor this industry tribute had made a single reference to her as a person or to her family.

At first I thought it was peculiar, strange behaviour. But then I believed that the rudeness was out of their own insecurity and lack of consciousness. It was just that the television cameras, the press, and all the other professional trappings elicited only behaviour dictated by the hype, their own egos, and fear of what others would think.

As John Wayne's voice continued to read off the names of companies, studios, television networks, craft unions, independent producers, actors' unions, and even the studio cleaners, I realized that I didn't fit into any of these categories. Since there was no recognition of family, there was no category for family. I waited until the very end, when the rest of the theatre was already standing. At last John Wayne added: 'Friends and others.'

That was an appropriate category, so my husband, stepson, and I stood during the very last minute of the tribute to my mother, Joan Crawford, under the designation of 'Friends and others'.

That was it. The show was over. The television cameras were turned off and the full house lights went on. A publicity man and a fan from New York with his family said hello to us on our way out of the theatre. We spoke with no one else.

As the three of us walked out into the cool night air, I held on to David's hand and thought, God Almighty, at last it is over. I have survived. It is time for us to go forward with vigilance, honesty, and love.

'. . . for reasons which are well known to them.'

THE BEST IN BIOGRAPHY FROM GRANADA PAPERBACKS

Dirk Bogarde

A Postillion Struck by Lightning	£1.50	☐
Snakes and Ladders	£1.25	☐

Elizabeth Longford

Winston Churchill	£2.50	☐
Wellington: Pillar of State	£1.95	☐
Wellington: The Years of the Sword	£1.25	☐

Jasper Ridley

Lord Palmerston	£1.50	☐

Han Suyin

The Morning Deluge *(Volume I)*	£1.75	☐
The Morning Deluge *(Volume II)*	£1.25	☐
Wind in the Tower	£1.75	☐
The Crippled Tree	95p	☐
A Mortal Flower	£1.50	☐
Birdless Summer	£1.25	☐

Kim Philby

My Silent War	£1.50	☐

Dusko Popov

Spy/Counter Spy	£1.25	☐

P22481

THE WORLD'S GREATEST NOVELISTS
NOW AVAILABLE IN GRANADA PAPERBACKS

Iris Murdoch

A Word Child	£1.25	☐
The Unicorn	£1.95	☐
An Unofficial Rose	£1.25	☐
The Bell	£1.95	☐
The Flight From the Enchanter	£1.95	☐
The Nice and the Good	£1.25	☐
Bruno's Dream	£1.50	☐
The Red and the Green	£1.25	☐
A Severed Head	£1.50	☐
The Time of the Angels	£1.95	☐
Henry & Cato	£1.25	☐
An Accidental Man	£2.50	☐
The Sandcastle	£1.25	☐
Under the Net	£1.25	☐
The Sea, The Sea	£1.95	☐

THE BEST IN BIOGRAPHY FROM GRANADA PAPERBACKS

P29481

THE WORLD'S GREATEST NOVELISTS
NOW AVAILABLE IN GRANADA PAPERBACKS

Ernest Hemingway

The Old Man and The Sea	95p	☐
Fiesta	£1.50	☐
For Whom the Bell Tolls	£1.95	☐
A Farewell to Arms	£1.50	☐
The Snows of Kilimanjaro	£1.25	☐
The Essential Hemingway	£2.25	☐
To Have and Have Not	£1.25	☐
Death in the Afternoon (non-fiction)	£1.25	☐
Green Hills of Africa	95p	☐
Men Without Women	95p	☐
A Moveable Feast	95p	☐
The Torrents of Spring	95p	☐
Across the River and Into the Trees	£1.95	☐
Winner Take Nothing	£1.50	☐
The Fifth Column	95p	☐

Richard Hughes

A High Wind in Jamaica	£1.25	☐
In Hazard	60p	☐
Fox in the Attic	£1.50	☐
The Wooden Shepherdess	£1.50	☐

James Joyce

Dubliners	£1.50	☐
A Portrait of the Artist as a Young Man	£1.50	☐
Stephen Hero	£1.50	☐
The Essential James Joyce	£2.50	☐
Exiles (play)	95p	☐

P3481